Roads and Rails of Birmingham 1900-1939

32
CLEANS
The Birmingham Mail

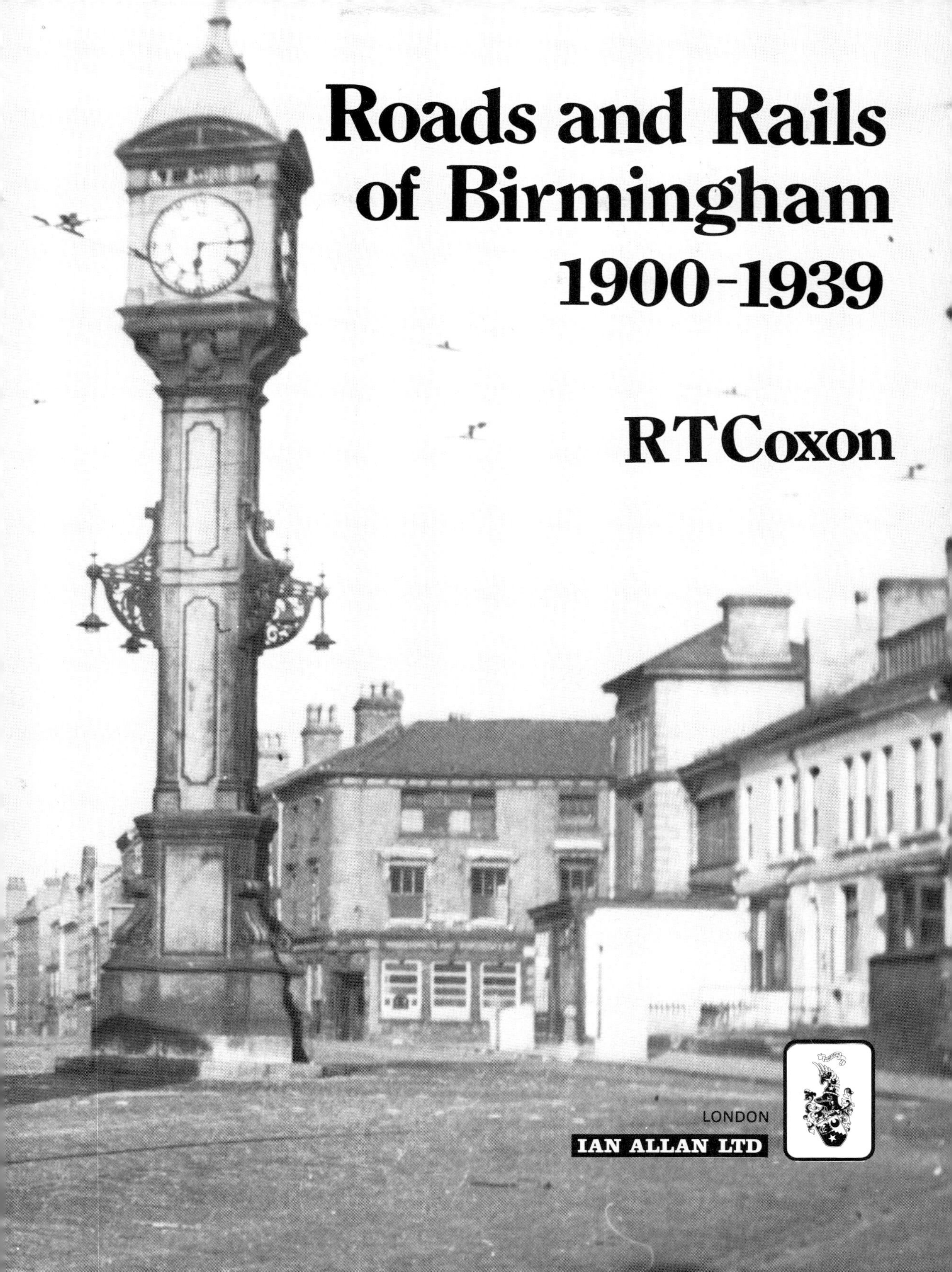

Roads and Rails of Birmingham 1900-1939

R T Coxon

LONDON

IAN ALLAN LTD

First published 1979

ISBN 0 7110 0913 9

Published by Ian Allan Ltd, Shepperton, Surrey; and printed in the United Kingdom by Ian Allan Printing Ltd

Contents

Above: City of Birmingham coat of arms.

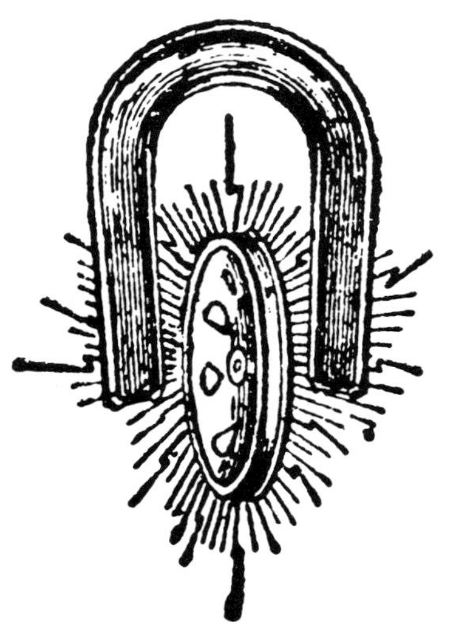

Above: British Electric Traction (BET) wheel-and-magnet device.

Acknowledgements

It would have been impossible to assemble a book such as this entirely on one's own. I have been very fortunate in having the help of a very devoted team, foremost among whom I must mention my wife, who typed the script from my original draft, if such a mass of bits and pieces could so be called. My 'crash-box' style of typing would have daunted most people, but Helen now has an almost inbuilt capacity for dealing with it.

I am indebted to many photographers, known and unknown, for the illustrations. Where known, individual acknowledgement has been made, and every effort has been made to trace the origins of pictures, but in some cases it has proved impossible. In these cases, should anyone recognise an unacknowledged photograph as his, I hope he will accept this as acknowledgement; the book would certainly have been the poorer without some of these photographs, taken by people unknown, who happened to be in the right place at the right time.

Special mention must be made of Arthur Whitehouse for preparing the photographs; he went to very great trouble to get the best possible prints from, in some cases, very doubtful negatives. 'Any photograph is better than no photograph' has to be a maxim for transport enthusiasts, but that is not acceptable to Arthur, who, with Stan Letts's assistance, has produced some quite remarkable results.

I have to thank the Midland Red Omnibus Company Limited, successors to the BMMO Co Ltd, for permission to reproduce the black-and-white illustrations which used to adorn their timetables and public notices. Each new BMMO type featured as an illustration in their publicity, and these are now used as chapter-headings. It seemed a good opportunity to put on permanent record these very fine illustrations as a series.

Many people have given assistance in one way or another with the book, and to list them all would be impossible. I must especially, however, thank Arthur Camwell, Peter Hardy, Alec Jenson and Stanley Webb for their part in getting this book on the road. I am no less grateful to all others who in any way have helped.

Ray Coxon

Roads and Rails of Birmingham and District

Above: Birmingham and Midland Motor Omnibus Co Ltd (BMMO Co Ltd) Tilling-Stevens TS3 bus 1920, OE 6165.

By the time this book reaches the public in 1979 it will be 25 years, give or take a little, since the last trams ran in Birmingham. During that quarter-century Birmingham, like so many other places, has changed (one would have reservations about saying improved) out of all recognition, but there are still bits of the place which, to me, look wrong without trams.

That, of course, is because I grew up with the trams already there; as a child begins to take notice of his surroundings and build up his own particular personal background, he assumes that what he sees at, say, age three or four years has always been there: the fact that places are always changing is not realised until rather later, though perhaps today children accept this idea much earlier, as the rate of change is so much greater. Places have always changed, even if imperceptibly in former times, but today not just individual buildings but whole streets and areas disappear almost overnight and something else is there next weekend, usually based on the idea that Big is Beautiful. Beautiful or not, we are stuck with it; perhaps present-day children grow up realising that things are always changing, whereas I and my generation tended to think that everything stayed put.

One of my earliest memories is of Colmore Row, Birmingham, the terminus for some of the tram services serving the Handsworth area. My route was Oxhill Road 26, which loaded from a kerbside shelter opposite the Grand Hotel; the site is still used by buses which traverse the anti-clockwise city centre one-way system. This one-way system dates from 1933, but 40 years later I still expect to see trams heading up Colmore Row to the Cathedral terminus. It all seemed so solid and permanent, as solid as the Grand Hotel, the Cathedral and Snow Hill station, but the trams left the Cathedral terminus in 1933 and used the Livery Street loop with the rest of the Handsworth routes until the whole of the Hockley group ceased operation in 1939. Now, incredibly, Snow Hill station is no more, but there is still that bit of Colmore Row which, looking towards the Town Hall, retains something of its appearance of the first quarter of this century. Only the trams are missing. Incidentally my father came home one night when I was about 10 with a story of a very narrow escape at the Cathedral terminus. As the conductor of the 26 tram hauled down the trolley-pole when the car stopped, the trolley-head, about 28lb of phosphor-bronze, came down and hit the ground between my father, who was first in the queue, and the conductor. Had it hit either of the two men it would obviously have done him a lot of no good; it gave them both a nasty turn.

This book is not a history — though care is being taken that the facts presented are correct — but a record of impressions and reminiscences of a period rapidly passing into history. The detailed history of the district's transport is being assembled by the Birmingham Transport Historical Group, and Stanley Webb has covered the Black Country Tramways in his masterly two-volume work of that title; it must be said that he leaves not one granite sett, not one wood block unturned to give a truly comprehensive picture of a system of which it seemed, because it suffered an early demise, many of the facts were already lost. This book, therefore, while not strictly a history, will of necessity be historical in character, and will attempt to present a picture of travel around Birmingham by rail, tram and bus up to the beginning of World War II. I myself date from 1917, so the pre-World War I material will not be first-hand, but in the inter-war period I shall be writing largely of things as I saw them myself.

The Landscape

Above: BMMO Co Ltd SOS 'S' charabanc 1925, HA 2436.

Before beginning any actual survey of the road and rail services of the area, it might be as well to look at the physical and social framework of Birmingham and the Black Country. The set-up is very different from London, as Birmingham, the largest borough, is not in the centre of the conurbation (ghastly word!) but to the south, and in the period we are considering, largely detached from the Black Country proper. Only since World War II has the gap between Handsworth and West Bromwich been built up on the south side with factories, the north side still being Green Belt, the former Sandwell Hall parkland, now known as the Sandwell Valley recreational area, which still drives a wedge of near-country between West Bromwich, Handsworth and Walsall. On the Smethwick road is a more solidly built-up situation, but leaving Birmingham by either the Smethwick (A457 Dudley Road) or West Bromwich (A41 Soho Road) roads one is soon aware by the differences in dialect that one is entering new country. The A41 enters West Bromwich through what was once a good residential area (Beeches Road-Birmingham Road), the heavy industrial area lying beyond Carters Green in the Dudley and Wednesbury directions. The road passes through Moxley and Bilston, leaving the centres of Wednesbury and Darlaston to the right, with great industrial complexes like the Patent Shaft and Axletree, Rubery Owen and many more before reaching Wolverhampton. Wednesbury and Wolverhampton are towns whose history antedates Birmingham's by several centuries, as does that of Dudley whose ancient castle still dominates the ridge of hills which begins south-west of Wolverhampton, beyond the Fighting Cocks, rises through Sedgley, on through Dudley and Rowley Regis above Halesowen to Romsley and the Lickey — the 'Birmingham Plateau' which all routes to Birmingham from the south and west have to climb — witness the Lickey Bank on the Midland Railway and Tardebigge Locks on the Worcester Canal. These hills — best known as the Rowley Hills — divide the Black Country into two distinct regions, and are penetrated by three canal tunnels (Dudley Old Tunnel, Netherton, and Wasthills on the Worcester Canal) and two railway tunnels, Dudley and Old Hill. On the western side the dialect and culture is quite different from the Wednesbury-Bilston side. The language of Brierley Hill, Kingswinford and Stourbridge has much more sing-song about it, with more than a touch of the true Worcestershire speech which would have prevailed around here three centuries ago. From the upper reaches of the Wolverhampton-Sedgley-Dudley road, semi-rural even today and looking not at all like a tram and later trolleybus route, one can see the Wrekin and the Clees, miles away to the west, and to the east the industrial sprawl across Tipton and Wednesbury to Walsall and Cannock Chase. Walsall, another ancient town, is a name to remember as the first operator, under South Staffordshire Tramways Company auspices, of overhead electric trams in the Midlands. Its Bloxwich and Walsall Wood termini represent the northern and eastern limits of the Black Country tramways. South of Walsall towards Sutton Coldfield and Birmingham lies pleasant residential development in country still retaining something of a rural aspect; Walsall trams did not get beyond the Bell Inn on the Birmingham road, and Birmingham's No 6 route did not go further north than Perry Barr. Midland Red began a bus service just before World War I and the projected tramway connections never materialised.

The area covered by this book is therefore from Stourbridge in the west, through Dudley, Sedgley and Wolverhampton to Willenhall and Walsall in the north, with Oldbury, West Bromwich and Smethwick roughly central and Birmingham to the south. Almost everything in the way of passenger transport has been seen in the area, and the set-up at the beginning of our period, 1900, was certainly varied enough. Now might be the point at which we can look at Birmingham in rather more detail.

Birmingham today is a sizeable place with over a million inhabitants. Its history as a city does not extend back very far, unlike, say, London, Bristol or York. Its expansion took place very rapidly in the 19th century, and in consequence its city centre is disproportionately small. It became the centre of the canal system, the interchange of the London and North-Western and the Midland Railways with the Great Western competing with both, the crossing-place of three important roads (the present A34 Winchester-Manchester, A38 Derby-Bodmin, and A41 London-Chester) and the starting place of many more — A45, A47 etc, and today is at the centre of the motorway system. Towards the end of last century it absorbed a number of neighbouring areas, which were really no more than villages, and this process continued in the early years of this century, so that today Birmingham includes Yardley, Moseley, Kings Heath, Kings Norton and Northfield on its southern side, Harborne, Edgbaston and Handsworth to the west and north-west, and Aston, Erdington and Stechford to the north and east. Of these perhaps only Yardley and Kings Norton retain their village flavour, the rest having become suburbs. It is a quite different situation from London, where many of the constituents of the Greater London Council retain their air of being separate towns, with various bits of common land and different levels of development occurring before meeting the next former individual borough. In Birmingham the individuality has been much more overlaid, perhaps because in the Edwardian period Birmingham went in for large-scale municipalisation of public services — transport, water, gas, electricity, not forgetting the Municipal Bank, whose motif — a key with *Birmingham Municipal Bank* on the wards appeared in ground glass on the sliding bulkhead doors of all Birmingham trams — perhaps a better achievement than on the Manchester trams where the injunction *Spitting Prohibited* in gilt transfer on one of the glazing bars appeared above a circular sticker on the glass itself — *Use the Manchester Ship Canal.*

Birmingham's small city centre has had a limiting effect on its transport services which is still felt today, though with the opening of the Queensway Tunnels and the Inner Ring Road, through traffic is taken out of the centre streets — until a pile-up occurs in the tunnels and then we do have fun. Even so, cross-city bus routes are in the minority and the attempt to run cross-city tram routes was abandoned well before World War I. Although Birmingham has no major river like the Thames dividing the city, the canal system which brought about the explosion of Birmingham's boundaries last century imposes many traffic restrictions even today due to lack of crossings. Along the Birmingham Canal (to Wolverhampton) to the north-west, bridges are far apart, as can be seen from a journey along the Stour Valley railway line which keeps the canal company almost all the way to Wolverhampton. Similarly, the Birmingham and Fazeley Canal to the east suffers from a lack of bridges which has had its effect on the traffic plan of Birmingham right down to date. 'Spaghetti Junction' at Gravelly Hill is so located to take the A38 traffic into Birmingham. Salford Bridge Junction, where three tram routes converged, on the original A38 (Lichfield Road) is where it is because of the Salford Canal Junction, where the Birmingham and Fazeley, the Tame Valley and the Birmingham and Warwick Junction Canals meet — and the canals join there because of the confluence of the River Tame and Aston (Hockley) Brook, with the Rea adding its quota a few hundred yards downstream. Certainly what Birmingham's rivers lack in size they make up in pollution, and they present the same sort of crossing problems as the Lea does in East London.

The city centre stands high, so that all roads except the Hagley Road (A456) from the West have to climb to reach the centre. Curiously, this western approach, via Broad Street, was the one main entrance which was not used by trams, though a concrete bed for double track was laid, but never used. The tram termini were scattered round the perimeter of the central massif, rather like the City termini in London, and there many of the present-day bus services continue to terminate. One gets a good idea of the elevated position of the centre of Birmingham when approaching New Street station from London. As the Grand Junction line comes in from the Aston direction to the right and the old Curzon Street station of the London and Birmingham Railway is seen, the Central Hall tower in Corporation Street is seen among all the empty office blocks, before the train dives into the New Street tunnels. Even the trams only came part-way up the Bull Ring before swinging right into Moor Street, but more of the city termini later. A brief description of Birmingham's suburbs is now perhaps called for.

Immediately surrounding the centre was a ring of industry and slums — Hockley to the north, Aston and Duddeston on the east, Bordesley and Balsall Heath to the south, and Ladywood to the west. In among the Victorian slums one could come across once-gracious Georgian houses engulfed by the industrial explosion; the ghosts of Georgian Birmingham probably still foregather in St Paul's Square, Hockley, in the Jewellery Quarter. The church dating, from 1777, strongly suggests St Martin's-in-the-Fields, and a few houses still remind one that this area, for a few years before the Fazeley Canal changed the scene in 1785, was Birmingham's new fashionable area. Then came the canal, and all the fashionables moved out to Edgbaston. Though much rebuilt, Edgbaston is still Birmingham's top suburb. At the period we are concerned with Moseley, Erdington and Handsworth Wood were also 'good addresses'; this term would hardly apply today. Between the inner factory zone and the exclusive outer suburbs were the artisan suburbs of Rotton Park, Handsworth, Perry Barr, Witton, Stockland Green, Erdington, Washwood Heath, Bordesley Green, Small Heath, Acocks Green, Sparkhill, Kings Heath, Stirchley, Bournville, and Selly Oak. One had better not include Harborne and Edgbaston under the heading of 'artisan' — not at this time, anyway. After World War I and to the end of our period an enormous amount of municipal housing was undertaken, with vast estates at Perry Common, Pype Hayes, Yardley, Hall Green, Weoley Castle and many more; from the amount of dual carriageway with centre reservations put in at this time one imagines that sleeper-track tramways were envisaged; the improvement in the motor-bus in the 1920s changed all that. By the time our period ends, the trams had already begun to give place to the bus, but as it begins the buses in Birmingham were horse-drawn and the overhead electric tram had still to make its belated appearance. In 1900, however, the suburban railways were still on to a good thing, and as Birmingham was on the country end of the first British main-line railway, we might first take a look at the railway scene in the West Midlands in 1900.

Rails of the West Midlands

Above: BMMO Co Ltd SOS 'FS' bus 1925, HA 2500

It is something of a curiosity that Birmingham, the terminus of the first two main lines — the London and Birmingham and the Grand Junction Railways — should have a relatively uncomplicated network of railways compared with, say, Manchester; it is equally curious that Manchester, where the canal age began with the Bridgewater Canal, should have little in the way of a canal network. There is certainly nothing to equal the convolutions of the Birmingham Canal Navigations in these islands; I imagine the BCN could give points to most continental canal systems. The creation of the Birmingham canal system was an undertaking of great boldness, especially as regards water supply. The Birmingham plateau lies at an average height of 450ft above sea level, with no great ranges of high country to supply water, and pumping on a large scale was the rule from low level back to the summits. The ruins of some of the pump houses — Smethwick for one — can be seen from the train today. The reason, then, for the not very dense railway network was that the canals were already in business and the Black Country was literally in full blast when the railways arrived. There are no important early tramroads such as those on Tyneside. Everything went by water. The London and Birmingham and the Grand Junction were passenger rather than freight lines, to begin with at all events. The railway freight business, of course, soon established itself, overtaking and buying up the canals, but well into the 1920s there was still plenty of business on the BCN.

The London and North Western Railway — formed in 1846 by the amalgamation of the London and Birmingham and the Grand Junction companies — had by 1900 built up a well-established passenger and freight business to London (Euston) and the North-West and North Wales via Crewe; if the LNWR constituents were first on the site they soon had company in the Birmingham and Derby Junction and the Birmingham and Gloucester Railways, soon to become the Midland Railway, using New Street station with the North Western. New Street was at first a dead-end station, but with the opening of the so-called Stour Valley line to Wolverhampton via Smethwick and Dudley Port, it became a 'through' station for the North Western, the Midland doing likewise when the old Birmingham

Above: LNWR New Street station about 1900. Webb Radial 0-6-2T on very clean set of six-wheel suburban stock at No 3 (Down) Platform.

West Suburban line from Lifford alongside the Worcester canal to Granville Street (off Broad Street) was transformed into a double main line down through the Five Ways tunnels in 1885 into the south side of New Street station (which the MR liked to call Station Street, as though to suggest no connection with the firm next door — as indeed was the case for years after both companies had become part of the LMS). To the east of New Street, access for the Midland trains from Derby had been improved with a burrowing junction at the Proof House under the LNWR, so that North Western and Midland trains could enter and leave New Street at each end without crossing each other on the level. Not to be outdone, the LNWR 'flew' its approach from the Aston direction over what had now become the goods lines into Curzon Street, the original station; the result of these burrows and flyovers was to present some tricky gradient profiles to trains coming in from the east, with a final down-and-up at 1 in 58 under the Great Western at Moor Street — the result of Captain Huish's strong-arm tactics in finally driving the GWR (Oxford and Birmingham) into Snow Hill, where it met the new line from Wolverhampton Low Level; Captain Huish of the North Western had outsmarted himself and created a competitor which, during our period, really gave the North Western and the LMS something to think about.

The gradients at the Western end of New Street on both the LNWR and the MR are severe, 1 in 77 straight off the platform, through a difficult maze of points and crossings and then into

Monument Lane (LNW) or Five Ways (MR) tunnels; exit by either route could be slow and painful. The North Western side operationally was obsolete from the start; its main down platform could take only about nine bogie coaches, any longer train either leaving its tail fouling the other platform approaches or having to overrun and set back into the fish dock — there was always an aroma of oil-gas and old fish about New Street, either side. In practice, eight or nine coaches was about the usual loading for the Euston trains, most of which only ran on to Wolverhampton. Most of the north traffic from Euston had from 1846 used the Trent Valley line from Rugby to Stafford via Tamworth — just as well, as Birmingham certainly could not have handled it. However, New Street was one of the most impressive of all stations in our period. A footbridge, open to the public, ran across it from Stephenson Street to Station Street, and all platforms were reached from it by staircases; the old No 3 (North Western Down Main) and No 4 (Midland Up Main) could be reached from Queen's Drive, the roadway dividing what were really two stations, while No 6 (Midland Down Main) could be reached on the level also from Station Street. The North Western side, with its great all-over roof, had a compelling if dingy grandeur about it. Descending the steps from the Stephenson Street (New Street station, either side of it, wasn't in New Street) booking office on to the footbridge was something like viewing a cathedral from the triforium; the resounding echo of a North Western 'George' or 'Experiment' blasting off under Navigation Street bridge (one-TWO-three-four, one-TWO-three-four) could sound like an infernal organ recital. Across Queen's Drive on the Midland side, things were quieter. Midland engines went woof-woof instead of hell-raising, and in addition the Class 2 4-4-0s played most melodious little passages on their coupling rods. Moreover they were a sight cleaner, even in the depressed late twenties and early thirties. Operationally, the Midland side was less inefficient than the North Western, but the whole place was bedevilled by the footbridge access to the platforms; ticket collection was out of the question, and all local trains had to stop for ticket collection at Monument Lane, Vauxhall, or Adderley Park on the North Western, or Five Ways, Saltley or Camp Hill on the Midland, imposing long waits and reducing line availability. If one booked a single from the stations mentioned to New Street, one was given an excess slip, not a card ticket. The ticket, if such existed, would go straight to the audit office.

Up to about 1930 New Street had changed little since 1900; in 1900 the LNWR trains would have been worked by 'Precedent' 2-4-0s and 'Lady of the Lake' 2-2-2s, with the Webb Compounds in evidence only rarely. Local trains were in the hands of the Webb 2-4-2 and 0-6-2 Radial and Coal tanks. By 1930 the 2-4-0s were no longer about — though in September 1932 I saw 'Director' No 5011 haring through Tamworth double-heading a 'Claughton' — and the small tank engines had been joined, but not ousted, by the 4-4-2 'Precursor Tanks' and the Bowen-Cooke 4-6-2Ts, and the 4-4-0 'Precursors', 'Georges', and 4-6-0 'Experiments', 'Princes', and an occasional 'Claughton' represented the tender classes — the few 'Renowns' were finishing their days on the North Wales main line, and I never saw one. The flavour was still very definitely North Western on that side of the station, although the Midland Compounds had taken over the Euston two-hour trains (their advent nearly causing a strike among the LNW loco men). Crewe seemed in no hurry to remove LNWR loco number plates or paint coaches in Midland Red; I recall seeing as a child plenty of goods trains banging up through Handsworth Park on the 1 in 75 with locos

Above: LNWR Soho Road station, about 1908. New Handsworth UDC Power Station extreme right, Ivy House pub in background. 'Precursor' class 4-4-0 No 2007 *Oregon* at island platform. Station closed in 1941.

Left: LNWR Handsworth Wood station about 1900. 'Problem' or 'Lady of the Lake' class 2-2-2 double-heading a 'Precedent' class 2-4-0. The last 'Problem' was withdrawn in 1907, but the 2-4-0s lasted into the 1930s.

Below left: LNWR Handsworth Wood. 'Precedent' or 'Jumbo' 2-4-0 arriving on Walsall-Birmingham train. Wooden platforms later replaced by brickwork and flagstone edging. Station closed in 1941.

still sporting LNWR brass number-plates, though the only positive memory is of No 7, which I thought must be a very old engine. In fact it was a relatively modern 'Precursor', later LMS No 5276 *Titan*. Suburban coaches in particular were still around in LNWR colours until at least 1930. The station itself retained its personality until the great roof was taken down in 1952. It remained gas-lit, and was perhaps best seen on one of those winter days in the coal age when it never really got light in the morning; by mid-day night descended on the city. Shops lit up, so did trams and buses, but street lamps, being on time-clocks didn't. At New Street, station staff were sent round at the double turning on the gas lamps, which put up a brave show against the fog, but never really stood a chance. And through this Stygian murk the 'Precursors' and 'Georges' and Radial tanks cautiously felt their way. On such a day, New Street was something to remember, and a departure through Monument Lane tunnel with the engine slipping like crazy and only just master of the train was quite hair-raising and claustrophobic. Once out of the tunnel by Monument Lane Loco one dropped the window and gulped in some of the relatively fresh, life-giving air straight from the ash-pit. I do not seem to have suffered any permanent detriment, however — I imagine the effects of diesel exhaust would be a different matter.

Services retained their overall pattern during our period; the grouping did not materially alter them. Long-distance services were, on the North Western, Euston-Birmingham-Wolverhampton HL; Birmingham-Stafford-Crewe to North Wales; Liverpool; Manchester; Carlisle and Scotland. Some Manchester trains ran via Stoke. The Midland had its important York-Derby-Birmingham-Gloucester-Bristol route, and important cross-country semi-fasts to Nuneaton, Leicester and the Eastern Counties. Local services on the North Western were the Harborne Branch, the Perry Barr-Soho Road circular, Walsall and Rugeley via Perry Barr or Soho Road, Sutton Coldfield and Lichfield, some trains running on to Burton, Coventry, Kenilworth and Leamington, Wolverhampton via Dudley Port; the dense network of lines round Walsall and Dudley was served by push-and-pull sets darting in and out between the coal trains around Bescot Junction; there was some

Left: LNWR New Street in LMS days. 'Precursor Tank' 4-4-2T standing at No 2 Platform, with LNER Gresley saloon in background. These engines, dating from 1906, were much in evidence in our period, particularly on the Sutton Coldfield-Lichfield turns. Photograph taken 1936. */ L. W. Perkins*

Below left: LNWR New Street in LMS days, with Bowen-Cooke 4-6-2T No 6957 in early LMS paint style with large numerals on tank sides. These engines came out in 1910, and were very quick off the mark and fast-running. Aston shed had some of them and so did Stafford, but there were fewer of them in the Birmingham area than the 4-4-2 tanks. Photograph taken in 1936. */ L. W. Perkins*

Above right: Midland Railway. New Street, Midland side, with Johnson 2-4-0. The MR at this period, about 1900, printed 'BIRMINGHAM' (Station Street)' on their tickets.

Right: Midland Railway Kirtley 2-4-0 No 18, a regular in New Street until the early 1930s, built 1866. */ The late W. L. Good*

pretty smart working in this area before the Walsall trams and Midland Red buses began to make their impact. The circular service via Soho Road was over the avoiding line built in 1885, the Stechford-Aston spur being part of the same scheme, so that goods traffic could reach Smethwick and the Black Country by taking the Stechford-Aston Spur, then the Soho Road line, thus avoiding New Street. Goods trains were not seen in New Street except perhaps on Sundays if engineering works were afoot somewhere. No stations were built on the Stechford-Aston line, but two, Soho Road and Handsworth Wood, were built on the Perry Bar-Winson Green (Soap Works Junction) line; this had gradients of 1 in 75 and 1 in 66, and a bank engine (two at night) was stationed at Perry Barr.

Midland local services were another circular — New Street, Selly Oak, Lifford Curve, Hazelwell, Camp Hill, New Street; only a few peak-hour trains ran round the circle, which by-passed Kings Norton, an important western suburb and the junction of the West Suburban line with the Camp Hill line. Most of the services on these lines were provided by trains running to and from Redditch, Evesham and Ashchurch. The Midland also operated local services to Walsall via the Sutton Park and Aldridge line, pushing on to Wolverhampton via Short Heath, with a branch from Aldridge to Brownhills, and stopping trains over the main line to Tamworth and Burton and over the Nuneaton-Leicester line. In the earlier part of our period these

Above: MR Class 2 (Rebuilt) and Class 3 (Oil-burning) 4-4-0s Nos 494 and 723 near Kings Norton.
/ The late W. L. Good

Above left: MR rebuilt Johnson 4-4-0 No 531 at Castle Bromwich. Note leading clerestory restaurant car on six-wheel bogies.
/ The late W. L. Good

Left: MR rebuilt Johnson 4-4-0 No 405 at Kings Norton, 1921. The splashers ahead of the leading bogie wheels were to prevent water from the scoop of the leading engine (MR expresses were usually double-headed) reaching the bogie bearings of the second engine. These splashers and the bogie brakes on MR 4-4-0s were soon removed by the LMS.
/ The late W. L. Good

suburban services were run by the Johnson 0-4-4 tanks and various 2-4-0 and 0-6-0 tender engines, but in the twenties and thirties the small tanks, unlike the North Western side, had been ousted by the Class 3P 0-6-4 tanks based on Saltley and Bournville sheds. One met the 0-4-4 tanks pretty well everywhere else on the Midland division of the LMS, but not around Birmingham. The 0-6-4 tanks — which we called 'clockwork engines' or 'hole-in-the-wall tanks' because of the gap in the side-tanks (which reached right to the smokebox) for access to the motion — did some very smart work in and out of New Street, the 1 in 77 up through Five Ways tunnels apparently troubling them not at all, and then very suddenly they were withdrawn. One of them was involved in a derailment between Evesham and Ashchurch, and the engine was blamed because of water surging in the half-full very long tanks. The inspecting officer mentioned at the inquiry that he put his walking-stick through one of the sleepers, so if the track was in that sort of condition the 0-6-4 or any other engine could hardly be entirely to blame for unsteady riding. However, they suddenly left the scene, except for some which were relegated to banking goods trains up through Camp Hill, and were replaced by ex-Tilbury 4-4-2 tanks which had been displaced by new Stanier three-cylinder 2-6-4 tanks. We heard that this was a temporary measure, but temporary or not, the Tilbury tanks were around for a long time and did well — but then, they have some gradients on the Tilbury. Stanier 2-6-2 tanks appeared on the Midland section towards the end of our period, and were highly unpopular in the Birmingham area due to insufficient boiler capacity. Like other early Stanier designs, such as the 'Jubilees', they improved as time went on, but at first they were not the equal of the Fowler 2-6-2 tanks (at first Nos 15500-69, later 1-70), some of which went new to Walsall and replaced the LNW

Radials on the Walsall-Birmingham and associated services. These were very competent engines and were regarded covetously by the Bournville men who made no secret of wanting the Tilbury tanks back.

Bristol main-line trains in the earlier years were worked by Kirtley and Johnson 2-4-0s and Johnson 4-4-0s and 4-2-2s. The Singles continued well into LMS days on piloting (' "M" is for Midland, with engines galore; they have two on each train, but they hanker for more') and Kirtley 2-4-0s Nos 2, 18, 19 and 60 were to be seen at New Street on stopping trains from the Derby direction into the thirties. For a long time the biggest engines on the Bristol turns were the Johnson Class 3 4-4-0s, numbered in the 700s. The Compounds did not go down to Bristol due, I understand, to weight restrictions on Stonehouse viaduct — for which reason the GWR trains running over the Midland were restricted to the 'County' class 4-4-0s — and one saw more of the LMS-built Compounds on the LNW side, on the Wolverhampton-Euston expresses, than on the Midland side of New Street. Eventually this restriction was removed and Compounds and Stanier Class 5 4-6-0s appeared on the Bristol turns, the latter livening things up in no uncertain manner, particularly up the Bromsgrove Bank (the locomen's term for the Lickey incline). Oddly enough, when No 2290, the Lickey banker, went to or from Derby Works, for some reason — could be line availability or could be clearances — she ran via New Street instead of the more obvious Camp Hill line. I saw her pass through on more than one occasion — and it was an occasion when No 2290 appeared, with no little squealing on the severe curves through the tunnels. It would have been a very pretty situation if No 2290 had climbed the rail and 'dropped down on

Below: MR Johnson Class 3 (Oil-burning) 4-4-0 No 766 approaches Halesowen Junction, 1921. / *The late W. L. Good*

Right: MR Class 2 No 519 at wartime Northfield (Halesowen Junction) platform south of the junction, 1921. / *The late W. L. Good*

Below right: MR Class 2 No 522 passing Halesowen Junction (Halesowen line to right) wartime platforms beyond footbridge, 1921. / *The late W. L. Good*

Above: MR Class 2 No 518 leaving Cofton Tunnel, opened out in 1929. Skyline now dominated by the Austin Works. / *The late W. L. Good*

Old England' in Five Ways tunnel — ! With the advent of the bigger engines on the Bristol turns the Class 3 4-4-0s were quickly withdrawn, though the Class 2 4-4-0s, both the Johnson and Deeley rebuilds were around for much longer. Seasonal visitors on the Midland side were some North Staffordshire New L Class 0-6-2 tanks from Stoke, which ran the extra trains to Castle Bromwich for the British Industries Fair, performing very smartly and adding a touch of variety with their deep-toned whistles, a change at any rate from the mournful wail, as of a lost and disembodied soul, of the Midland whistle. At New Street, the Midland wail, particularly at the west end of the station was punctuated by the horn-signals of the shunters; they carried small brass horns, rather like hunting horns, and some of them were real virtuosi with some of their calls to drivers to set back, etc; one would never had been surprised, when standing — as we did by the hour — at the very top end of No 1 Bay, to see a fox pursued by the pack with a Midland 0-6-4 tank in rear heading away into Five Ways tunnel. One was never surprised by anything on New Street.

An outstanding memory for me of New Street was the exhibition in No 3 Bay in 1927 of 'Royal Scot' No 6149, then without name, but later *Lady of the Lake*. It was certainly a good publicity stunt, and to me a never-forgotten thrill to climb up into the cab. The fire had been dropped, and I was astonished to see brickwork — the brick arch — inside the firebox. However, I was to learn fast about locomotives. No 6149 at that date had the huge numerals on the tender, Midland style. This practice was soon after dropped and the number carried on the cab side. Apart from this, one rarely saw the 'Scots' in Birmingham. The LMS named its more important expresses, but only two named trains ran through Birmingham, the 'Pines Express' and 'The Devonian'. The 'Pines' came off the Midland Division and on to the Western Division at Birmingham, and one might get a 'Scot' on this turn to Manchester. Much more likely would be a 'Claughton' or even a 'Prince of Wales'. It is still a puzzle to me why the LNWR did not rebuild the 'Experiment' 4-6-0s into 'Princes' in like manner to the superheated 'Precursors', which were brought into line with the 'George the Fifth' class 4-4-0s. The saturated 'Precursors' were a good engine in their own right, if expensive to run, but the 'Experiments' were outclassed from the start. The 'Princes', a superheated, piston-valve version of the 'Experiments', were a very good engine indeed, smart at getting away, good uphill and fast on the level, and were very much part of the New Street scene. By 1930 the 'Experiments' had been severely thinned out; Walsall had a few, so had Bletchley, and a regular Saturday night working was a Stoke 'Experiment' leaving at 7.30pm. A small clique of us would spend Saturday afternoon on Snow Hill, up to the arrival of the West of England express with a Bristol 'Saint' or 'County', then hare across to New Street to see what Stoke had turned up. Other visitors from Stoke at one period around 1930 were two K class 4-4-2 tanks, LMS Nos 2182 and 2186, which I used to see stepping it out smartly through Great Barr at about 6pm. Another less likely North Staffs loco turned up at New Street one day in 1933, B class 2-4-2T No 1459, to work the 4.08pm to Harborne. I just had time to book a ticket for the train and rode behind her, my only trip behind a North Staffs engine apart from the 0-6-2Ts on the BIF specials. What the Stoke engine was doing on the Harborne train instead of a Monument Lane Radial I never found out. I mentioned the Midland side hunting-horn effects; on the LNW side the engines put up their own sound effects. Apart from their clangorous exhaust beat, the LNWR engines played quite complicated, in fact contrapuntal tunes on the rods, due I believe to the Joy valve gear which was rocked by the connecting rod instead of by eccentrics. Though one could hear this unmistakable LNWR sound anywhere on the system, it was heard nowhere better than at New Street under the great glass roof. It was a quite different sound from the sonorous roll of Midland coupling rods slightly loose on their pins. If the LNW engine had a leaking gland as well it could sound just like a pig being killed.

For many years the station shunters on the North Western side at New Street were a Webb coal tank from Aston at the east end, and a Webb 2-4-2 tank from Monument Lane at the west — almost invariably Nos 6671 or 6672. When not actually dealing with 'tail traffic' they sat on a loop at the top on No 1 Bay, from which platform most of the 'Harborne Expresses' departed.

Frequently, before backing down on to a train in the bay, the North Western engines would stop at the ash-pit in the loop between Navigation Street and Hill Street bridges, and the fireman would knock open the dog-catches securing the lower half of the smokebox door, then, using a fire-iron, knock open the main central wheel-and-lever catch, hastily stepping clear as the smokebox door swung open to reveal the smokebox full to the top of the blastpipe with near white-hot cinders. One was well aware of these cinders when travelling behind a 'Cauliflower' or Radial tank; they could be heard raining down on the carriage roof, and at night seen going past the windows like a 'Brock's Benefit'. Those which didn't go up the chimney got left in the smokebox, and New Street Stour Valley Bay loop was one of the places where they were removed. Photographs reveal that most LNW engines had the lower half of the smokebox door with the paint scorched off, which is not surprising. One of the 2-4-2 tanks from Walsall came to grief one morning about 1935, when it crossed over to the Midland side to use the turntable where the signalbox now stands. The approach road to the turntable was on a steep gradient, and the table was not set for No 6755. Probably due to greasy rails, the brakes picked up and No 6755 high-tailed it into the turntable pit.

Commuters fared rather better for rolling-stock on the Midland than on the LNW. The Midland ran bogie sets with semi-elliptical roofs, but on the LNW side there was a very mixed bag. The three-coach sets were not of uniform stock; one of the brake-thirds might be a low-roof LNW bogie with huge torpedo-ventilators, the compo in the middle an LMS Midland style coach, the other brake-third a LNWR elliptical roof, of rather severe but solidly comfortable appointments, or it might be a new LMS steel-panelled job. At peak hours would emerge some 'Birmingham Strengthening Sets' — more low-roof LNW specimens dating from the very early days of bogie coaches. One exception was a close-coupled set of elliptical-roof six-wheelers which always worked on the Sutton line; these were of relatively modern build, and I believe similar sets worked on the North London services and out to Watford. Possibly this set was one displaced by the Watford electrification.

In the 1930s I used Handsworth Wood station, on the LNWR circle, and did a good deal, in the way of unofficial canvassing and booking of tickets, to keep the station open. By that time the last train to call at Handsworth Wood was the 6.05pm from New Street, generally worked by a 'Cauliflower' 0-6-0, with anything at all for rolling-stock. Generally two coaches, the best it ever achieved was a Caledonian 'Grampian' 12-wheeler, which I, of course, rode in, but sometimes one of those villainous Lancashire and Yorkshire horsehair-seat gaslit bogies turned up; anything could and did run on the 6.05pm. Even a Highland bogie made an appearance one night. On one occasion the driver of the 5.37pm from New Street forgot about Handsworth Wood, slapped the brakes on too late and overran into the tunnel. The guard shouted out, 'Anybody for Handsworth Wood?' and on my answering shout of 'YES!' the driver reversed the 'Precursor', No 5250 *Faerie Queene*, up out of the tunnel and set me down. After that I missed No 5250, a New Street regular, but saw her most improbably later that year in a forlorn row of LNW engines lined up at Llandudno Junction waiting her call to the graveyard. That was the year when I covered all the LNWR branch lines in North Wales (1934) and got in a trip over the Welsh Highland and the Festiniog for good measure. That holiday began from Handsworth Wood, and to my great delight the engine on the first 'leg' to Bescot was an 'Experiment' — No 5508 *Buckland*. If it was to be a North Western holiday, how better to start than with a North Western engine! The 'Experiments' may not have been world-beaters, but they looked good and I liked their names.

Since New Street saw no goods traffic, one had to go elsewhere to see what was going on in that less glamorous department; I was already a hardened cyclist, and quite a few of the 'miles in the legs' were covered between Birmingham and Tamworth or Lichfield Trent Valley, or to Bescot or Bromford Bridge on the Midland. Bescot Junction shed was almost entirely LNWR 0-8-0s, with a few Coal Class 0-6-0s and some of the 19in goods 4-6-0s (a mixed traffic version of the 'Experiment', but much more lively in performance). In store out in the open with the chimneys covered over were two 0-8-2 tanks, Nos 7885 and 7886, which didn't move for years. There was always something on the move at Bescot, apart from the passenger trains on the Grand Junction main line and the South Staffordshire line to Walsall. 0-8-0s would come wheezing in from all directions, with a fair sprinkling of Hughes-Fowler 'Crab' 2-6-0s. These engines by the 1930s were now in black, whereas when new the first of them had come out in red with tender numerals. Such was the state of things in the early thirties that many LMS engines, particularly the LNW 0-8-0s, had the number chalked on the cab side as the painted number was illegible under the grime. I doubt if any other class of engine anywhere would have run at all in the condition of the Gs and G1s, but they kept going regardless, and eventually outlasted all other LNWR engines in service. On the Midland around Birmingham, Bromford Bridge was the place. Again, always something moving — endless coal trains — literally, running 'Permissive Block' on the goods lines, the engine of the next train hard behind the van of the last — with anything from Johnson 2F and 3F 0-6-0s to the 4Fs and the Garratts, sometimes with one of the L and Y 0-6-0s from Saltley adding some variety (about six of the Lankies were at Saltley). The coal trains were for Saltley Gasworks or Nechells Power Station, the wagons lettered 'City of Birmingham Gas Department' or 'Electric Supply Department', with, of course, hundreds of private-owner colliery wagons — ELSECAR, WATH MAIN, HAUNCHWOOD, and legions more, all adding something to the railway scene which today is absent. Those

Above: GWR Snow Hill station, about 1900. 2-4-0 No 197, ex-West Midland 6ft 0in class 106-111, built by Beyer-Peacock 1862, completely rebuilt by GWR at Wolverhampton and renumbered 196-201. No 197 withdrawn 1914. Old Snow Hill station, with Pugin's St Chad's RC Cathedral in background. Note gas-wagon for recharging gaslit coaches.

colliery wagons taught me quite a bit about topography, as I have always hankered after locating place-names: some of those pits took a great deal of locating.

Towards the end of the period, the trains were changing considerably; locomotives of Stanier design were appearing thick and fast, and end-loading steel-panelled coaches with large flush windows were appearing in numbers on the best expresses — beautiful vehicles they were, too — but right up to World War II the pre-grouping flavour had not been dispelled. Apart from Walsall station, which was given a new facade, the stations in the area remained North Western and Midland; bridges showed their L and B or GJR origins in their cast or wrought iron railings — some do to this day — and signals showed their pre-group ownership, even if upper-quadrant semaphores were becoming common. The LMS adopted the LNW style of signal post as standard, but Midland signals, with their distinctive finials, continued to survive, and some still do. A portent was the closing of the Harborne branch to passenger traffic in 1934, though this was not the first closure in the district, as the Midland Walsall-Wolverhampton via Short Heath service had been taken off in 1931, and a number of stations had closed during the LMS era, such as Church Road and Somerset Road on the West Suburban line. So, despite the inroads of the Stanier régime, one could say that the Victorian aura still lingered on the LMS around Birmingham right up to 1939 — and after.

Very different was the scene on the Great Western when I got really acquainted with it in the late 1920s. There was much more precision and snap about the whole thing; Snow Hill was lighter, cleaner and far more efficiently run than New Street, and if you asked for information, you got it — none of the 'No connection

Above: GWR No 1132 *Prince of Wales* 7ft 0in 2-2-2 built 1875 and named in 1896. Snow Hill old station, north end, showing unusual design of roof end-screens, originally glazed. Probably the glass screen offered too much wind resistance and trapped smoke and steam under the already dark unglazed roof.

with the firm next door' here. Although a smaller station in area than New Street, Snow Hill handled almost as many trains, with the goods traffic using the centre roads as well. Points and signals were electrically operated from two large boxes, and all concerned really put a jerk into things.

Snow Hill had not been quite like that in 1900. A good enough station for the traffic then obtaining, but the 1900 GWR service to London was via Oxford and took three hours, and there was no Bristol service. The then 'train shed' was about 30 years old, with a single through passenger platform and through goods line in each direction, and bay platforms each side at the north end. The Birmingham and Oxford line was originally to have run into the LNWR Curzon Street station, but, as previously noticed, Captain Huish's tactics backfired on him and the Oxford line went into Snow Hill, meeting the Birmingham, Wolverhampton and Dudley Railway with access to Shrewsbury and Chester — all becoming part of the GWR — but the LNWR insisted on the viaduct approach from Bordesley to Curzon Street being built, though they well knew it would never be used — could not, in fact, as their New Street line cut it at almost a right-angle near Curzon Street; to this day parts of the Duddeston viaduct still stand as a memorial to the 'ill-conditioned spite of a great railway company against a victorious rival in the old fighting days' (McDermot).

In 1900 the initials 'GWR' were rudely interpreted as 'Great Way Round' in Birmingham, but this was not to remains so. Having got rid of the broad gauge in 1892, the GWR really began to liven things up, all over the system. In the Birmingham area, this involved the rebuilding of Snow Hill, quadrupling the Bordesley viaduct of 56 arches and bringing into use of Moor

Street station in July 1909 for the use of the trains over the North Warwickshire line from Stratford, opened in July 1908. North of Snow Hill the line was quadrupled as far as Handsworth Junction, where the Stourbridge line parts company with the Wolverhampton (Low Level) tracks. Much later, in the early 1930s, the line was quadrupled south to Rowington Junction, so that, Snow Hill tunnel excepted, there were four tracks from Rowington to Handsworth Junction.

The North Western had commenced running two-hour trains to Euston in 1905. They were soon to have competition. With the opening of the new line from Ashendon to Aynho, near Banbury, the distance from Paddington to Birmingham Snow Hill was reduced from 129 to 110 miles, and the GWR put on a two-hour service from July 1910 to the newly rebuilt Snow Hill. They had a far more difficult road, with the gradients through the Chilterns around Risborough and Hatton Bank to contend with, and their trains mostly ran through to Chester and Birkenhead, so the Birmingham service saw the GWR's big 4-6-0s of the 'Saint' and 'Star' classes, with later the 'Castles' and 'Kings', of which latter class six were stationed at Stafford Road, Wolverhampton. The old Birmingham loco shed at Bordesley was replaced by a new shed and works at Tyseley, but as Wolverhampton was the engine-changing point, Tyseley's allocation was mainly goods and passenger tank engines.

In 1900 the Birmingham services were mostly in the hands of various 2-2-2 and 2-4-0 tender engines, the double-frame 4-4-0s of the 'Duke', 'Bulldog' and 'City' and 'Flower' classes being required for the Paddington-West of England services. As the new Churchward engines rolled out of Swindon, however, the 4-4-0s moved up to the Midlands and the 2-4-0s gradually vanished or moved up on to the Cambrian. One occasionally saw a 'Barnum' sandwich-frame 2-4-0 on an Engineer's coach, and a few of the 5ft 2in 3201 and 3501 classes still lurked around Wolverhampton, as late as 1933. One of the 'Barnums', No 3210, staged a remarkable come-back in 1934 when, overhauled and repainted green at Tyseley, she was put to work on the 4.10pm Snow Hill-Stratford, which train had previously worked to

Below: GWR No 363, Armstrong 'First Lot' 0-6-0 built 1866, on Up local train leaving Tyseley about 1920. Note rebuilt Gooch tender and mixed four-wheel stock. Loco withdrawn 1933. */ L & GRP 17714 — Courtesy David and Charles Ltd*

Bristol with a Churchward 'County'. The antique-looking 'Barnums' outlasted the 'Counties' by three years, Nos 3210 and 3222 surviving until 1937. I am glad now to remember that I got in a short ride behind No 3210, but just as glad to remember my first-ever footplate ride (unofficial) around Snow Hill on No 3809 *County Wexford*, the station pilot — and a rough ride it was! The station pilot at Snow Hill was always a big engine which could take on any train in case of a failure — usually a Churchward 'County' or 'Saint'. The very last 'County', No 3834 *County of Somerset*, also staged a memorable come-back when she took a train via Oxford to Paddington in 1933. I happened to be on holiday in London at the time and saw her going past Old Oak. The bush telegraph swung into action, and there was quite a turnout on Paddington, to see her go back to Birmingham — nobody ever expected to see a 'County' in Paddington again, but

Below: GWR No 1195, one of the last survivors of the Armstrong Standard Goods double frame 0-6-0s, built in 1876, in Oxley shed. Withdrawn 1934.

Bottom: GWR No 3210, 'Barnum' class 2-4-0 with sandwich frames, at Tyseley after overhaul. She then made a most unlikely return to virtually express working on the 4.10pm Birmingham-Stratford. Withdrawn 1937.

No 3834 made it. The 'Counties' were always rough-riding engines, which is not surprising with a 30in stroke, outside cylinders and a four-coupled wheelbase. As they ran their mileage out they got even rougher, and one driver told me that his engine was so bad that once he had got away from a stop and had the engine linked up he stood at the front of the tender instead of on the footplate. They are on record, however, as having performed at times quite brilliantly; by Great Western standards they were perhaps not the best engines on the line, but other companies would have been very glad of them. As already mentioned, they were the optimum power units on the GWR Birmingham-Bristol and West services until the restriction on the Midland line from Standish Junction to Yate, over which the GWR had running powers, was lifted in, I think, 1931. Then Bristol 'Saints' appeared for the first time in Snow Hill, and the 'Counties' were quickly withdrawn. However, one evening there was yet another come-back — the 'Penzance' came into Snow Hill, right time, behind one of the few remaining 'Badminton' 4-4-0s, No 4115, formerly *Shrewsbury*.

By the outbreak of World War I there was thus a very different situation on the GWR in the Birmingham area from that obtaining in 1900. In those few years the whole railway was transformed, certainly as regards its main lines (GWR branch lines in some instances remained absolutely idyllic until BR days). As to Birmingham, what had been little more than a provincial out-station was now a first-rate centre competing on equal terms with the LNWR for the London and Chester traffic and with the Midland for the Bristol and West routes, and the new Snow Hill station was a showpiece and remained a fine station until killed off by BR. G. J. Churchward, and C. B. Collett after him, provided the magnificent engines for the new services, which always seemed masters of their work. After the first few staccato barks to get the train on the move, the drivers shut the regulator (with those engines with lever reverse this was necessary anyway), reduced the cut-off and opened up again and speed built up quickly and, by comparison with the LNW, quietly; the outstanding feature of the GWR loco sound was the tick of the vacuum brake pump, particularly on the Churchward 2-cylinder engines were the pump was slung below the offside running-plate. Snow Hill, like New Street, was a good place for sound effects, and I know of no station where a train could make such an entrance, particularly on the Down Main. On the Down Side locking bars, each about 60ft long, were placed in series on all three roads — two platforms and the central goods line — and the flanges of the entering train would send these bars crashing down one after the other in highly theatrical and compelling fashion. The approaches being practically straight, trains entered out of the Moor Street tunnel still with quite some way on them, so that the entrance was sudden and dramatic. I suspect that these locking bars, an early form of track circuiting designed to protect trains standing on the tracks in question, were retained long after they could have been replaced by conventional track circuits probably because someone in the Signal and Telegraph Department, if not someone much more highly placed, liked that bit of stage-management at Snow Hill. Certainly all heads swung round to see what was arriving with such panache. The practice was for Down expresses, travelling at anything up to 80mph, to shut off steam at Tyseley and roll the rest of the way to Snow Hill without touching the brakes until the actual platform pull-up. Still doing a nice speed over Bordesley viaduct, the 1 in 45 of Moor Street tunnel would bring the speed down further; standing on the platform end one could see, if the tunnel was clear, the two headlights suddenly come up over the top of the gradient in the tunnel and the train would enter the station still at the canter; just a touch of vacuum and the engine would stop just clear of Great Charles Street bridge, the girders of which were extended upwards between the tracks. More than once I have seen a 'King' pull up in Snow Hill with a pheasant (a brace of pheasant on one occasion) on the headlamps. These stupid birds would play at being 'last across' somewhere between Leamington and Birmingham. One bird was too badly mangled to be of any use and went on the fire, but the other went in the fireman's lunch box and doubtless came in handy for the week-end.

There was also a short but steep approach to Snow Hill from the north side, of 1 in 50 from the skew bridge under Livery Street up to the platforms, past the signalbox perched high up on a cantilever girder structure. I do not claim that this was unique, but I cannot call to mind any other such box. Thus the exits from Snow Hill were the reverse of those at New Street, the down gradients making for easy getaway with a retarding effect in the other direction. It occasionally happened that an up train was brought to a halt under Livery Street bridge at the bottom of the 1 in 50, and then there were some sound effects. One rarely heard a 'King' really opened up — they didn't have to — but this was one case where they did.

Before the great transformation of the pre-1914 period in the Birmingham area, photographic evidence suggests that the atmosphere would have been much more akin to that which prevailed at Bristol Temple Meads until the great extensions there in the 1930s. On a journey down to Weston-super-Mare, which I did fairly frequently, Bristol was the place to see the real Victorian Great Western, with 2-4-0 and 0-4-2 tanks and Dean 0-6-0s which we only saw in Birmingham rarely, usually heading south for Swindon on their last trip of all. Photographs suggest that in the Birmingham area many local trains were worked by 0-6-0 and 2-4-0 tender engines as much as by tank engines, though the 3600 2-4-2 tanks and the 3900 class, 2-6-2 tanks rebuilt from Dean 0-6-0 tender engines, were represented. The saddle-tanks, whose numbers were legion, were everywhere, of course, and did nearly everything. Most of them, by my time, were rebuilt as pannier tanks, but several of the

Wolverhampton-built 1901 class were still around as saddles. While it was the Churchward and Collett engines which caught the eye, both tender and tank, there would occasionally come sidling into Snow Hill visible reminders of the GWR of Dean's and Armstrong's time, such as the astonishing appearance of No 354, the last survivor of the Beyer-Peacock double-frame 0-6-0s, as pilot on the down Bournemouth one day in 1931. This engine, stationed at Leamington, was the bank engine for Hatton Bank. On this occasion there was apparently trouble with leaking brakes on the Southern stock on this train, and the driver of the Chester 'Saint' required assistance up Hatton. Old 354 came on the front and ran right through to Wolverhampton, returning later that afternoon with the crew, rightly, looking very pleased with themselves. Other double-framed Armstrong 0-6-0s were at Oxley, Nos 22, 1094 and 1195. No 22 was often on a pick-up goods down to Handsworth and Smethwick, and the last I saw of 1195 was a performance even more incredible than 354's — double-heading a 'King', no less, on a down London express to Wolverhampton, through Handsworth Junction and going a sight faster than it had probably ever run before. If the old engine shook all the rivets out of the frames on this trip, what a glorious way to go! Another of the Beyer-Peacocks, originally No 359 but renumbered 323 when rebuilt as a tank, was at Stourbridge Junction, and there was a fair scatter of the Armstrong double-frame 0-6-0 tanks in the district. I saw No 1080 of Tyseley propelling 60 wagons in Small Heath sidings, quite a load for any engine. Tyseley had some of the auto-fitted Armstrong tanks, with fully-enclosed cab, for the Snow Hill-Dudley via Great Bridge motor-trains — the 'Dudley Moke'. These were Nos 1061, 1147, 1169, 1234, 1256 and later 1567. No 1234 was the favourite, and I recall some very unparliamentary language on the part of the crew when a new purpose-built auto-fitted pannier tank, No 5407, appeared on the train in 1932. The 54s were not man enough for the Dudley job, and were soon replaced by the 6400s with 4ft 7½in wheels instead of the 5ft 2in of the 54s. The 64s were better, but the Tyseley men said that compared with the Armstrongs they 'wouldn't pull Pussy'. But the old double-framers really had shaken themselves to pieces and were seen no more, and the 6400s had quite a long innings on the Dudley Moke.

Two other *revenants* from an earlier age were to be seen daily in Snow Hill in the thirties. Each afternoon an empty train of close-coupled four-wheel coaches ran through from Tyseley round to Old Hill and then over the Halesowen line to Longbridge for the Austin works. The engine was usually No 2714, one of the larger Dean saddles now rebuilt as a pannier tank but still with no backboard to the cab, or if not this engine then 2716 or 2753. (This class was the basis for the 5700 class panniers built by the hundred from 1928 onwards.) Why these ancient four-wheelers could not have been left at Longbridge, or Halesowen, or even Old Hill after the early morning trip is a mystery; as the running costs for the empty working all the way back to Tyseley and then out again for the evening trip must have more than cancelled out any earnings from the passengers. I once rose very early in the morning, walked to Handsworth and Smethwick and caught a local to Old Hill and then rode the Austin works train to Longbridge. This was on 31 January 1936 — I still have the ticket, a workman's grey card printed OLD HILL AND LONGBRIDGE and Back. As I would have had to wait at Longbridge until late afternoon, I rode home on a Bristol Road tram, the much-prized ticket going into my collection. I didn't see a thing from the carriage windows, of course, at that hour of a January morning, apart from the unbelievable state of the atmosphere in the compartment. I just have no idea what they were smoking, but the memory lingers on. The other *revenant* was either Nos 3529 or 3557, one of the tiny 4-4-0s rebuilt from, in some cases, broad-gauge 0-4-4 tanks by literally turning the boilers the other way round on the frames and attaching a tender in rear. Some, in addition, were given domeless coned boilers, but Nos 3529 and 3557 carried the domed Belpaire variety. With their sandwich frames they really looked archaic, and we were inclined to be scornful of them, but I like to think now that I knew them well. They came from Kidderminster, and had very small tenders so that they could just get on the turntable at Kidderminster. Their daily appearance at Birmingham was to work a train to Hartlebury and then up the Severn Valley line, and I regret that I never

Below: GWR No 3529, a 3521 class 4-4-0 rebuilt from an 0-4-4 tank, arriving in Snow Hill to work to Hartlebury and the Severn Valley line. Note diminutive tender. Withdrawn 1931. / *The late W. L. Good*

Left: GWR No 3809 *County Wexford* on Up Wolverhampton-West of England express passing Handsworth Junction, where the Wolverhampton and Stourbridge lines converged. Loco withdrawn 1931.
/ L & GRP 17679 — Courtesy David and Charles Ltd

Below left: GWR No 3819 *County of Salop*, a Bristol engine, shunting stock in Snow Hill before going on to the turntable to return with the 4.10pm Bristol and Weston-super-Mare train. Loco withdrawn 1931.
/ The late W. L. Good

travelled behind one of them. Small and slightly comic, perhaps, but they could step out smartly.

For a long time the semi-fasts over the Old Hill line to Stourbridge and Worcester were worked by the 'Bulldog' 4-4-0s. I believe there was a restriction in Old Hill tunnel on any of the big engines, later relaxed. One service over this far-from-easy road was glorified by the title BIRMINGHAM SOUTH WALES EXPRESS, with roof boards to that effect, even if the stock was usually Dean clerestories and the engine a Worcester 'Bulldog'. (To see the Worcester 'Stars' we had to go to Stourbridge Junction or Wolverhampton.) One of the 'Bulldogs' was No 3414 *A. H. Mills*, later renamed *Sir Edward Elgar* — why Swindon had to remove the original name when there were plenty of nameless 'Bulldogs' was never clear — and I had a vague notion that Elgar was something to do with music; the notion became an article of faith when one Wednesday lunch-time I went into Birmingham Town Hall, to shelter from the drenching rain. G. D. Cunningham was giving one of his mid-day recitals on the Town Hall organ, and on the programme was Elgar's Organ Sonata. *Then* I understood; since then the GWR always seemed Elgarian, rather than Edwardian, to me. There is, indeed, a certain facial likeness between Elgar and Churchward; but to me the Elgarian flavour attaches to the whole of the GWR, not just the locomotives. And at Stourbridge Junction, where the Black Country ends, one looked south-west under a bridge towards Elgar's Worcester; the Oxford, Worcester and Wolverhampton line of the GWR must have carried Sir Edward to and from the Faithful City many times. Quite right that a locomotive of his own day, No 3414, should have borne his name. The 'Castle', No 7005, belonged to a later age.

The Great Western was well aware of the existence of railway enthusiasts and catered for them. I have a copy of the 1923 *GWR Locos — Names, Numbers, Types and Classes*, which booklet continued through many editions over the years, together with the famous '10.30 Limited' and other books which certainly helped to create an enthusiast cult. One could keep up to date with the *GWR Magazine*, which also opened one's eyes to many other aspects of railway operation besides the loco side. It was much more difficult to get information about LMS locomotives; the *Railway Magazine* ran a long series of articles dealing with them, but there was nothing official. At Snow Hill, one of the first things to do on arrival for an afternoon's observation was to consult the blackboard in the Telegraph Office, visible through a glass door, where reports of trains running 'T' (Right Time) or how many minutes late were chalked up — and also any specials. Then to the platform kiosk where excursion bills were displayed, for anything new since last time. Sometimes there would be a special, perhaps off the Southern, for Cadbury's chocolate factory at Bournville. This would be met by a fleet of beautifully kept Leyland Lioness coaches in Cadbury's chocolate livery, waiting under Great Charles Street bridge, which coaches were normally used for taking visitors on a tour of the Bournville housing estate, part of the package tour of Cadbury's. The stock for the special, if off the Southern, was on occasions brought all the way up by the Southern engine, an LSWR 4-4-0. We looked at the stranger with a certain degree of unbelief that such a relatively small engine could cope with a 10-coach train up Hatton, but years later I was to see one of the small mixed-traffic LSWR 4-4-0s move a train of 18 bogie vehicles out of Southampton Central round to the Terminus station with no trouble at all. There were other occasions when Southern 4-4-0s ran up to Wolverhampton with relief portions of the Dover or Bournemouth expresses; the only other strangers seen in Snow Hill were some Hughes-Fowler Moguls off the Central Division of the LMS in 1933, when for some reason the LMS locos ran through to Snow Hill on excursions to, I think, Bournemouth. The Moguls then went to Tyseley and returned later. I have a record of LMS Nos 13011 and 13014 on these turns, and the return trip coincided with the departure on the Down Relief of a Worcester 'Bulldog' on the 'South Wales'. I saw the two trains coming up the 1 in 100 through Handsworth and Smethwick, the 'Crab' on the Down Main and the 'Bulldog' on the Relief, with the 'Bulldog' leading by half a train's length and getting the better of the situation, but with a lighter train and a crew who doubtless knew the road better than the visitors off the 'Lanky'. However, I more than once saw the 'Dudley Moke' on the Relief temporarily overhaul a 'King' on the Main until the bigger engine with its vastly bigger load had really got going; the 'Dudley Moke' would have been checked at Handsworth Junction where the four tracks became double-track only to Wolverhampton and to Stourbridge, but it was fine while it lasted.

Birmingham saw the three French Compounds frequently on the through expresses from Dover and Bournemouth, but they must have disappeared just before I became actively concerned. I am sorry to have missed them, though I probably did see them when much younger, but have no positive recollection. The Southern trains were worked by Oxford and Chester 'Saints', including the pioneer No 2900 *William Dean*, and I did get in a ride behind this notable engine, even if only as far as Wolverhampton. It came as a severe shock when the 'Saints' began to be scrapped early in the thirties — the scrapping of relatively modern engines like the 'Counties' was bad enough; we thought engines like that would go on forever, and only the small and ancient locos were for scrapping. On top of all this, news of the first 'Star' to go, No 4006 *Red Star*, really rocked us. From 1928, however, the 'Halls' were rolling out of Swindon in greater numbers even than the 'Castles'; initially they were in replacement of the 'Flowers' and 'Cities'; then the 'Saints' and 'Bulldogs' began to disappear, but many of both these classes survived World War II, the 'Bulldogs' in some cases staging a highly improbable comeback as 'Dukedogs', the first being

No 3265 *Tre Pol and Pen*, a former Snow Hill regular, reappearing with the straight frames from No 3365, but then migrating to the Cambrian section.

On two Sundays in 1932, 10 and 24 April, a pneumatic-tyred railcar, the 'Micheline' visited Birmingham, at New Street on the first date and Snow Hill on the second, presumably as part of a tour. I saw it at Handsworth and Smethwick on the 24th, where it made a special stop for a number of bowler-hatted gentlemen from the Birmingham Railway Carriage and Wagon Works to inspect it. As I was honorary platform staff at this station I was allowed on the platform, but a sizeable crowd had collected up at the cattle-dock roadway, which incidentally had a long steel fence built of old broad-gauge bridge rail. My recollection is of acceleration such as I had never seen before or since on the railway as the 'Micheline' took off (nearly!) in the West Bromwich direction. The GWR did not order any, but my guess is that it set them thinking, for not long afterwards the first of the GWR-AEC railcars came out.

Despite growing tram and bus competition, there was still increasing suburban traffic on the Great Western; the

Below: GWR No 3920, a 2-6-2 tank rebuilt from Dean 0-6-0 No 2502, on a train of Dean clerestory coaches leaving Stourbridge Junction. Loco withdrawn 1931.
/ L & GRP 17570 — Courtesy David and Charles Ltd

quadrupling of the line, already referred to, to Rowington Junction was accompanied by an allocation of new 5100 class 2-6-2 tanks to the Birmingham area sheds, which already had many of the Churchward 3100 series, now renumbered as 5100 class. They displaced the nearly new smaller 4575 class 2-6-2 tanks which had ousted the 3600 2-4-2Ts and the 3900 2-6-2Ts, a few of which were still around carriage shunting, however. The 45s in many cases moved to Bristol, so that Birmingham was almost entirely served by the 5100 class, than which no more competent suburban engine has appeared on any railway. With their moderate-sized 5ft 8in wheels and long 30in stroke one could feel them really getting into their stride by the pressure of the seat squabs in the small of the back — the motion could in fact be uncomfortable if the driver was a bit down and trying to get 'Right Time' again, but the 51s were a real investment.

Except for summer Saturdays there was plenty of goods traffic through Birmingham. Among the regular turns were the ironstone trains from the Banbury area going up to Stewarts and Lloyds, Wrexham, and the Brymbo steelworks. These trains were usually worked by the 2600 'Aberdare' 2-6-0s with double frames, not the prettiest engines on the GWR but good at their job. The GCR type ROD 2-8-0s took a share of this work — good engines, but not the equal of the GWR 2800 class 2-8-0s which were rather rare in Birmingham. The RODs were rated as equal to an 'Aberdare' by the men, though perhaps the LNER men with the same engines — the 04s in LNER parlance — would not have gone along with this. Around 1931/2 a frequent sight in an up goods would be one or two new 5700 class pannier tanks, being worked dead to Swindon from the makers, either Kerr Stuart or Bagnalls of Stafford, without coupling rods or motion, and at Handsworth and Smethwick one would see new Tube stock for the London Underground Group leaving the Birmingham Railway Carriage and Wagon works to be hauled south, or stock for foreign railways going up probably to Liverpool for shipment, after first being checked for clearance. One goods which the cognoscenti always waited for was 'The Meat' — its official title; the GWR named quite a few of its regular fast goods — from Birkenhead to Smithfield. This came up through Birmingham at just before 9pm and the engine would be a London 'Star' or 'Castle' even, or one of the 5ft 8in 4700 class 2-8-0s, running at not much less than express passenger speed. This, of course, was a fitted freight, and we thought the guard in the rocking van must have seen service in the Royal Navy, probably in destroyers, because no ordinary mortal could have withstood the motion. However, he would most probably be on the rear platform exchanging a wave with the signalman, apparently impervious to it all. A GWR guard during World War II in fact told me that the best place to be in during an air raid was the brake van of a goods in motion. There was so much racket from the van that you were entirely unaware of what might be breaking loose outside.

GWR publicity was always very good, but if they wanted to keep something quiet they were just as good at that. One Sunday morning in 1934 four 'Kings', running in two pairs abreast of each other on adjacent tracks were run at over 60mph over the new steel skew bridge over the Warwick Road, Olton, for deflection tests. Not a word leaked out; the first we knew of it was a photograph, somewhat touched up, in the *GWR Magazine*. Had the 'Buzz' got about, the whole district would have been crawling with people, and someone, of course, would have been injured or killed. But no one blew the story and the photograph shows an empty landscape.

With the completion of the quadrupling to Rowington, the GWR programme was complete. However, not only had track improvements taken place, but great improvements in handling goods traffic had been carried out, among which was the building of a fine depot and warehouse at Soho and Winson Green, and the extension of Hockley goods depot. There was a difference in coal trains on the GWR compared with all the other companies — the employment of GWR-owned 20-ton steel coal wagons, rented out to coal-owners, so that one saw less of the wooden-frame 10- and 12-ton private owner wagons than on the LMS. The GWR were also very keen on containers, and really pushed this traffic long before the present trend for putting everything into a container got under way. A detail of GWR Road Motor Dept practice is worth going on record — the employment of Karrier 'Cob' — or Scammell Mechanical Horse — three-wheel tractors to assist the heavy horse drays from the Parcels Department under Snow Hill station, up Snow Hill itself — quite a pull. It was then a granite sett road surface, and it was quite a sight to see one of these equipages nip out between the buses and trams with the horse striking sparks from the setts and the combined tractor and horse really attacking the gradient. If they got a clear run up they would swing round into Colmore Row where the 'assisting engine' would uncouple and run back light for the next load.

Below: GWR No 2867 entering Snow Hill past Northwood Street sidings up the 1 in 50. A post-World War II photograph, but apart from new signalbox on left unchanged from the interwar years. Original Cantilever signalbox still in situ. / *R. T. Coxon*

Churchward's progressive outlook was reflected not only in the Locomotive Department but also on the coaching side. Permanently-coupled suburban sets were the order before World War I, the Birmingham sets being of four coaches of the 'top-light' variety, some being 70ft examples, unique in suburban coaches. These were supplemented in Collett's time with steel-panelled bow-ended coaches of 57-60ft length; there were many of these sets, and there was a high degree of uniformity in the local trains serving the Birmingham area. The standard train was a 5100 class 2-6-2 tank on a four-coach set or two sets at peak hours. Business was particularly good on the Leamington to Birmingham service, and trains arriving at Snow Hill rapidly disgorged their load and were on their way either as empty stock to Northwood Street Sidings or reversed into one of the north end bays to go on to Stourbridge. Among the Snow Hill ticket collectors, stationed at the top of the wide flight of steps up from platform level, was one man, who, it is said, could detect someone with a 'bad' ticket — out of date, or defaced with intent to defraud — before the person even began to climb the steps. Something slightly over-casual in the approach, perhaps, but this man was their match; it took a real master-criminal to put one over him.

At Moor Street station, which catered mainly for the locals off the North Warwickshire line from Stratford-on-Avon, traversers were installed for the engines. A train having arrived, the engine would cut off and move on to the traverser which would then transfer the engine laterally to the adjacent road to run round the train. This took up less space, of which there was none to spare, than a crossover. Snow Hill had one of these traversers, though of the radiating variety, or 'sector-table', at the inner end of the two Down bay roads; I never saw it used — in fact, an old goods brake stood on it for the use of passenger guards and carriage examiners.

During the great post-Broad Gauge years before 1914, a very definite GWR style of architecture was evolved, red brick being the dominant material. Used for buildings great and small, it certainly stood the test of time, and among the new buildings of this period were the locomotive depots at Tyseley, Stourbridge Junction and Oxley, all being of the turntable variety, as were many other GWR sheds. Stafford Road, Wolverhampton, was not rebuilt, and a visit to this shed was a slightly ghostly experience — dark, and, for the GWR, decrepit. Not the sort of place to come across a 'King' — one would not have been surprised to see some of the 'Sir Daniel' 2-2-2s still around, or some archaic Shrewbury and Birmingham survival, long forgotten like some of the way-back examples at the far end of Swindon 'Dump' in the 1930s, which survived the breakers' torches for years because they never got near enough to the back end of the Dump before more locos from South Wales, etc, came into take the spaces occupied by the engines they had only just cut up. Across the Stafford Road were the Wolverhampton

Works, rebuilt in 1932 on very modern lines. Formerly a loco building centre, the last locos built there being the 4ft 1½in 4400 class 2-6-2 tanks and the first 20 of the 4500 class 4ft 7½in in 1905/6, it had since been used for repairs only. Now completely rebuilt, it could deal with all but the largest classes, though it continued to handle moderate-sized examples up to, say, the 4300 class 2-6-0s. There were usually some surprises there off the Cambrian section, and I even saw one of the ex-MSWJ 0-6-0s there from Cheltenham.

To conclude this survey of the railway scene, it should be said that on the Great Western there was progress along the well-established lines set by the great regeneration of the railway in the pre-1914 years, which the 1923 Grouping affected hardly at all — as a cartoon in the *GWR Magazine* of that period reflects, the subject being a GWR porter, the caption reading, 'Never even blew me 'at off!' The GWR was changing with the times, but to the GWR pattern. Over on the LMS, the task of unifying such a much bigger empire, with in some cases definite hostility between constituents, was a very different proposition, and the sort of changes which the GWR had instituted in the early 1900s were only just beginning to emerge in the late 1930s after the depression of the late 20s and early 30s. Certainly no one in 1939 could have visualised the railway scene of the 1970s, with Snow Hill and the GWR line virtually erased, New Street rebuilt out of all recognition and the Euston line electrified with the trains 'doing the ton' up to London in 90 minutes.

Below: GWR 'Hall' class 4-6-0 on Up train at No 7 Platform looking into Moor Street Tunnel. A post-World War II photograph included as it shows the scene unchanged from our period and vividly captures the atmosphere of this great but now vanished station.
/ *The late W. H. Perry*

Steam Tram Metropolis and Transformation Scene

Above: BMMO Co Ltd SOS 'QC' coach 1927, HA 3668.

The character of man is a mass of opposites and contradictions — the capacity for unlimited self-sacrifice and kindness, and for cruelty which leaves the most savage animals nowhere at all; infinite capacity for ingenuity and industry, and unbounded idleness on the other hand. There are many other facets of the human anima, but perhaps it is these two opposites of industry and idleness which are reflected in the passenger transport business. It could be said that passenger transport began with the introduction, who knows how far back, of the litter or stretcher — still with us today. This vehicle was surely the first conveyance by which one person was toted about by the efforts, under compulsion, doubtless, of two others; the whole history of the industry has been of improvement after improvement, and it is still going on. The fastest vehicle will usually win out, but in the long run it is the vehicle which will occasion least trouble and effort to the traveller which will come out best. When, nearly 150 years ago, the railways began to take shape, country people who would have had to walk 10 or more miles to the market town were glad enough to have to walk only two or three miles to a railway station; 50 years ago the buses began to penetrate to the villages and hit the country railway stations. Now most country people — and townsfolk — have their own transport and the country bus is well on the way to becoming a figure of history. And each successive improvement takes a bit more of the adventure of travelling away — indeed, to many travelling has long been no sort of adventure but a necessary bore — and if we ever arrive at the 'Star Trek' style of personal transport, 'beaming up' or 'beaming down', then all the adventure will have gone. 'To travel hopefully is a better thing than to arrive' — how right Stevenson was!

In 1900 Birmingham and the Black Country were the Steam Tram Metropolis. Lancashire and Yorkshire had quite a few steam undertakings, London and Bristol, after brief trials, would have none of it; it was Birmingham which made the steam tram its own. It was Edinburgh for cable trams and Manchester and Glasgow for electrics, far more so than London which despite having the largest electric fleet of over 2,000 cars had over 5,000 motor buses by 1930.

Despite being reputedly dirty and noisy — though not necessarily so — steam trams were faster and could cope with more passengers than horse trams or buses. It is on record that a Birmingham and Aston Tramways driver was booked for reckless driving with a steam tram, doing no less than 15mph on the Witton route — which would be quite alarming on one of those things, I imagine. And as usual, the people who had grown up with them preferred them to anything else, just as many today mourn the disappearance of the steam locomotive, despite the undisputed greater speed, efficiency and availability of electric and diesel traction. Today, the Bristol-Birmingham trains consisting of a diesel and 11 coaches come thumping up the Lickey unassisted, speed dropping to perhaps 40mph near the top, with most of the passengers not knowing or caring about coming up the famous incline. But the adventure has gone out of it! It was always the major thrill of the journey — witness the heads craning out of carriage windows on every train — to see whether it was 2290 or a brace of 'Jinties' coming on behind, then the crow whistles, and then blast-off; finally, out came the heads again at Blackwell to see the bankers drop off, and 18 or 20mph at Blackwell was good going. My father told me of touch-and-go trips on the steam trams on the Wheeler Street line to Lozells on wet nights, with the conductor throwing ash under the loco wheels to help get up the gradient if they had a full load up. Sometimes they did and sometimes not, in which case drop back and take another run at it! The electrics which replaced them, like the diesels on Lickey, took the gradient as though it didn't exist.

Birmingham in 1900 was predominantly steam, however, with horse trams on the Nechells route, battery-electrics on Bristol Road (1890) and cable trams (1888) from Colmore Row to New Inns, Handsworth. Although the original horse tramways to Handsworth and Bournbrook in the 1870s had been laid to the standard 4ft 8½in gauge, the 3ft 6in gauge was imposed by the

Below: City of Birmingham Tramways Co Ltd (CBT Co Ltd) Falcon locomotive and trailer at Hill Street, the loading point for Moseley. The kerbside loading arrangement was on account of the sweep of the curve from John Bright Street; this may well have influenced the Corporation's very early use of kerbside loading in the city Centre. / *Alec C. Jenson*

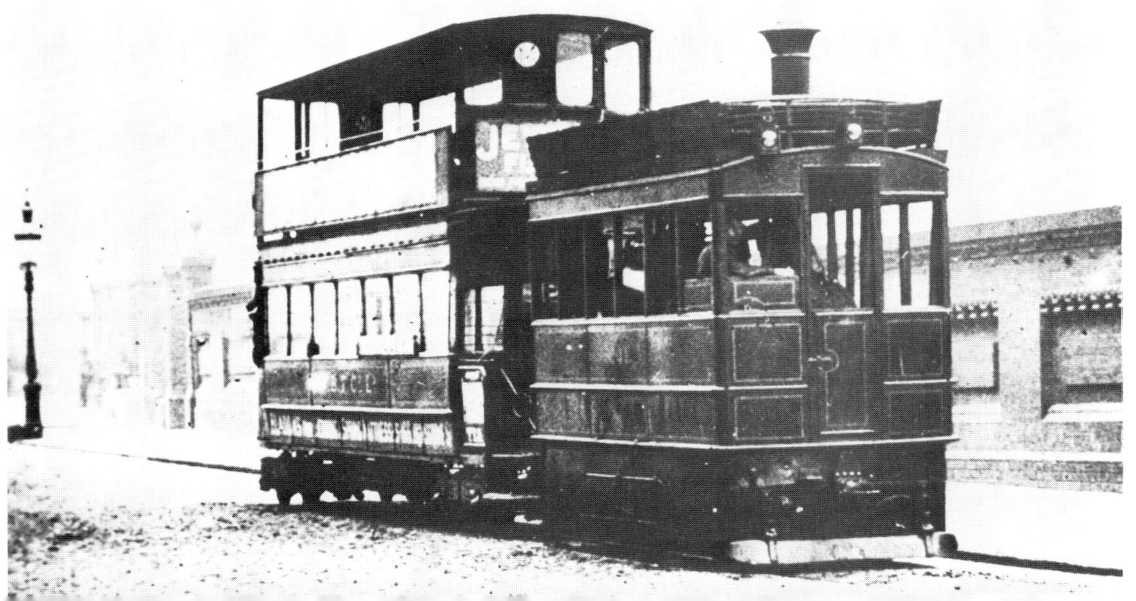

Above: CBT Co Ltd Kitson locomotive with two gas wagons for tramcar lighting, turning into Bradford Street from Smithfield Street. Drovers' Arms in background. Smithfield Street was part of a connecting line via Meriden Street and Park Street to Albert Street and the Nechells line.

Board of Trade for the Birmingham and Aston Tramways Company which began steam operation in 1882 and this became the gauge for all routes in the city, the horse lines being reconstructed when converted to battery and cable operation. The only other exceptions to the 3ft 6in gauge in our area were the Dudley, Sedgley and Wolverhampton Tramways Company. Its steam route and the Wolverhampton Tramways Company Limited horse tramways, were built to 4ft 8½in gauge but reconstructed to 3ft 6in gauge for electric traction, so that Birmingham, the Black Country companies and Wolverhampton and Walsall Corporation tramways constituted quite easily the most extensive narrow-gauge network in the British Isles.

In Birmingham from the outset the Corporation had been the owners of the tracks, operation being on lease to companies. By 1900 these companies were three in number, the Birmingham and Midland Tramways Limited, operating from Lionel Street (Parade) along the Dudley Road, and the City of Birmingham Tramways Company Limited running on most of the main roads, and the Birmingham and Aston Company. The days of company operation were numbered, however; Birmingham Corporation, having eventually agreed to overhead wires on the Bristol Road for the CBT Company in 1901, after years of arguments about conduit operation, itself went into tramway operation in 1904 on the Aston route with the 20 cars of the famous and well-loved 'Aston Bogie' class. Before the outbreak of World War I in 1914, Birmingham Corporation operated all tramway routes in the city.

By the turn of the century it had been realised in London that surface transport could not cope with the traffic, and the Tube network was beginning to take shape, and there was already a great suburban network of main-line railways, many of which were electrified and are still in business. Not so in Birmingham. The main-line railways in Birmingham for the most part do not lie convenient to main roads, and the first suburban stations out from New Street or Snow Hill were quite some distance from the city centre, Five Ways on the Midland being about the closest in. Although some suburban services did well, Birmingham has never been railway-orientated for its suburban traffic like London and some other cities. Instead, it took to the trams, even if there was a lack of connections in the centre. Even so, Birmingham's tram routes with only a few exceptions served only the main roads, unlike Manchester or Liverpool where there were much denser tramway networks and vastly better central connections. Nevertheless, Birmingham's trams dominated the scene until 1930, when No 843, the last new tram for Birmingham, entered service. By that time the Corporation bus fleet had built up to about 300 strong, and in the Black Country the company trams had given place to Midland Red buses or those of Wolverhampton, Walsall and West Bromwich Corporations, the Birmingham-Dudley and Wednesbury services, still operated by Birmingham trams, excepted.

What was Birmingham like in 1900? Photographs can do much to give us the flavour of those days; certainly there is now little visible evidence left of the Birmingham of nearly 80 years ago, but if one would develop further the picture of Joe Chamberlain's Birmingham, Marjorie Hessell Tiltman's 'Quality Chase' and the novels of Francis Brett Young — an author at present sadly neglected — will supply the necessary background apart from being first-class literature in their own right. In Brett Young's *A Man About the House* the trams of North Bromwich (Birmingham, of course) figure in the story, running along the Halesby (Hagley) Road. In *Dr Bradley Remembers*, the Black Country is marvellously written up, and there are countless other touches in Brett Young's very considerable output.

The steam trams seemed to fit the Victorian Gothic landscape of Joe Chamberlain's Birmingham admirably, equally so the cinderous murk of the heavy industry of the Black Country. In their 20-odd years' stint they did well, and the vagaries of the climate apparently troubled them little. Snow ploughs were unnecessary, as the heat from the ashpans of the locos kept the tracks clear of snow, and in fog — the kind described in the railway section — the drivers kept the bell going and pressed on. However, quite obviously, the smoke nuisance and the necessity of the engine running around the car at termini, or reversing round a triangle or where possible running around a loop terminal were drawbacks which set operators seeking for other means of mechanical traction, and the alternatives in Birmingham, the battery and cable cars, were at least cleaner and quieter. Of the two, the cable cars had the longer run. The electric motors and accumulators of 1890 were of limited efficiency and the weight of the batteries meant that a fearful dead weight was being moved around. Batteries today are heavy enough, but those of the 1890 era were far heavier, the weight making itself felt all the more as the charge ran down.

It was not unknown for batteries to run completely flat, leaving the car stranded until either freshly charged accumulators could be brought up or the car propelled to the terminus by one or more following cars — which in turn would 'cane' their batteries. Complaints from passengers about the acid fumes were frequent, some becoming quite ill, which is readily understandable, and altogether the Bristol Road accumulator cars were only a partial success. They did demonstrate, however, that the electric motor was an excellent means of propulsion, and doubtless the Leeds people and the South Staffs company took a good look at Bristol Road before deciding on the overhead trolley system, which had already made its debut in the United States in the late 1880s. It is rather odd that Bristol Road, a tree-lined and gracious thoroughfare of Georgian and Regency residences, should have been the venue for Birmingham's first public transport, the horse-bus of 1834, and one of the first horse tramways in 1876, running out to Bournbrook with nearly a mile of undeveloped country in those days before reaching the terminus at the Gun Barrels. There was some industry at Bournbrook, the Birmingham Battery Company, but the area was better served by the Midland Railway at Selly Oak than by the trams at the bottom of the hill.

The Handsworth cable line was to be the only example of its type in the Midlands. While on the whole reliable, it too had its disadvantages if any complicated junction work had to be negotiated, which in Birmingham was not the case. In this respect the cable system suffered similarly to the 'atmospheric' railway, in that pointwork was next to impossible. (In view of all the many crazy ideas put forward at various times for operating trams, it is odd that nobody to my knowledge thought of giving the 'atmospheric caper' another trial on street tramways. My father, who had something to do with the design of the zip fastener, always said that if that device had been available in Brunel's time the atmospheric South Devon Railway might have worked!) Cable track was costly to install and maintain, and as the cable wore out it became a problem. When a strand of the cable broke, it snarled up round the 'gripper' of the next car along so that the brakeman — he was hardly the driver — could not release the gripper and therefore could not stop the car. Before long he would be catching up with the car in front, unless his conductor had managed to reach a telephone — not many telephones in those days — and told the engineman at Hockley depot to stop the cable, and then the whole shooting-match stopped until a repair gang arrived, lifted the cable, unsnarled the gripper and spliced the cable, all of which might take several hours. Towards the end of their lease on the Handsworth line the

Right: The CBT Co Ltd Colmore Row (Grand Hotel) terminus of the Handsworth cable tramway, taken from the Blue Coat School.

Below right: CBT Co Ltd cable track-laying, Holyhead Road-Booth Street corner, 1888/1889. Although antedating our period, this photograph is included as of great interest. Note similarity in construction to the London conduit track.

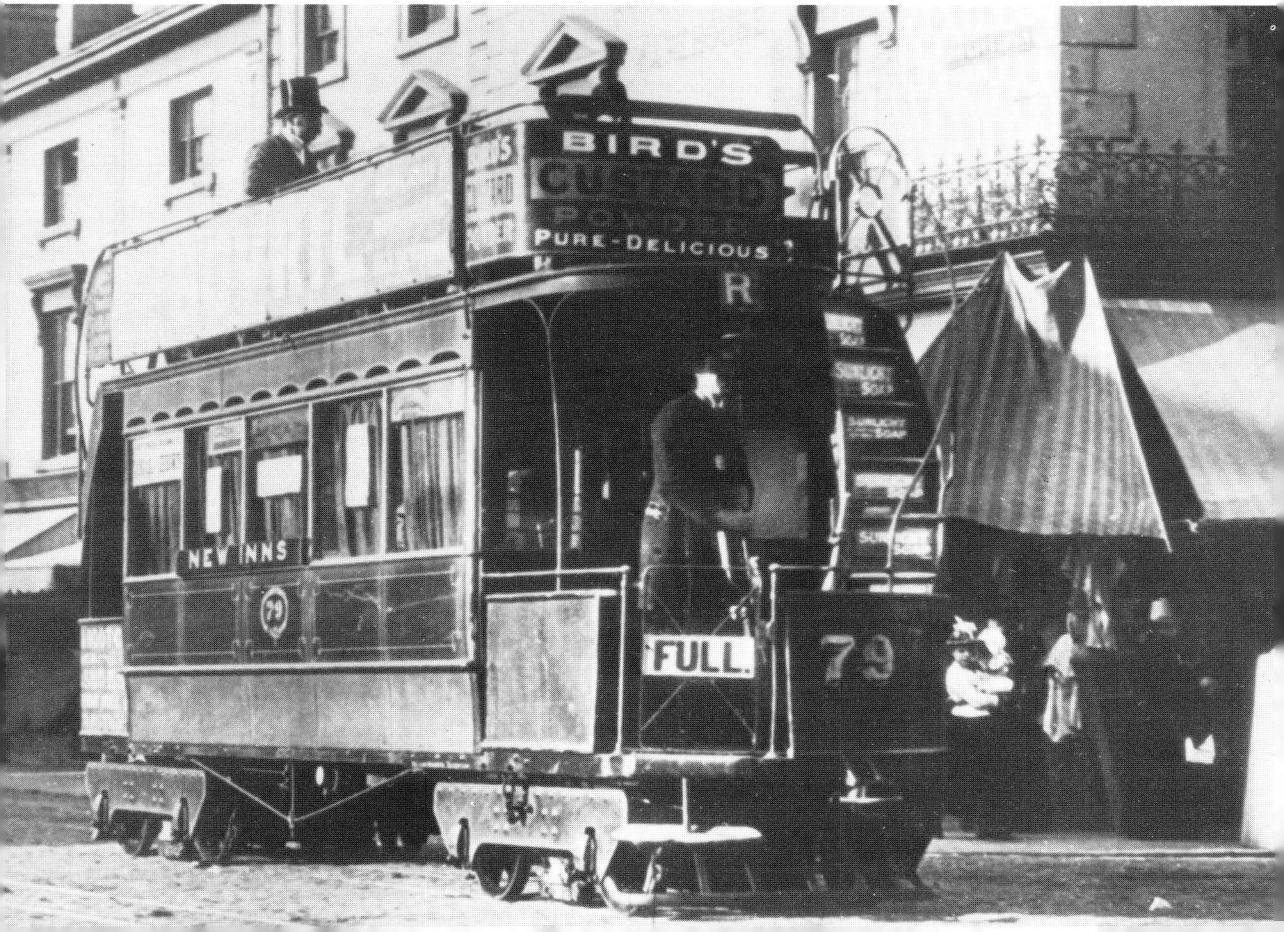

BIRD'S
CUSTARD
POWDER
PURE-DELICIOUS
R
NEW INNS
FULL.
79

Left: CBT Co Ltd cable car No 116 descending Snow Hill about 1900, before the rebuilding of the station had begun.

Below left: CBT Co Ltd cable car No 79 at Hockley Brook. Bogie details, including slipper brake, show up well in this photograph. The drawn curtains and top-hatted upstairs passenger impart an air of some mystery.

CBT Company, knowing their time was drawing near, were not going to the expense of a new cable and the service became very erratic.

The rolling-stock for the Bristol Road battery line and the Handsworth cable route was very similar. Both lines had bogie open-top cars with half-canopies over the platforms, the battery cars (CBT Nos 101-112, built by Falcon) having six bays, while the cable cars were slightly shorter five-bay bodies, Nos 75-94 being Falcon built and Nos 95-100 Metropolitan. These first 26 cars were for the Colmore Row-Hockley section opened in 1888, while for the extension to Handsworth New Inns in 1889 they were joined by Nos 113-118 (Falcon) and 119-124 (Metropolitan) these following the numbers of the battery cars. The bodywork style of these cable and battery cars could be described as short open-top versions of the steam trailers, with similar platform arrangements, the step being at the corner of the platform instead of at the side. Then followed 10 more cable cars, Nos 141-150, which, incredibly, were of single-deck cross-bench toast-rack design; a less suitable route for such cars would be hard to imagine, and they seem to have seen little service as cable cars. A photograph of one in Hockley depot yard shows it in rather forlorn state, and no commercial card showing one on the route has come to light, though plenty exist of the open-top cars. They were transmogrified into electric toast-racks for the Kinver Light Railway, and even there they underwent a third transformation, being rebuilt as solid-side conventional single-deckers and used mostly on the Kingswinford routes. Whoever thought up toast-racks for the Hockley route was an incurable optimist. However, more cars became necessary, and Nos 172-177, built by the CBT Company were put on in 1906, these being still short-canopy open-top bogie cars, but with four-bay bodies very closely resembling those of the Bristol Road overhead electrics Nos 151-171. This again is another minor mystery; one would have thought that some of the Bristol Road battery cars, replaced by the overhead cars in 1901, would have readily converted into cable cars — some at least ran as steam trailers, still open-top, and by 1906 the company would have been aware that their time was running out. Yet these six new cars were turned out with only a few years to go, and did not reappear, so far as anyone knows, rebuilt as electrics either on the Black Country system — where many ex-CBT cars migrated after company operation had finished in Birmingham — or elsewhere, such as the Devonport system where some CBT cars were transferred. Presumably they were broken up with the rest of the cable stock when operation finished in 1911, but I have always felt that there might be something more to be discovered about these six nearly new car bodies. A cable-car body has survived as a garden summer-house in Smethwick, and is now in the care of the Black Country Museum, but this is one of the five-bay cars.

For a time the Birmingham Corporation electric cars which took over from the cables continued to run over the cable tracks,

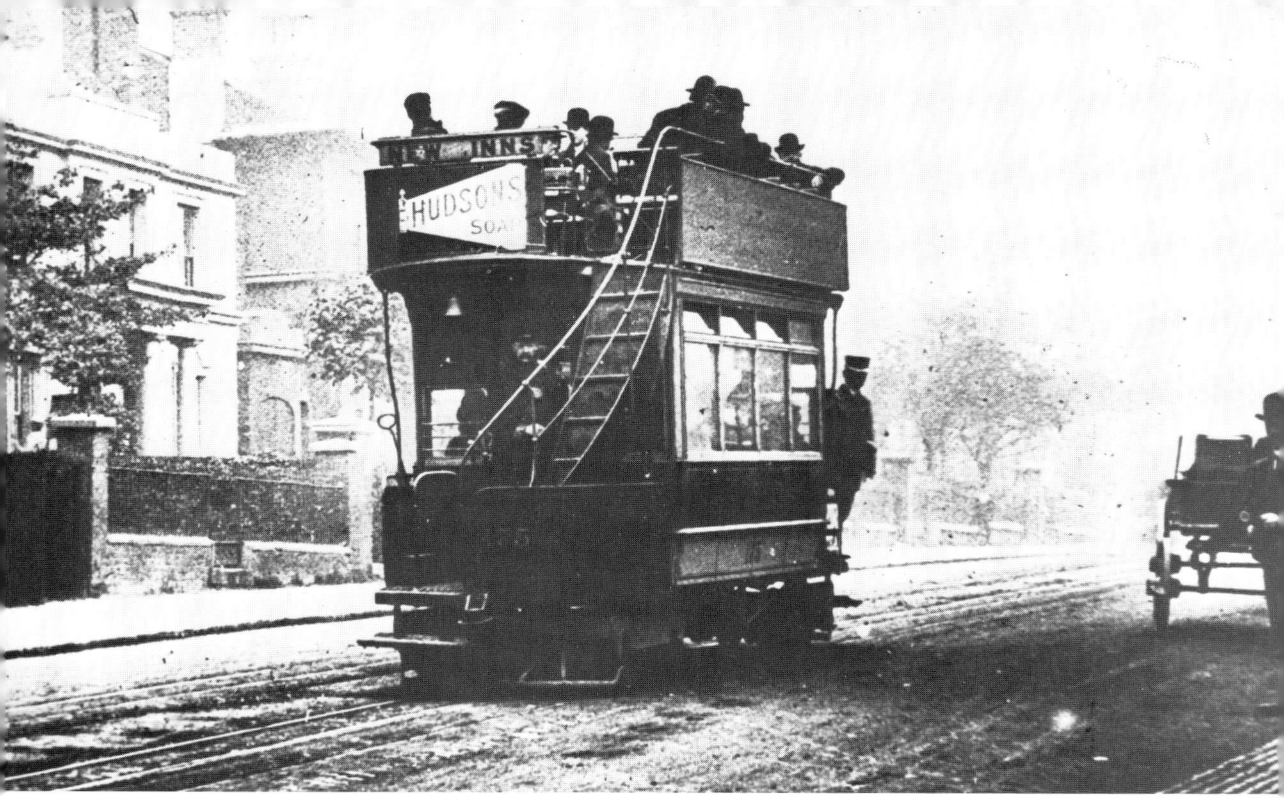

NEW INNS
HUDSONS SOAP

BAKER'S BLACK LEAD
IT RECOMMENDS ITSELF
BIRD'S
CUSTARD
POWDER
PURE-DELICIOUS
104

Left: CBT Co Ltd cable car No 175, one of the 1906 four-bay cars, at the Roebuck, junction of Soho Hill and Hamstead Road, then a good address.

Below left: CBT Co Ltd Bristol Road battery car No 104, still carrying BCT Co inscription, at Suffolk Street terminus. Overhead poles in position for the conversion of 1901. */ Alec G. Jenson*

with quite some problems over loss of voltage due to the unbonded joints. A photograph taken near the New Inns shows a Birmingham Corporation open-top 21 class car running on the cable track, with a track gang in the background evidently re-laying with all speed. The cast-iron yokes were left buried, and when only a few years ago excavations were being made at Hockley for the flyover, and at Snow Hill for St Chad's Circus, the contractors were highly puzzled by these cast-iron affairs which their drills kept encountering. Some Tramway Museum Society members were able to enlighten them, and one yoke — very similar to those for the LCC Conduit system — is in the Birmingham Museum of Science and Industry, while others found their way to the Tramway Museum at Crich. Hundreds more still lie beneath the A41 from Snow Hill to New Inns. The two cables were worked by steam winding engines at Whitmore Street Depot, Hockley, one for the Colmore Row-Hockley section and the other for Hockley-New Inns, it being necessary for the brakeman to jump the cables at Hockley Brook. The winding-engine building still survives, being the single-storey block to the east of the running sheds, easily visible today from the Hockley Flyover and used as the ticket and stationery stores of the Birmingham Corporation Tramways and their successors. The cars were shunted on and off the cable line into Whitmore Street by steam tram engines, some of which, of course, had to be retained for this purpose after steam operation finished at the end of 1906. It might have been possible for cars coming off service in the up direction, towards Birmingham, to run back by gravity over the trailing junction into Whitmore Street, but it was a sharp curve, and knowing from experience in the early days at Crich how much more effort is required to manhandle a tram round a curve as compared with a straight run, I rather doubt it. However, at the Colmore Row terminus, nearly opposite the Grand Hotel, the cars began the return run by gravity right round the corner into Snow Hill, picking up the cable at the top of that street, and the same applied at the New Inns where the terminus again was on a rising gradient. There would therefore have been little for the brakeman to do apart from keeping a general eye on things and executing the one jump at Hockley, as compared with the very great skill required in getting through junctions on the Edinburgh and San Francisco cable systems.

Before moving on to the next development, two other non-passenger (officially, anyway) cable lines ought to be mentioned, these being 2ft gauge colliery tramways of quite some length, one at Hamstead Colliery with two branches, and one from Jubilee Colliery to Sandwell Colliery. The Hamstead line had one branch running nearly to the top of Hamstead Hill to a coal-wharf just below where Vernon Avenue now enters Hamstead Hill, with a culvert under the LNWR, the other branch running up to the Tame Valley Canal and to the great spoil-bank which has now completely disappeared. The Hamstead Hill wharf was to save the horses the slog up Hamstead Hill, but motor lorries gradually put it out of business and the line closed in the mid-thirties when the Hamstead Hall estate went for building. I and a school companion who lived at one of the wharf houses used to ride illicitly on the empty tubs going back to the pit, but ready to make a smart getaway if we saw any miners walking up the track. On this line the cable ran on sheaves mounted on the sleepers, but on the Jubilee-Sandwell line, which passed under the Holyhead Road by the Sandwell Archway now preserved in the Motorway Interchange, the cable ran over the top of the tubs, so that if sufficient full tubs were not available, empties had to be put in to keep the cable off the ground. The line, after passing under the main road tramway route at Sandwell Archway, continued under what looked like a snow-shed (more likely to prevent looting of coal from the loaded tubs) to the long-closed Sandwell Colliery alongside the GWR, where the tubs discharged into railway wagons, or on to the Birmingham Canal near Summit Bridge where there were coal staithes for the boats.

Incidentally I have been told by an old Handsworth resident that the rumble of the tramway cable in its conduit was not unlike the distant rumble of the motorway, and could be heard quite some way from the tram route. At least the cable stopped after the last tram had run in, whereas the rumble of the motorway ceaseth not.

Evidently the CBT Company and Birmingham Corporation decided that one cable line was enough, though it gave good service for 23 years, better than the battery cars which did only 11. For all that, there was still some hankering after conduit electric traction despite all the upheaval involved, and it was not until 1901 that the overhead electric tram appeared on Birmingham's Bristol Road. By that time overhead cars had been operating on the South Staffordshire Tramways in Walsall since 1893, and more recently on the Dudley, Stourbridge and District Electric Traction Company Limited and the Wolverhampton District Electric Tramways Limited; other Midland overhead tramways were the Kidderminster and Stourport and the Coventry tramways, and more distant installations at Leeds and Bristol, so that there was now a fund of experience to draw on, and on balance the overhead cars were coming out well, especially in adverse weather conditions. Conduit and cable cars were apt to strike trouble in snow and ice, but the overheads seemed to enjoy it. Objections to the overhead wires at all events proved less strong in Birmingham than in London, where the LCC Tramways were forced to adopt the conduit system at enormous costs both of installation and operation, and doubtless Mr Alfred Baker, who came to Birmingham from the LCC Tramways as first general manager, after having set the LCC cars on their way, was mightily relieved at having no more to do with the conduit.

The first Birmingham overhead cars, CBT Company Nos 151-171, if late on the scene were quite advanced cars for their time,

Above: CBT Co Ltd overhead electric car No 163 of 1901 on the Bristol Road route at Priory Road. Note rigid suspension of trolley wire to the bracket arms. These poles, after conversion to span-wire suspension, lasted to the end of the Bristol Road routes.

with canopied platforms and reverse stairs. Ten of them became Birmingham Corporation 502-511 in 1912, but unlike the other CBT cars were not modernised with top-covers and vestibuled cabs in the 1920s, probably because they would have come out too high with top-covers. They were originally on Peckham Cantilever trucks, later replaced by Brill 21Es, and would have seen little passenger service with Birmingham Corporation before being replaced on the Bristol Road by the new 301 class top-covered cars which could pass under Selly Oak bridge. Nos 502-511 were relegated to Engineering and Permanent Way cars, and it was as such that I recall two of them, Nos 505 and 507 as PW 8 and 9, still as open-top cars with reverse stairs and the top-deck seats in position, but with water-tanks inside. They were still in what I presume was the old CBT red, then (early 1920s) looking very tatty; the battered appearance of these two cars frightened me as a small boy, though I was drawn to them because they reminded me even then of the Weston-super-Mare trams whose acquaintance I had made about 1921 — and indeed, they were virtually 3ft 6in gauge versions of the Weston cars. (Our family holidays alternated between Weston and Rhyl, with one disastrous exception at Morecambe; but at least I have a positive recollection of travelling on the Morecambe horse-trams. Of the other two places, I gave Weston a high rating

Above: CBT Co Ltd car No 185 of the 'Yardley Bogie' class 181-188 at Small Heath Park, departing for Yardley, during the period between 29 March 1904 and 23 February 1905. On the latter date the steam trams (see background) gave place to electric through cars Station Street-Yardley. The coke yard entrance for the steam trams can still be seen opposite Small Heath Park.

because it had trams, Rhyl almost no rating at all but for the miniature steam railway around the Marine Lake.) One of the CBT Bristol Road cars lasted almost to the end of the Birmingham tramways, however, this being 166 (BCT 509) which became the trailer to the single decker No 451 and later the second PW 9, lasting until June 1952. Others of the Bristol Road cars went to the South Staffs Company, and some found their way to Devonport and eventually Plymouth Corporation.

After the Queen's death in 1901 the Victorian Gothic flavour was suddenly 'out' and the Edwardian neo-classic 'in'. King Edward's request to the LNWR to make the new Royal Saloons 'as much like a yacht as possible' would seem to have brushed off on to the tramcar industry as well, for the new Edwardian electric trams were much more commodious and attractive vehicles than the late-Victorian predecessors, and to me there is a slightly nautical smack about reverse stairs, which were the 'in' thing for a few years until it was realised that they cause bunching of passengers from both decks on the platform, and obstruct the driver's nearside view. This did not matter at first when the electric tramcar was the fastest vehicle on the road, but when motorcars in increasing numbers began passing the trams on the nearside they went out of favour and in many cases reverse-stair cars were rebuilt with normal stairs. However, the CBT Company's next three cars, built at the Kyott's Lake Road works at Sparkbrook, were large five-bay cars on Brush 'D' equal-wheel bogies, numbered 178-180 and having reverse stairs. It is believed that these three cars were intended for the Aston

Above: 'Aston' type car No 242 of CBT Co Ltd on Pershore Road route to Stirchley. Car bears paper stickers 'Stirchley and Breedon Cross'. The line opened to Breedon Cross on 20 May 1904. Car became BCT No 472 in 1912.

service, running jointly with BCT's 'Aston Bogies', but it is not clear where they operated; no photographs have come to light showing them in service, and the two which came to BCT in 1912, Nos 178 and 180 (BCT 451 and 452), were out of service with no motors or equipment. The other car, No 179, went to the South Staffs as their No 16. These were followed by CBT Nos 181-188, again reverse stair bogie cars but with shorter four-bay bodies by Brush for the Yardley-Small Heath Park service. These again were on Brush 'D' bogies, but probably owing to the bogies being too close together showed a disposition to de-rail and were put on Conaty single-trucks. Plymouth Corporation years later made the same mistake with their bogie cars, which showed a similar inclination to go straight ahead when the line went round a corner, and were 'singled'. After car No 188, the CBT Company went in for normal stairs and adopted what Stanley Webb aptly calls the 'Aston' type of four-bay single-truck as standard. On these cars, the windows were square, the bodies being 16ft over bulkheads, the same as the Preston three-bay type of car. The CBT cars were of Brush and CBT manufacture and were also built for the associated Black Country companies, and many of them, not taken over by Birmingham Corporation in 1912, went to the Black Country system. For some reason Birmingham only rebuilt four of the larger Yardley cars with top-cover and vestibule cab, but almost all of the 16ft cars were so treated. To revert to the early 1900s, electrification was now well under way, with, in 1904, the Corporation on the Aston route and the Birmingham and

FOR FURNITU
SMALLHEATH PARK
TO
STATION St
34

Midland on Dudley Road — with BCT appearing here in 1906. The Small Heath-Yardley electric service was extended into Station Street, replacing steam, in 1905, while 1904 had also seen electric trams to Cotteridge (CBT Company) and extensive developments in the Witton and Lozells areas. The same year saw, up at the Handsworth-West Bromwich boundary, something of the sort of confrontation which occurred in the early days of railways, when the South Staffordshire Company, having electrified their line through West Bromwich, desired to run through to the New Inns to meet the CBT cable cars and eliminate the half-mile or so of remaining steam operation between the Woodman at the boundary and New Inns. Current for this section was supplied by Handsworth UDC, then enjoying the reputation of being one of the most awkward local authorities in the country, and South Staffs were unwilling to accept Handsworth's terms. However, the day before the electric service was to start, South Staffs ran a trial car down to the New Inns, upon which the Clerk to the Handsworth UDC ordered the council's steam roller to be driven up to the boundary, placed squarely across both tracks and the fire dropped. This was on 8-9 September 1904, and there the roller remained until South Staffs gave in and the service began on 1 October 1904. These were the days, and no mistake!

Left: Birmingham Corporation Tramways (BCT) 'Aston Bogie' 1-20 class car No 13 at Steelhouse Lane terminus about 1906. Car was top-covered in 1907. The imposing new Wesleyan and General Assurance Society building still stands in Colmore Circus, but all else on this photograph has vanished. Steelhouse Lane was Birmingham Corporation's first and last city terminus.

Below: BCT car No 54 of the 21-70 class passing Small Heath Tavern en route for Station Street about 1909. Board indicator on balcony grille, canopy roller blind box empty, no route letter.

Enough has been said about the development of overhead traction around Birmingham for it to be realised that the development was indeed around Birmingham rather than in it at this period. The districts in which the overhead cars were now running were outside the city boundary — Witton, Erdington, Yardley, Kings Norton, and the Black Country via Smethwick and via West Bromwich. In Birmingham itself the steam nucleus was to remain until 31 December 1906 when most of the CBT Company's leases expired. The following day nearly 200 Birmingham Corporation overhead cars, Nos 21-70, open-top three-bay Preston cars on Brill 21E 6ft trucks, some of which had entered service in 1905, and Nos 71-220, top-covered open-balcony four-bay Preston cars on Mountain and Gibson Radial trucks, took over operation on the already prepared routes, with new routes to Bolton Road, Small Heath, and to Stoney Lane in addition to the former steam routes. The Nechells route, operating from Martineau Street, was also inaugurated with the cars running outwards along Nechells Park Road and returning via Long Acre to Nechells Green. In readiness for all this a large and handsome power station had been built in Summer Lane.

This was a tremendous operation; as the steam trams finished their run each was worked away to Ward's scrapyard at Wednesbury, in Lea Brook Road, and the details of just how this was done remain a mystery to this day. It is presumed that they would have gone via Six Ways, Aston, Wheeler Street and Great Hampton Row and then on over the junction with the cable line and reversed, with in the first place a spare engine to take the trailer off the engine which had just entered Constitution Hill, that engine then moving up to take the next trailer and so forth; at Wednesbury, temporary connections must have been put in to get the steamers into Ward's yard, but extensive research at Birmingham and Wednesbury has failed to establish any facts. Whatever happened, all the steam trams had to be out of Birmingham for the next day's electric takeover, and by all accounts it was a very smooth operation. Weather was evidently favourable; had it been otherwise a very bad situation might have resulted. Some steam cars perhaps ran via Navigation Street, the Ladywood route (opened October 1906) Smethwick, Dudley and Ocker Hill, but again, no definite facts have come up. One loco burst a boiler tube at Silver Street depot, Kings Heath, and could not be moved. It remained there for long afterwards, but that apparently was the only non-starter. Birmingham Corporation Tramways were now really in business, and 70 more cars of the 21 class were added between March 1907 and April 1908, bringing the fleet strength up to 330 cars. (Seven of the Radials, 208-214, apparently did not arrive until 1908, but the rest were in service at the end of 1906 or very early in 1907.)

Thus from 1 January 1907 Birmingham Corporation Tramways were operating on all routes in the city except Bristol Road, and Pershore Road (Cotteridge) where the CBT Company electric cars ran until the lease ran out in 1911, and the Handsworth cable route due to expire in the same year. As the Ladywood cars and the CBT Company Bristol Road cars used the same tracks in Suffolk Street, Navigation Street and John Bright Street a separate overhead wire, insulated from the CBT wire, was put in for the Ladywood cars round this loop terminal, and this was to remain in position to the end of the Ladywood tram service. As only a run-through frog was needed instead of a moving drop-lever or 'poker-frog', the Overhead Department evidently decided there was no great advantage in taking out the separate wire when BCT took over the Bristol Road, but many people were puzzled over many years by the two wires where one would seem to have been sufficient.

Apart from electric tramways, there were signs and portents that the Greater Birmingham was beginning to shape up. In readiness for the great boundary extensions of 1911 when Handsworth (until then in Staffordshire), Aston, Erdington, Yardley and Kings Norton and Northfield became part of Birmingham, the Council House Extension was built in Birmingham on the Congreve Street-Great Charles Street-Margaret Street-Edmund Street site, connected to Yeoville Thomason's Council House in Victoria Square by a handsome bridge across Edmund Street. This extension housed additional rooms for the Art Gallery, the Education Office and the Tramways Department, among others, and was built to deal with the extra work involved when the additional areas came into the city in 1911. Handsworth's imposing Council House on Soho Road then lost its original function and became the Library, and the same applies to the other local authority offices.

Right: BCT car No 261 of the 21 class (221-300 series) outside Moseley Road depot about 1908. Canopy roller box displays TRAFALGAR ROAD via LEOPOLD STREET, balcony board shows MOSELEY ROAD via LEOPOLD STREET. No route letter. After arrival of the 401 class the 21 class cars were prohibited on Leopold Street.

Below right: BCT car No 226, operating from Miller Street depot, running over the cable track just below the New Inns, Handsworth, immediately after electrification in 1911. Observe track gang in the background relaying with all speed. Canopy roller indicator now removed.

The area around Edmund Street, Colmore Row and Congreve Street during our period with most of the buildings in Italian Palazzo style had quite a touch of the City of London about it — nothing so imposing as Westminster, but, yes, quite a hint of the City, enhanced by Archer's St Philip's Church of 1725 (which became the Cathedral in 1905) and this flavour remained up to 1939. This is not the place to discuss what has happened since.

The terminus for the Dudley Road services was Edmund Street, with the cars making a complete circuit of the Council House Extension. The Edmund Street track, originally central, was moved to the kerbside, and the Council House, the Extension, and the Bridge created a vast echoing vault which brought out the distinctive two-tone motor note of the Radial cars quite memorably. No other cars I have ever met made quite the same sound. The M and G Radial trucks as such did not last long. Like most such designs, after a little wear the radial gear failed to restore both axles to the parallel state, and the gear was soon made rigid — which about describes the riding characteristics of the 71 class, hard, noisy and unyielding even on good track, while on the not so-good company track beyond the Grove Lane city boundary, up Cape Hill, they were something to be endured. When re-trucked in the mid-twenties on Peckham P35 trucks the contrast was quite unbelievable. They rode the outworn single-and-loop stretches in the far wilds of Tividale, on the Dudley via Oldbury route quite effortlessly and comfortably — curiously the same trucks under the Manchester 'Pilchers' gave anything but a comfortable ride, but admittedly I only knew the Pilchers under wartime conditions. Reverting to Edmund Street, cars on the Dudley Road group tended to be kept in very good nick, even if they were some of the oldest in the fleet; they had to pass Head Office every trip, and a tatty car very soon had someone ringing up!

Apart from the original 20 'Aston Bogies', Mr Baker had ordered single-truck cars for the Birmingham fleet, and this was to be the case for the next two orders. A hundred more cars were needed for the 1911 extensions, and these were the 301-400 class on United Electric 7ft 6in Swing Yoke trucks, a few of which had been put under some of the 71 class. The swing yokes, which permitted some lateral movement of the axle when entering a curve, soon proved troublesome and the trucks were made rigid, but without the punishing effects of the Radials. The UEC trucks rode excellently and these cars ran up some big mileages, in some cases, such as the preserved example 395 in the Birmingham Science Museum, exceeding the 1,000,000 mile mark. The bodies were an advance on the previous top-covered cars, the Radials, as they had ventilating lights on the top deck, and were of lower overall height, 15ft 7½in to trolley plank as against 16ft 0in of the Radials, and could pass under Aston and Selly Oak railway bridges which the Radials could not pass. They appeared to be bigger cars than the Radials, but this was deceptive. They were fractionally longer, 17ft 9in over bulkheads

Right: BCT car No 156 of the 71-220 'Radial' class as built on Mountain and Gibson trucks, but with canopy roller indicator removed. Outside Kyotts Lake Road works with obviously new canvas dodger rigged up, which could not have been fitted with the canopy box in position.

CORPORATION TRAMWAYS
156
ROAD

Above: BCT car No 331 of 1911 in Kings Heath, as built. Nos 301-360 were delivered with vertical handbrake wheels, but soon had these replaced by normal brake handles, involving blanking off the offside cab-window with the characteristic Birmingham 'pocket'. Observe overhead wires to Silver Street (old CBT Steam) depot.

as against 17ft 6in of the Radials, but looked much longer probably due to the lower overall height and the top deck ventilating lights. They had vestibule cabs from new, the first in the fleet, and at first had the 'Ackley' type hand-brake with a vertically mounted wheel, with three windows of equal width facing forward set in an 'angle-dash', whereas previous Birmingham cars had all been round-dash cars. The vertical hand-brake wheel did not go down at all well, and was replaced by the normal horizontal brake-handle, though this had to be shorter than standard and the controllers had to be repositioned. To allow room for the driver's hand, the lower portion of the offside vestibule window had to be blanked off and a slightly bulged pocket put in, and this has been a feature of all Birmingham cars from this time, even on PW cars. Other operators have sometimes included this feature, including Northampton, Stockport, Middlesbrough and Warrington, but it was a very distinctive part of the Birmingham cars and gave them a perhaps rather fanciful look of winking an eye. (If trams can be said to have a face, the Birmingham cars had a cheerful face.) On cars 361-400 the platforms were made 3in longer, these cars being built with normal handbrake, and therefore coming out at 29ft 9in overall as against 29ft 3in of 301-360. The balconies on 301-400 also had a wing-window on the offside, which made the corner balcony seat quite cosy even in bad weather, but in the forward direction caused a scooping effect of air which sent a cold draught down the stairs on to the driver's head. The stair-

Above: BCT car No 314 on Slade Road, Erdington, with offside cab window fitted with pocket for handbrake, but no sunblind.

well therefore had to be fitted with a trap-door to mitigate the draught, and seemed to work well.

A detail feature of Birmingham cars, the sunblind over the driver's half-drop cab window, was not included at first on the 301 class. A photograph of No 314 on Slade Road shows the offside window rebuilt with the handbrake pocket, but no sunblind. I am not sure if Nos 361-400 had sunblinds from new, but certainly the next new cars had them. It is surprising how much this small detail adds to the quite distinctive 'Birmingham' look of the cars; for a long time I was puzzled by the 'something missing' look of my models, and then I got it. Making the dummy sunblind fixtures was a fiddly job, but they made all the difference. On the open-cab round-dash cars an elaborate lash-up of canvas dodgers was rigged up, very probably designed by someone who had been in the Royal Navy. This included a top blind, and doubtless early representations were made about the lack of them on the first of the 301 class. From a careful study of photographs of other tramway undertakings, I know of no other system which included this feature on its cars. The blinds were useful in snow conditions as well as when running into the sun.

One of the very few serious accidents involving Birmingham trams probably had something to do with the order for the next 50 cars, Nos 401-450, which were identical with Nos 361-400 as to bodies, but the trucks this time were Mountain and Gibson marque, most being 7ft 6in wheelbase with a few 8ft 6in examples, with a United Electric and a Peckham for good measure.The accident in question was to car No 22 on 1 October 1907, on the Lodge Road route. The driver had doubts about the brakes, and at the Chamberlain Clock at the corner of Frederick Street and Warstone Lane said as much to an inspector who happened to be there. Warstone Lane descends from this point to Icknield Street by quite a steep and sharply curved gradient. The driver apparently refused to take the car down the hill, whereupon the inspector took the car over, to find — too late — that the driver was right and the car was running away. It overturned on the sharp right-hand curve at the bottom of the hill with dire consequences.

The 401-450 class were specially fitted with the Spencer-Dawson oil and air brake, pressure being maintained by an eccentric-driven pump worked off one of the axles. These cars went new to Moseley Road depot for the Leopold Street service, the steepest gradient on the Birmingham system, and remained there for the whole of their service. Only the bogie cars with the 401 class, were allowed up or down Leopold Street, with passengers aboard anyway. The 21 class was prohibited entirely, not even the various illuminated cars (266 and 63) running that way. A photograph taken about 1909 shows No 261 outside Moseley Road depot showing a Leopold Street destination board, so evidently this ban did not come into force immediately, but with the arrival of the 401 class the 301 class, some of which evidently went there new, were transferred away to Bristol Road to replace the CBT cars and to Miller Street for the Erdington routes, previously served only by open-top cars due to restricted clearance at Aston station. From this time began the programme of top-covering the 21 class, not quite completed by World War I. Miller Street must have had a busy time about 1911/1912, as they were called upon to work the Handsworth routes, via the double-track junction from Steelhouse Lane to Colmore Row, until the cable tram depot at Hockley had been rebuilt for electric cars. Two photographs of this period exist showing 301 class cars on Soho Road, Handsworth, but when the new Hockley depot received its quota of new bogie cars of the 512 class, the 301 class returned to Aston and were very rarely seen, even for football specials, on Hockley again.

Doubtless as a consequence of 22's accident, many of the 21 class were fitted with the Maley brake, operated by a large brass wheel below the normal handle on the brakestaff — certainly all those for the Lodge Road were so fitted. There was no question of prohibiting them on this route, as by reason of sharp curves and tight clearances no cars of greater length could pass. They were 27ft 6in overall, and though two Radials of 29ft 0in could just pass on test, it was too close for comfort, and long after the 21 class had disappeared from other depots, a fleet of them had to be kept for Lodge Road. Even with these cars, care had to be taken on the curves when running with snowploughs, and in practice the cars did not pass on curves. The 21 class were smart, quiet-running and nippy little cars and certainly earned their keep on Lodge Road.

So far the Birmingham Corporation cars had arrived in nice round numbers up to 450; we now come to the addition to the fleet of the City of Birmingham Tramways Company Limited rolling-stock, 61 cars coming into Corporation stock, a very odd number indeed, and throwing out forever the nice round numbers by one. They were numbered 451-511, all being open-top and all except the first two being single-truck, mounted on either Conaty ex-radial trucks or Brush 'Flexible Wheelbase' trucks, both of 8ft 0in wheelbase. Being non-standard and already outdated they were now used for spare duties only, and most retained their CBT colours until modernised in the 1920s. The first two cars, however, 451 and 452, were used for trials of the Burnley bogies in 1912. Mr Baker had evidently decided that larger cars were now necessary, and one imagines that he would have looked at current LCC practice, where the E1 bogie cars were building by the hundred. Perhaps the slight rock-and-roll imparted by the centre (or near-centre) pivoted bogies of these cars caused him to look for alternatives; there were already 20 Birmingham cars on Brill 22E bogies, which rode well enough but had a tendency to frame fracture. The Maguire bogies of the LCC 'D' class had proved rather troublesome. At all events, two sets of Burnley bogies were assembled at Kyott's Lake Road and put under 451 and 452, then still in open-top reverse-stair condition, but as I understand repainted in BCT colours. In the Burnley bogie, the pivot is not central, but in line with the driving axle, so that the entire body weight is taken over the driving wheels, the pony wheels taking the weight of the motor and acting as guides. It appears that the idea was developed from the Simpson and Parke Radial truck, a pair of which were put under Burnley Corporation single-deck car No 47. These trucks, with a spiral spring on each side of the axlebox, looked suspiciously like a Burnley bogie without the pony wheels, and certainly No 47 later had Burnley bogies, Nos 451 and 452 ran their trials on the Bordesley Green route, where their massive proportions compared with the little 21 class Brill cars apparently somewhat scared the local folks who gave them the nickname of 'Titanics' — this puts a date on things — which name stuck to them for the rest of their time. Much was to happen to these cars later, but that is for a later chapter. The trials were a success, and in November 1913 the 512-586 class open-balcony bogie cars began to take the road. These cars, with United Electric bodies, were on Burnley bogies of Mountain and Gibson make, and were the same over bulkheads as the Aston bogies but with longer and, of course, vestibuled platforms, being 33ft 6in overall. As the pivot-points of the bogies were well apart, there was no 'hunting' movement with these cars, even on the fearful Black Country track which some of them were to encounter. They were ideal on street track, but tended to punish the sleeper track somewhat, but more of that later. They were hardly ever afflicted by wheelspin, with so much weight on the driving wheels, even when their original 40hp motors were replaced by 63hp or 70hp units, and they were good uphill. London found it necessary to use four-motor cars, the HR2s, for the Dulwich routes with the famous Dog Kennel Hill. The Birmingham cars had worse hills than the Dog Kennel to cope with — Holloway Bank, Wednesbury, and Griffins Hill on Bristol Road among them, but the Burnley bogies proved equal to their task. Those with 2×70hp motors were equal in power to a 4×35hp London HR2, but that again really belongs to later on. The last few cars did not arrive until November 1914, some having first-class appointments in the lower saloon for the Hagley Road route, where the trams had met with intense disapproval from the local residents — who were glad enough to have them, however, when petrol rationing caused the more patrician motor-buses to disappear. Perhaps 1914 would be a good point to leave Birmingham for the moment and review the scene in Walsall, Wolverhampton, and the Black Country, first, however, recalling that in 1900, where this chapter began, there were no overhead electric cars in Birmingham. In the decade and a half covered by the chapter, over 500 cars were in service, operated by the municipality which in 1900 had simply been the owners of the tracks over which the various types of company-owned trams ran.

Below: BCT car No 535 of the 512-586 bogie class of 1913 at Hagley Road (Kings Head) terminus; the stencilled 34 on the headlamp dates the photograph as 1915 or later in the war. Some of these cars ran with lower saloons 'First Class' when the route opened, but the war soon put an end to that, and the Hagley Road residents were very glad to have their trams.

By Tram through the Black Country

Above: BMMO Co Ltd SOS 'QL' bus 1928, HA 3786.

Well before the first overhead electric cars began to operate along Birmingham's quite exclusive Bristol Road in 1901, electrics were rolling in the Black Country. As already mentioned, the South Staffs Tramways had been running electric cars in Walsall, to Wednesbury, Darlaston and Bloxwich from 1893, these being quite tiny open-top uncanopied four-wheel cars, with swivel-head trolleys for side running. The Dudley to Stourbridge route was electrified in July 1899, followed quickly in 1900 by the partial opening of the Dudley-Sedgley-Bilston service of the Wolverhampton District Electric Tramways Limited, the Netherton-Cradley and Scotts Green-Kingswinford-Brettell Lane lines of the Dudley, Stourbridge and District Electric Traction Company Limited. Without going into further details, which have been admirably covered by Stanley Webb, it can be said that by 1907, with the opening of the Dudley-Tipton-Wednesbury line, the Black Country network was complete. No further new mileage was opened, and any further schemes never saw the light of day.

Although so close to Birmingham, the quality of life in the Black Country is altogether different, even today, rather like the differences one can observe in the various cantons of Switzerland. Black Country towns, in many cases, are simply large villages strung out along main roads, with little in depth behind the main roads, such as Brierley Hill and Sedgley. Only Walsall and Wolverhampton were big enough and closely-knit enough to develop and operate their own tramway undertakings. Dudley was an important tramway centre, where indeed all four of the Black Country tramway companies met, but was not an operator, and the same applied to West Bromwich, where the heavily trafficked South Staffs services to Dudley and Darlaston were supplemented by the two local routes to West Smethwick (Spon Lane) and Oldbury (Bromford Lane). The pattern for the Black Country tramways was therefore one of long routes serving the communities strung out along those routes, the almost 'interurban' touch being strongly brought out at Stourbridge with the Kinver Light Railway, one of very few such lines in this country — Burton and Ashby, Grimsby and Immingham, Sunderland District, the Llandudno and Colwyn Bay and the

Above: Dudley, Stourbridge and District Electric Traction Co Ltd (DS&DET Co Ltd). One of the 1899 Brush cars which survived up to 1939 as a rail-grinder at West Smethwick depot. / *R. T. Coxon*

Dearne District just about completing the tale of them. Only in Walsall and Wolverhampton was there the true town pattern of radiating urban routes with the conventional town types of tram. The rolling stock of the Black Country companies was by no means conventional, and I would go so far as to say that nowhere else was there so much variety of cars in what was a relatively small fleet, despite the ponderous titles of their four owning companies. (This is, of course, the usual case, vide the Taunton Company — Taunton and West Somerset Electric Railway and Tramways Company Limited, with one mile of track and six cars — and the incredible number of actual or hypothetical American Railroad companies, X-Y-Z and Pacific which never got within a thousand miles of the Pacific.) The 1893 Walsall SST electrics were of steam-trailer section, though open-top and very short. The 1899 Dudley-Stourbridge cars, though built by Brush at Loughborough, had a decidedly transatlantic look about them, being single-deckers on Peckham Cantilever trucks, with turtle-back roofs and of 'closed-combination' construction — that is, the bulkheads were one bay back from each end, the end seats being semi-open, though the sides were solid throughout, unlike the Manchester single-deckers of 'California' type. One of these cars survived as a rail-grinder at West Smethwick depot until the Birmingham-Oldbury-Dudley route closed in 1939. Some were built as trailers, but I imagine with the pretty fearsome hills on the Dudley-Stourbridge route the idea of trailers was soon dropped and they were equipped as motor cars. There is a difference in levels of about 300ft between Stourbridge and Dudley, though the climb is not continuous but rather undulating, and the motors of the D and S cars would have been pretty warm on reaching Dudley Market Place.

Let no one imagine that the Black Country was all black (today, with the Clean Air Bill and so much rebuilding, it is not easy to see why the name applied). Even on the main D and S route, there were parts where the houses, furnaces and factories ceased and one could get glimpses of the still green country behind; around Netherton and up on the Rowley Hills farming was still carried on, and one met with real cows, pigs, and, of course, the inevitable 'mokes', for donkey traction was very much a part of the Black Country economy. They were much in use by the gipsy communities, of which there were many in and around the Black Country. There was plenty of waste land where they could pitch their camps and vehicles, and until comparatively recently one could come across the remains of long-derelict gipsy caravans; they seemed particularly strong around Gornal (where, according to legend, the donkeys are made) and Bloxwich, to give two examples, and it was from the latter town that Pat Collins, in the great days of steam fairground rides, built up the great showman's business which still bears his name. The mokes travelled far and wide with their little carts, their owners' trade being the sale of bar salt (probably brought from Cheshire down the Shroppie by canal-boat) and clothes-pegs. I remember more than once my mother buying salt which she did not really want ('Go on, lady, 'ave arf a bar!') as the only way of dislodging the very persistent pipe-smoking gipsy lady from the doorstep, and this in Handsworth, a long way from the moke's Black Country home. I also recall in West Bromwich seeing a gipsy setting about his (presumed) wife outside a pub in Spon Lane. A man went to her assistance, whereupon both gipsy man and woman set about him and gave him quite a going-over, the woman the while informing her would-be rescuer that if her bloke wanted to belt her that was none of his .... business. This was near the canal, and they may have been canal folk, but that was a long time back. I was on my first bicycle following the tramlines down Spon Lane, hoping to see a tram. I was too late. They had gone, and the route was being operated by the West Bromwich Corporation Dennis 'E' buses, one of which, No 32, can fairly be said to have changed the course of my life, but more of that later. I do, however, have a quite distinct earlier memory of the single-deck trams on Spon Lane. The gipsies were very much part of the Black Country scene, and even today one will see, particularly on Saturdays, it seems, horse-drawn totters' carts bringing in the scrap. I doubt if the gipsies used the trams very much, as being the 'travelling people' they have always had their own means of getting around.

The Dudley, Stourbridge and District would seem to have had the most difficult routes to operate, with Castle Hill and Queen's Cross, Dudley, the long climb up Cinder Bank to Queen's Cross

Above: DS&DET Co Ltd 'Kinver' toast-rack crossing the plate girder bridge over the Staffs and Worcs Canal, which replaced the original timber bridge, at the Stewponey. From Kinver to Stewponey the line was on private reservation alongside the canal; from Stewponey to Wollaston it was on roadside reservation. The wooden overhead poles are still in use today.

Above left: Birmingham and Midland Tramways Joint Committee (B&MTJC). A DS&D single-decker, converted as the Kinver milk-van, and a Tramways Parcels Express van, both on Lord Baltimore trucks, in the yard at West Smethwick depot where they stood for years. Pile of material from cut-up CBT cars in 1938. */ R. T. Coxon*

Left: 'Cradley' bogie car of DS&DET Co Ltd approaching Kinver alongside the Staffordshire and Worcestershire Canal.

on the Cradley route, the Old Hill-Blackheath branch corkscrewing its way up to Blackheath among its hazards, but other companies all had some hills to contend with — the climb from Fighting Cocks up to Sedgley on the Wolverhampton District, Holloway Bank on the South Staffs-Wednesbury route, and Cape Hill, Smethwick on the Birmingham and Midland (Birmingham District Power and Traction Company Limited from 1912). However, a DS and D driver apparently had some bad moments when taking one of the long 'Cradley' bogie cars to Moseley Road depot in Birmingham for a tramwaymen's outing to Kinver, the Cradley bogie running empty from Hartshill depot to Moseley Road. The driver took the car up Leopold Street to reach Moseley Road, but flatly declared he wasn't going back that way and returned via Bradford Street. One would have thought that after Queen's Cross and Castle Hill, Leopold Street would have been chicken-feed, but apparently not so. A pity no one photographed the Cradley car at Moseley Road! This was probably the furthest penetration into Birmingham by a Black Country car, though special workings to Kinver loaded at the Parade on the Dudley Road route, and Kinver cars are known to have come down to the New Inns, Handsworth, for Sunday school outings, but again, no photographic evidence. Hundreds of such outings must have worked over the Kinver Light Railway, for churches and chapels of every marque were another part of the Black Country scene, many indeed still surviving, though as elsewhere some have disappeared. It was an old tram-driver, I think, who a long time ago told me of his lay-preaching work, conducted unusually from a canal boat. 'Ar, we 'ad one of the coal-boats out, we put a deck atop on 'im, and whitewashed it up, and went round preachin' the Werd. We said, "If the Lord Jesus Christ con 'ave a boat out to goo preachin', we con 'ave a boat out an' all". ' Perhaps this might be the moment to 'feature' the story of two men waiting near Hartshill depot for a tram. The Dudley-Stourbridge company, it will be recalled, began the service with single-deckers, but on this occasion one of the large open-top bogie cars, Nos 39-42, came in sight, the first double-deck car ever seen by our two men. 'Ay, mate, see what's a-comin' ? It's a new 'un, ay it?' said one.

'Ar, it am a new 'un an' all,' replied No 2.

No 1 boarded the car and went up aloft, but No 2 went 'inside'.

'Ay yo' comin' up 'ere, then?' said No 1.

'I'm a-gooin' inside', said No 2.

'Yo goo on up if yo' want'.

The tram moved off, but after two stops No 1 came below and rejoined his friend.

'What's a-matter wi' yo' then?' said No 2.

'It ay bloody right, mate', said No 1. 'I ay a-stondin' fer that lot. There's no bugger a-drivin' up theer.'

Well, the story may date back to 1901, but if it's new to some, then worthwhile putting it in. As in other industrial areas, the Black Country had its quota of pubs, many being of some antiquity, and all with their own individuality, particularly the canalside pubs. Some to this day — a few only now — are 'home-brewed' houses, and like the chapels, many have gone, but many pub names were part of the tramway lore — 'Cape of Good Hope' and 'Blue Gates', Smethwick, 'Boat Inn', Tividale, 'White

Below: The main Stourbridge-Birmingham road before 1914, with a DS&DET Co Ltd 'Peckham' single-decker leaving Lye Cross for The Hayes. Views of the Lye route are very rare, and this is included to show the kind of roads the Black Country Tramways had to fit into. Not a spare inch even on the 3ft 6in gauge!

Horse', Wednesbury, 'Brown Lion', Pleck, 'Handel Hotel' at Blackheath terminus, and many more. The houses along the routes varied enormously, of course, and if some of them were not a planner's paradise (we know too well today what that means) the letter-box and door-knob and step-plate were usually brass or copper, and polished, even if there was no front garden. Some of the churches were and are landmarks — Dudley 'Top Cherch' and 'Bottom Cherch', also Sedgley and Wednesbury, and, isolated, rather aloof and looking to me rather haunted, the blackened tower of Netherton church in its graveyard on a hill-top overlooking the canal.

Perhaps one very strong reason for the success of the Dudley-Stourbridge route was that the railway stations of those two towns were both inconveniently located. One first had to take the steam railcar from Stourbridge Town up to the Junction, and at the Dudley end had to make one's way up Castle Hill to the town, and as remarked in the opening paragraph of the Steam Tram chapter, it is the vehicle which occasions least trouble to the passenger which will come out best. In this instance the trams certainly had the edge over the railway, and I imagine most of the passengers on the Stourbridge Town-Junction railmotor were for the Birmingham or Worcester directions. The Great Western Railway did not take things lying down, however, and ran very competitive services on all their Black Country lines, even opening up a new line to Wolverhampton via Wombourn in the mid-twenties with steam railcars. This never really caught on, however, and I recall seeing the railcar at Oxley Junction obviously carrying no one but GWR employees.

There were plenty of contrasts on the D and S main line, from

Below: High Street, Cradley Heath, in the early 1920s. A DS&DET Co Ltd 'Tividale' single-decker may be dimly discerned in the background. The view is included to illustrate the fearful, but typical, Black Country track. The Cradley line did not figure in many photographs!

Above: Wolverhampton District Electric Tramways Limited (WDET Ltd). Brush bogie car No 15 on Willenhall-Darlaston route in Church Street, Darlaston, pre-1914. The only known photograph of a car actually on this route.

Right: WDET Ltd Brush bogie car No 14 with stairs altered to normal at Darlaston Bull Stake. Probably 1918-1920. Note clock-faces on tramway pole to indicate departures of next cars. / *Via S. Griffiths*

the two market towns at each end to the impressive Round Oak Steelworks, with glassworks at Amblecote, brick and tileworks along Brettell Lane, railways, canals, pubs, and unexpected vistas of distant Shropshire, but perhaps the route offering the most contrast was the Wolverhampton District main route from Dudley to Bilston via Fighting Cocks — becoming Dudley-Wolverhampton in later days. Once clear of Dudley, in tram days the line was rural to a degree; in Dudley itself there is little heavy industry, as the town was there centuries before the Industrial Revolution, and gracious architectural examples of earlier ages are still to be seen. The town stands high, and the WDET route runs along the ridge to Sedgley, which still retains its village character, and then begins the long drop to Fighting Cocks. This section of road puts me in mind of the Rochdale to Halifax road in places, except that the canal is missing. Even in trolleybus days the rural flavour persisted, and though much of it is now built up, this is of very modern date. The sight of the very large WDET bogie open-toppers, of the 14-30 class, must have been rather incongruous on this quite remote road. They were really a 3ft 6in version of the six-bay bogie cars favoured by the London United, Metropolitan, and Manchester tramways, though with canopied platforms and reverse stairs, and similar cars, except for gauge, ran on the Greenock and Port Glasgow tramway. They — and four slightly smaller cars on the D and S — though undoubtedly large cars were in fact the same overall length as the South Staffs, five-bay open-toppers Nos 10-27, namely 34ft 6in, and only 1ft longer than the Birmingham 512 class. One would have thought that single-deckers would have been more suitable but other sections of the WDET probably gave the big bogies plenty of custom. Between Fighting Cocks and Bilston the contrast set in without a doubt, with steelworks and Thompson's boiler works at Ettingshall, and on this section the trams quite often had to sort it out with a steam traction engine, or a pair of them — one of them probably fitted with a crane out in front, known locally as a 'steam hook' — hitched on to a huge low-loader boiler trolley. Usually when it came to 'sorting it out' a tram had the advantage in weight, but not even a WDET big bogie would be able to take on a traction engine with a power station boiler in tow! The through service on the WDET main line had begun on 13 November 1902, from Dudley station via Stafford Street to Sedgley, Fighting Cocks and Bilston, but because of congestion in Dudley Market Place — which certainly had not been laid out with tramway operation in mind — it was cut back to Dudley Post Office in 1905, the Stafford Street line being retained simply as a connection with the DS and D. As a result, the line always had a rather 'out-on-a-limb' flavour, even in Wolverhampton Corporation trolleybus days, as even in Wolverhampton the Snow Hill terminus was also isolated. Eventually a junction with the Wolverhampton Corporation line was put in at Fighting Cocks and some WDET single-truck cars were equipped with 'Lorain' surface-contact skates so that they could work over the Corporation's Fighting Cocks-Snow Hill line and a through service from Dudley to Wolverhampton could operate. This was one of the first cases of inter-running between a municipal undertaking and a company in the area, but more were to follow. Birmingham Corporation and the Birmingham and Midland Tramways Company Limited were running jointly on the Bearwood and Soho routes, Walsall Corporation and the South Staffs at length began joint running Walsall Bridge-Wednesbury and Walsall Bridge-Darlaston in 1907, and later, in 1912, South Staffs cars operated into Birmingham over the electrified Handsworth route from Darlaston to Colmore Row.

It was at Pleck, on the Walsall-South Staffs Joint, that the episode of Inspector Cooper's whistle took place, and as a result, Inspector Cooper always saw to it that whatever dress, summer or winter, he was wearing, his whistle was always on the outside

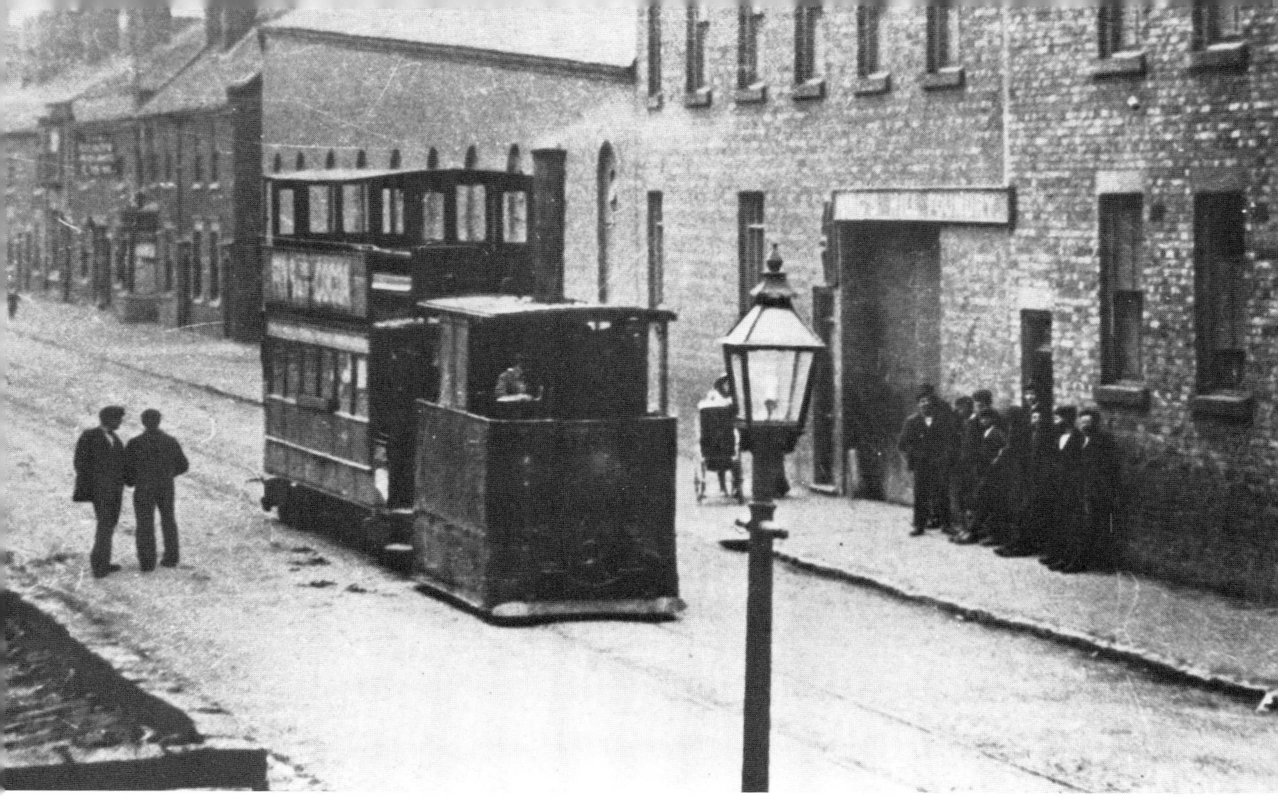

Above: South Staffordshire Tramways Co Ltd. Steam tram from Wednesbury to Darlaston passing Kings Hill Foundry about 1900.

and ready to hand. There was a reverse curve on the double-track line between the 'Brown Lion' and the beginning of the slight climb over the railway, and Inspector Cooper — then on the South Staffs — was watching a company car pass him en route for Walsall. The driver had thrown off the power on the slight down gradient; as the car pitched gently round the curve, the trolley developed quite a 'whip' on the too-slack wire, left the wire and by some freak chance re-wired itself — on the other wire! The driver then began to put one or two notches of power on to get over the railway bridge, and sure enough, the power was there, but from the wrong wire — the overhead was bracket-arm construction with both wires close together. Inspector Cooper reached for his whistle, but as it was a cold day he was wearing his greatcoat and the whistle was underneath, attached to his tunic. By the time he had located his whistle the car was out of range, and after thumbing a lift on a coal-lorry, when he caught up with the offending tram its trolley had successively dewired two Walsall Corporation and one South Staffs cars going the other way. When I knew Inspector Cooper 40 years ago he was with Birmingham Corporation at Hockley depot — and always with the whistle at the ready! This tendency for slack wires persisted at Walsall into trolleybus days, certainly up to World War II, as I recall seeing a Bloxwich trolleybus coming down Bridge Street, as they then did, with both trolleys 'whipping' in contrary motion to the extent that I fully expected to see a flashover and the trolleyheads weld themselves together.

Above: Confrontation! September 1904. Handsworth UDC Steamroller across both tracks at Handsworth Boundary, with SST (Lessee) Co Ltd bogie car and baffled officials behind. The service eventually began on 1 October 1904.

While in the main the South Staffs had some very heavily trafficked routes, their Dudley-Wednesbury via Tipton route was another 'out-on-a-limb' line, though it did connect at each end with other services, at Dudley station and at Dudley Street, Wednesbury, though this was short of the centre of the town. The route itself wandered about all over the place. At the Dudley end there was at least the view of the Castle on its tree-clad hill, and the Wren's Nest, before reaching the built-up area of Tipton; perhaps 'near Tipton', in the manner of the LCC route 28 'Near Willesden Junction' might be more accurate — that is, if Owen Street is the real centre of Tipton. The line crossed the Birmingham Canal by the beautiful little cast-iron Factory Bridge, where the original Brindley contour canal is joined by the straight-running Telford canal. The bridge, now replaced, has gone to the Black Country Museum, or at least its outer decorative spans have. From here to Princes End is quite a switchback, and to judge from the alarming angles taken by some of the buildings along this section — though they have been like that for years — keeping the track anything like level must have been a headache, though it would seem that the authorities concerned didn't try too hard. (On the Dudley-Stourbridge route from Dudley to Kingswinford, where a section of road just beyond Scotts Green Junction subsided, a section of rail was relaid at each end of the subsidence forming ramps and the trams kept going.) In the Black Country one has to live with colliery subsidence — and no one knows where some of the

Left: While the SST (Lessee) Co Ltd was in dispute with Handsworth UDC, electric cars had to be towed out of the Boundary depot by steam tram locos beyond a section-breaker into West Bromwich territory. Here is No 13 being hauled 'dead' by a Beyer-Peacock loco.

Below left: SST (Lessee) Co Ltd car No 6, top-covered and with temporary windscreens on joint SST-Walsall Corporation service at Oakeswell End, Wednesbury, in early 1920s.

ancient uncharted workings went — and it was the logical thing to do. Princes End certainly had some interesting specimens of subsidence at one time, and one hopes that the people who have cheerfully built high-rise creations in recent years are quite sure of what they are doing. Beyond Princes End comes a quite sharp drop over a crazy-looking canal bridge down Wednesbury Oak Road through a landscape which at one time looked like one of Bruce Bairnsfather's 'Old Bill' cartoons of World War I, but which looks very different today. At Ocker Hill ('Ocker Bonk') are houses, shops and schools again, the line still dropping down Lea Brook Road, past Ward's scrap-yard, under the Great Western Railway, then a short climb past the Patent Shaft and Axletree steelworks to the Dudley Street junction with the Wednesbury-Bilston line. Scenically the route had little to recommend it, though to anyone who likes industry (and I for one do) then there was plenty of interest, but photographs of this route are notable for their scarcity. Initially, the line was worked by the small three-bay uncanopied open-toppers, known to SST drivers as 'submarines' — could this be a rather far-fetched comparison with the Blackpool Dreadnoughts? — the large five-bay bogie open-toppers being kept to the Dudley-Handsworth service. These were certainly hefty cars, as well as very handsome ones; as already mentioned, one of the three CBT company five-bay cars, No 179, which was almost identical, came to the SST in 1912 in replacement of No 16. None of them were top-covered, some in fact being cut down to single-deckers. The Dudley service at first terminated at the New Inns, Handsworth, but when Handsworth became part of Birmingham in 1911 the terminus became the Woodman Inn at the boundary. This was probably because Birmingham insisted on top-covered cars running into the city, and certainly the through Darlaston-Colmore Row service was always operated by top-covered SST single-truck cars. These were very tall cars which could not pass under the Ryland Canal Aqueduct at Dudley Port; had the bogies been top-covered they also would have come out too tall. (CBT Nos 178 and 180, which became BCT Nos 451 and 452, were not allowed beyond Carter's Green when top-covered due to their height of 16ft 3in.) The bogies remained open-top and the luckless Dudley passengers had to change at the Birmingham boundary. Their luck changed when Birmingham took the service over, but more of that later. The Dudley-Birmingham traffic was catered for by the alternative route of the Birmingham and Midland Tramways, later the Birmingham District, via Oldbury and Smethwick to Edmund Street, Birmingham, and this route was certainly not without interest. It made an end-on junction with the Birmingham system at the bottom of Cape Hill, Smethwick, at Grove Lane; at the top of this quite long but not unduly steep hill the Bearwood route took off to the left, opposite Windmill Lane. This, though BD territory, was always worked by Birmingham as service 29, to balance the mileage of the BD Dudley cars working over

Above: SST (Lessee) Co Ltd car No 50 at Darlaston terminus on Birmingham (Colmore Row) service. Temporary windscreens, and some temporary-looking overhead. / *The late J. Aston*

Left: Birmingham and Midland Tramways Company Limited (Birmingham District Power and Traction Company Limited from 1912). Car No 47 in Congreve Street, just after leaving Edmund Street for Dudley about 1911. Council House Extension (1909) still looking very clean.

Birmingham track; Birmingham likewise worked the Soho 31 route, the end of which was also BD area. Company cars occasionally did a trip to Bearwood, but I think not to Soho. A few yards from the Windmill Lane junction towards Smethwick was an electric sub-station, on the site of 'Windmill Lane' steam tram depot, which was in fact quite some little way from Windmill Lane; track and overhead led into the yard and was doubtless used by the tramways Parcels Express, but in later days was simply retained for feeder purposes, the same applying at Tividale works almost at the other end of the route, where track and overhead remained *in situ* right through the period of operation by Birmingham, long after the tramcar works had closed. The line continued through a quite pleasant residential area of Smethwick (some parts of which are very attractive despite the view one gets from the railway) and then became more scattered before reaching Spon Lane, West Smethwick. Between here and Oldbury the area becomes industrial — Chance Brothers Limited glassworks to the right, with some very interesting early industrial buildings still extant, and a complex of the chemical works of Albright and Wilson to the left. The atmosphere just around here could be very interesting at times. Oldbury Carriage Works at Broadwell were on the right; a childhood memory of mine is of being awakened one night by the sound of many factory hooters or 'bulls' going and seeing the glare in the sky as, we later found out, Oldbury Carriage Works burned. A short, quite steep climb into Oldbury involved the negotiation of a piece of double track in Birmingham Street where the tracks were too close together for cars to pass and which was operated as single track by means of trolley-actuated signal lights.

Beyond Oldbury one entered more sparsely populated country — this still applies, though less so today. At Brades Locks, where a flight of three locks linking the Birmingham and Wolverhampton levels of the canal passed under the tramway, was Brades Hall farm, where farming was in fact continued until relatively recently. On to the Boat Inn, Tividale, and one became conscious of the hills crowding in from the left. At Groveland Road the line passed over Netherton Canal Tunnel, though this was not obvious to the tram passenger, but if one knows where to look the tops of the ventilator shafts could be seen striding over the hills. Tividale Works now came up on the left, and at one time a great deal of activity went on here. During World War I, when most tramway undertakings were in no position to take on new construction, Tividale built quite a number of standard double-deck cars for the Birmingham and Midland Tramways Joint Committee, these being an improved version of the Brush 'Aston' type car of the CBT Company, with balcony top-covers and semi-vestibules — windscreens rather than full vestibules, and the celebrated 'Tividale' single-deckers. It seemed that the BMTJC was all set to re-equip their tramways when hostilities were over with these high-speed single-deckers, and certainly quite a fleet of them was built. Wolverhampton Corporation had some Brush-built cars of virtually the same pattern, and so did Barrow Corporation, while one car went to the Potteries for evaluation. Certainly the cab layout influenced another BET operator, the Gateshead and District Tramways Company Limited, whose large bogie single-deckers (No 5 survives at Crich and No 10 at Beamish) could be described as enlargements of the Tividale car. However, the war over, the 'transformation scene' on the Black Country tramways never took place. The Committee, or the companies, were not masters in their own house; they did not own their tracks, but only leased them, and as the leases ran out the motor-bus, in particular the motor-buses of their associated Committee member, the Birmingham and Midland Motor Omnibus Company Limited ('Midland Red') seemed a more attractive proposition. When the BMMO Company began building its own vehicles, of SOS design, it was 'curtains' for the Black Country trams, and except for the routes which Birmingham Corporation trams continued to operate until 1939 — Colmore Row to Wednesbury (75) and Dudley (74) and Edmund Street to Dudley via Oldbury (87) the trams left the stage. Sections of track and overhead lingered for years, depending on how tidy-minded various local authorities were; along Brettell Lane, Stourbridge, the tramway poles were sawn off short and converted to lighting poles, while on the Wolverhampton-Dudley route which became part of the Wolverhampton trolleybus empire the familiar poles with the BET 'Wheel and Magnet' device cast into the pole-base, survived until the end of electric operation. Doubtless a major factor in the early disappearance of the Black Country tramway system was the enormously increased costs of track renewals after World War I, which the local authorities were

Below: The prototype B&MTJC 'Tividale' single-decker designed by Richard Humphries of 1917, at Tividale works. (SST No 2).

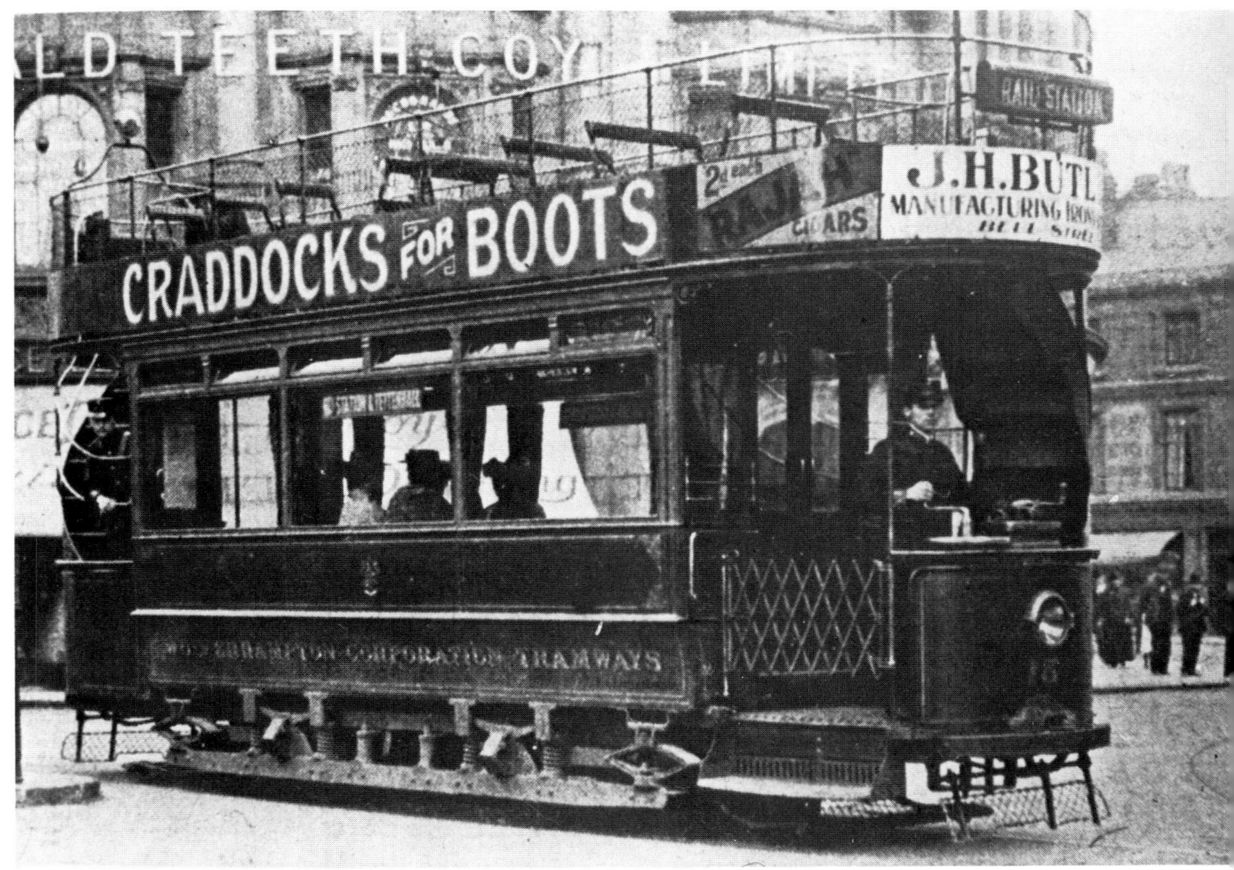

unwilling to carry out, coupled with road improvements which had to wait many years — in many places they are still waiting — to be carried out. It was not just a case of new trams; the whole road system on which they operated needed re-thinking, and the BMTJC had little if any say in this. The trolleybus and more so still the motor-bus with its almost unlimited availability were the easy way out. However, it had to be a good bus to work in the Black Country, and Wyndham Shire's SOS Midland Reds were all that and more, and as the tram routes one by one succumbed, the Black Country became a Midland Red stronghold; by 1930 company operation was all over.

Above: Wolverhampton Corporation Tramways Car No 15 on Dupont surface-contact truck at the railway station terminus of the Tettenhall route.

When Wolverhampton Corporation set about electrifying its tramway routes, the system of current collection adopted was the Lorain surface-contact system, whereby studs laid centrally between the running rails came into contact with a skate underneath each car, the skate being long enough to span two studs. The skate in fact was an electromagnet when the car was in motion, though batteries had to be employed to lift the studs when the car was stationary. When not in contact with the skate, the studs lay flush with the road surface and were, or should have

Above: Walsall Corporation car No 27, at Pleck, on Darlaston-Walsall service. This is the location of the episode of Inspector Cooper's Whistle.

Left: Walsall Corporation car No 27 again, top-covered and vestibuled, on Birmingham Road (Bell Inn) route, about to begin the descent into Walsall. Photographs of this route, replaced by buses in 1928, are very scarce.

been, electrically dead. As the car progressed, the magnetic skate lifted the next stud in its socket, thereby making it electrically alive and maintaining the supply, while the stud just left behind dropped back into its socket and became dead again. Of all the surface-contact systems adopted in this country — the Dolter system was tried at Torquay and the Griffiths-Bedell briefly in London, the Lorain had the longest run in Wolverhampton, and the original cars had Lorain single trucks — the only examples, I believe, in this country and of typical continental appearance. The London experiment used bogie cars, and I imagine that a skate under a bogie car, presumably attached to the body, would have presented difficulties. The Wolverhampton Lorain cars worked well for many years, many of the three-bay open-top cars being rebuilt with open-balcony top-covers, while some new cars with vestibule cabs were added after World War I. Owing to a low railway bridge on the Wednesfield route, single-deckers had to be used for that service and, as already mentioned, some new single-deckers of the 'Tividale' pattern were also added. It now became apparent that the Lorain system was worn out, and that some of the studs were alive when flush with the road; I believe this was discovered when a Great Western Railway horse came to an untimely end by stepping on a live stud, and there was a rapid conversion to overhead in the early 1920s. Some of the studs survived in Cleveland Road depot, and a few years ago were dug out and built into a section of track at the Crich Tramway Museum. At this time there was a renewal of interest in trolleybuses — still called 'Trackless Trams' at this date — Birmingham having converted the Nechells route in 1922, and Wolverhampton became interested. By 1930 the town had gone over to this form of traction with both single- and double-deck vehicles, and had moreover taken over the Wolverhampton District Electric Tramways Company routes and converted them to trolleybus, so that the light green and cream Wolverhampton trolleys ran to Dudley, Darlaston, Willenhall to Fighting Cocks, and to Walsall via Willenhall, Walsall Corporation also investing in a few trolleybuses for this route. Wednesfield still had to be restricted to single-deckers, until 1943 when the road was lowered under the GWR and double-deckers just squeezed under the bridge, some quite modern single-deck trolleys then being sold. Both Sunbeam and Guy trolleybuses were made in the town, and it can certainly be said that Charles Owen Silvers' trolleybus installation was the model for the widespread adoption of these vehicles elsewhere.

Walsall Corporation's trams had gradually been 'phased out' in the 1920s, being replaced by motor buses of Guy and Dennis manufacture until the turn of the last route to Bloxwich in 1933. In the pre-1914 period Walsall had been early off the mark with top-covers, the first with uncanopied balconies, something between the Liverpool 'Bellamy' roof and the 'Magrini' type as fitted in Hull. There the Magrini roofs were deeply curved at the sides, but the Walsall top-covers had a much shallower curve. Walsall went further, and some cars had a fully-enclosed top-cover, with later some cases of enclosed cabs as well, so that Walsall had fully-enclosed cars long before Birmingham did. One of these, No 16, lost most of its glass in a Zeppelin air-raid. Fully-enclosed cars on the narrow gauges were disapproved of by the Board of Trade, however, and these cars had disappeared well before the end. The cars which ran the Bloxwich route at the end were four-bay open-balcony single-truck cars with angle-dash enclosed cabs very similar to the Birmingham 301 class, with perhaps a touch of the Bradford cars about them. They were replaced in this instance not by motor but by trolleybuses, 15 new Sunbeam six-wheelers coming into the fleet. The very interesting period of Walsall's trolleybus expansion under Edgley Cox lies outside our period; but at least it can be mentioned that the Walsall tradition of rebuilding and modernising vehicles, dating from early tram days, was fully maintained. As Walsall was one of the very last trolleybus operators, the vehicles in fact having passed into the hands of the West Midlands Passenger Transport Executive, the town's place in the history of electric road traction is a very important one.

Below: Walsall Corporation car No 25 with full-enclosed top-deck at Walsall Wood, the north-easterly extremity of the West Midlands tramway complex. Pre-1914. / *Via J. Haddock*

Perhaps due to being a hybrid vehicle, the trolleybus never quite achieved the affectionate regard of the public that the tramcar did, and trolleybus stories are not met with so frequently as were tramway ones, but I witnessed the following scene in Wolverhampton outside the High Level station at Victoria Square. This was the terminus for the Tettenhall trolleys which swung right round the square and back up Lichfield Street. The Whitmore Reans-Darlaston route also traversed Victoria Square, but continued via Pipers Row towards Darlaston; the overhead junction frogs were manually operated by a rod on a traction pole — they may have been replaced later by automatics, but I am not sure on this point. At all events, on this occasion the conductor of a Darlaston-bound trolley whose duty it was to pull the rod tangled with some other traffic and by the time he reached the pole, the trolleys had passed the junction but, of course, had taken the Tettenhall direction. Both trolleys dewired, got enmeshed with span wires, some of which broke, and the whole installation sagged down nearly on to the roofs of those trolleybuses within range. The Darlaston driver got out of his cab — he was a burly man, the conductor somewhat undersized, so there was something of a Laurel and Hardy situation. The driver came wearily round to the back of the bus

Below: Walsall Corporation car No 16 at Birchills depot with most of the glass blown out in a Zeppelin raid. Car fully enclosed. / *Walsall CT*

Above: Walsall Corporation car No 32 at Darlaston Bull Stake, looking towards Walsall. Open-balcony top-cover, vestibule cab. Observe trolley-pan on overhead, to minimise flashing at night during air-raids. Clock-faces on pole now removed (see WDET car 14). / *The late J. Aston*

and said, 'I might a' known it. I might a' known I'd 'ave some bleedin' bad luck if I 'ad yo' on the back. I'd rather see a cross-eyed 'ooman than tek yo' out for the day.' As the incident took place near Cleveland Road depot, there was a tower wagon on the spot in a very short time and everything was strung up and going again very expeditiously, the service actually continuing at the caution once the trolleybooms of the Darlaston vehicle had been retrieved — no running wires broke as luck would have it. Dewirements on the Wolverhampton system were very rare in my experience, but it seemed that whenever I visited some other trolleybus towns there were always some trolleybooms waving in the breeze when they should have been on the wires.

It is perhaps difficult today when public transport is taken for granted — where it is not in fact fighting for its life against competition from private transport — to realise what an extension to the boundaries of everyday life was conferred by the tramcar 70 years ago. It gave mobility at very cheap rates to people whose lives had hitherto been confined to their own locality, and made it possible for them to work at distances from their own homes which would have been impossible on foot, even in those times when people walked distances, as all in the day's work, which today would require sponsorship as being something highly unusual. Marketing and pleasure excursions by tram quickly became part of urban life, and any town of any pretentions at all had its trams. With hindsight, we can see that only a very few years separated the arrival of the electric tram and the motor bus; had the latter vehicle become a viable proposition a few years earlier than it did, the trams would never have been, involving as they did so much fixed equipment such as power stations, cables, track — with its concomitant road upheavals. When the Black Country Tramways took shape in the early 1900s the motor bus was a music-hall joke — which joke

Above: Wolverhampton Corporation's first trolleybus, of Tilling-Stevens manufacture.
/ *Wolverhampton Library*

sometimes backfired when nasty runaways like Handcross occurred — and were not to be taken seriously against the already proven electric tram. The end of World War I saw the tramways everywhere in a sorry and run-down state, and those in company ownership in particularly vulnerable situation. The motor bus had come through the war period — in the case of the London General 'B' type, through the war itself — toughened, hardened and reliable. During the 1920s the bus developed into a fast and sophisticated vehicle against which the more elderly tramcars made a poor showing; but even in 1920 buses were coming into service which were a formidable opposition to the tram. Really, there were only about 20 years in it — but for those of us who grew up with trams, what a slice of life would have been missing without them! They were, of course, blamed by those who always complain anyway for causing delay and congestion; they did — any public vehicle will necessarily do so. But let it be categorically said that on the whole they did NOT cause the same degree of congestion that today's one-man double-deck buses 8ft 2in wide, and 36ft single-deckers do, but there is, of course, now a generation gap between the drivers of the bull-nosed Morris Cowleys of the 1920s, cursing the tram loading in the middle of the road and the young driver of today who lives with congestion anyway (and for whom trams were something his parents went to school on) stuck behind a front-loading one-man bus with its back end out across the road, due doubtless to a car parked at the bus stop. Perhaps he accepts the fact that he and his fellow motorists are part of the congestion of today, the underlying principle being if-you-can't-beat-'em-join-'em. One aspect of the tramway period deserves to go on record, certainly applying to the Black Country system — that for shifting the crowds, the trams had no rivals. They still have not been surpassed.

Enter the Motor Bus

Above: BMMO Co Ltd SOS 'QLC' coach 1928, HA 4835.

Above right: Birmingham Motor Express Co Ltd Milnes-Daimler motor bus and CBT Co Ltd horse bus at the Ivy Bush, Hagley Road, 1903. Despite the 'New Street' display the bus is bound for the Kings Head. The tradition of wrong destinations in Birmingham dates back a long way!

Right: Birmingham and Midland Motor Omnibus Co Ltd (Midland Red) Tilling-Stevens TTA 1 petrol-electric bus of 1912 at the Bear Hotel, Bearwood. The bus carries the BET wheel-and-magnet device on the side panel, and was in fact B and MT property for BMMO use. Later batches carried the Midland fleet name. This vehicle later became Birmingham Corporation property.

If the overhead electric tram made a late appearance in Birmingham, the motor bus was there early. In 1903, the same year in which the Great Western Railway set upon the roads of Cornwall some Milnes-Daimler buses, running between Helston and the Lizard, the Birmingham Motor Express Company Limited began bus operation in Birmingham, with a quite varied though small fleet of Napier, Milnes-Daimler, Wolseley, Durkopp and Thornycroft vehicles, working from a garage in Ladywood Road. Bus services in Birmingham at this period were, of course, of the horse-drawn variety operated by the British Electric Traction (BET)-controlled Birmingham and Midland Tramways and City of Birmingham Tramways Companies, and to counter the competition of the new motor buses a new BET company was set up in 1904, the Birmingham and Midland Motor Omnibus Company Limited, whose initial fleet consisted of some Brush open-top buses with 40hp engines. The Express Company had only a short run, and in 1905 was taken over by the BMMO Company, who continued to operate the combined fleet for another two years but then decided that this was no way to run a bus service and went back to horses, the motor buses being transferred to the Deal and District Motor Services. The Birmingham company, however, retained the word 'Motor' in their title.

It has always seemed to me a little odd that in Birmingham, of all places, such a debacle should have taken place. The GWR, whose Helston-Lizard experiment was to find out if road motor traction could save the expense of branch line or light railway construction, went on to extend greatly their road fleet of passenger and goods vehicles until they became a sizeable bus operator, with long runs like Oxford to Cheltenham, while as far back as 1905 the GWR inaugurated a motor bus service from Stourbridge to Hagley, Belbroughton and Bromsgrove, and put some Clarkson steam buses on a Wolverhampton-Bridgnorth service, much later to be taken over by Wolverhampton Corporation buses. Perhaps the BET, knowing their days as tramway operators in Birmingham were numbered, were not prepared to expend vast sums of money on motor buses just for prestige reasons; by all accounts the horses gave a better service

MILK
NEW STREET

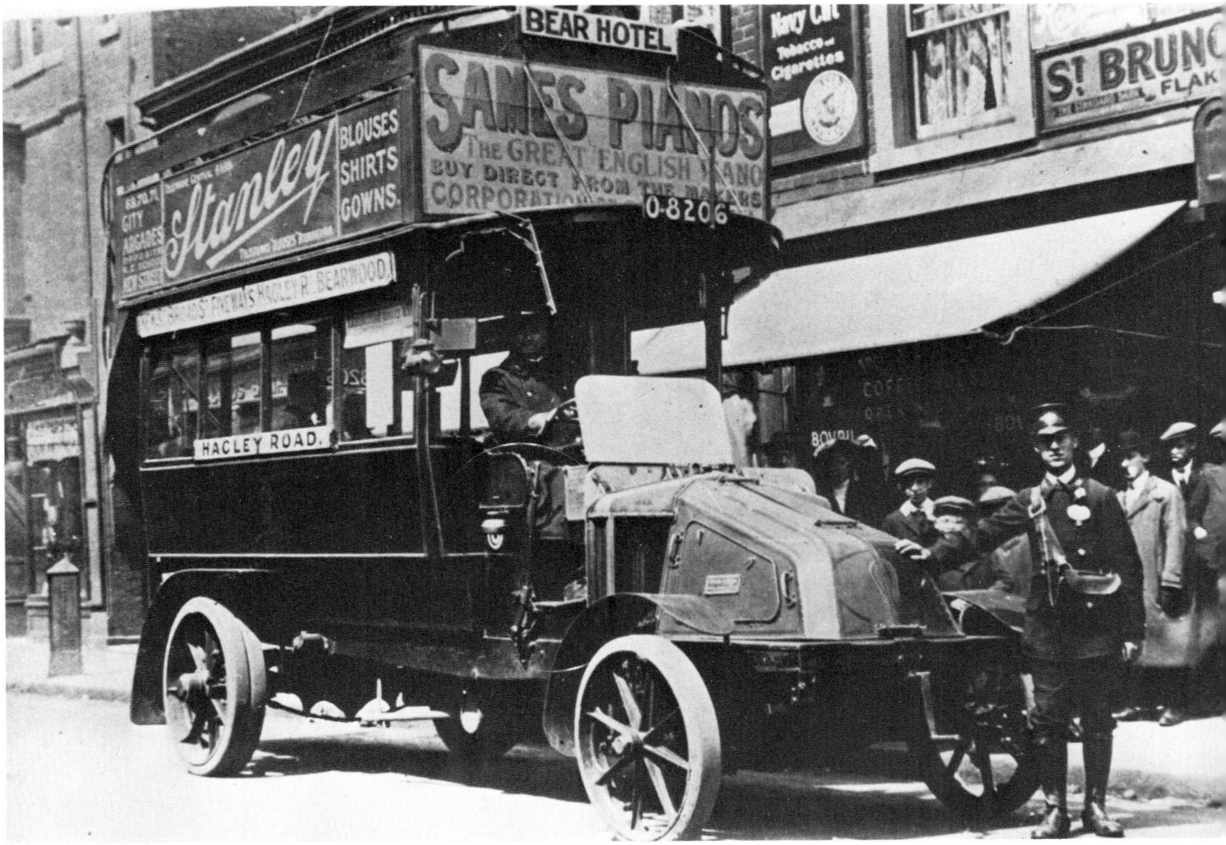

BEAR HOTEL
SAMES PIANOS
Stanley
CITY ARCADES
NEW STREET
BLOUSES SHIRTS GOWNS.
0-8206
HAGLEY ROAD.
Navy Cut
Tobacco and Cigarettes
St BRUNO

and at least got you there. With the motors it was anybody's guess. Whatever, there was this hiatus until 1912 when the Tilling-Stevens petrol-electric TTA 1 model became available, and this altered the aspect very considerably. There had been an experimental Daimler petrol-electric on demonstration in 1911, embodying some very advanced thinking indeed, but I believe this remained a 'one-off'. The fact is, however, that Birmingham, to become one of the main centres of the motor industry, turned its back on the motor bus during this period. Not far away Wolverhampton Corporation put a Milnes-Daimler on the road in 1903, and some Wolseleys followed in 1905, being discontinued in 1909 when tramway routes replaced them, but evidently they had been found useful in opening up new routes. Birmingham Corporation had nothing to do with buses until 1913, when 10 'Y'-type Daimlers with LGOC 'B' type bodywork appeared on Bristol Road, connecting with the trams at Selly Oak and running to Rednal and Rubery. By this time many operators all over the country were taking to the motor bus, and in London they were already outnumbering the trams. Birmingham was not alone among the big provincial cities in more or less ignoring the bus while promoting the municipal tramways — Liverpool and Manchester adopted similar courses; but whereas London was predominantly motor bus really before 1914, it was not until the late 1930s that the buses outnumbered the trams in Birmingham. Probably the explanation is that the first two general managers in Birmingham were tramwaymen and very good at their job; however, in L. G. Wyndham Shire in the 1920s Midland Red had an engineer who produced some of the most highly competent buses ever seen in this country, and in that decade the BMMO certainly made up for time lost before World War I.

In the early days of the motor bus there was trouble from all sides, and not the least was the difficulty of keeping the solid rubber tyres on their rims — wheels were then of wooden construction, and driven wooden wheels tended to shed their tyres very easily — it was not unknown anyway with trailing wheels, as all wheels on horse-drawn vehicles were, but a driving wheel was another matter. There were some very good petrol engines available by 1903; they were not trouble-free, and neither are the engines of today, but engine trouble was as nothing compared with transmission — clutch, gearbox and final drive. The Milnes-Daimler would seem to have been as good as any at this time, with final pinion drive on to a gear ring on each back wheel, noisy especially when worn but relatively reliable. One imagines the final drive would have to be frequently renewed due to wear from road grit and the like, but the Milnes-Daimler was built in quite some numbers and by all accounts did well by the standards of the time.

Standards? What standards? There can have been precious few in 1903 — doubtless plenty of regulations, but regulations are by no means standard. Standards in anything can only be established when there is a fund of experience to draw on, and there was little of that commodity in motor-bus work in 1903. One looks back in awe at those men of 1903 who took out those heavy (and they were!) early motor buses with only the most primeval brakes, in some cases only an upgraded horse-bus brake acting on the rubber tyre, of little use if the driver missed his gear when down-changing on a steep gradient, or if the gear-stick flew 'out of cog' on a descent. The engines of those days had not the reserve of power to do what a driver I used to know did on one occasion when, nearing the end of his country route, he had a straight but steep descent to a narrow river bridge, then an equally steep ascent to the terminus. On beginning the descent, he felt the brakes on his Leyland Tiger TS II go completely limp; he already knew the handbrake was of only nominal value. He stepped on the gas down the grade, offered up all the prayers he knew that nothing would be coming through the bridge the other way — and his prayers were answered — and charged up the 1 in 8 the other side, and swung her round into the pub yard terminus at the top; here at least the handbrake just about held the bus, though he scotched the rear wheels before telephoning his depot to the effect that he wasn't bringing it back until somebody had been out to fix the brakes — all of them. I may say that this incident did not take place in the Midlands; all came out well because there was plenty of power in reserve. When such situations arose in the early days, as they are known to have done, the chances were not so good. Those early bus-men learned fast, though not in Birmingham; as recorded elsewhere, by 1910 Metropolitan Police requirements had put them on their mettle,

Below: Tilling-Stevens TTA II, O 9938, of BMMO Co Ltd at Chester Road tram terminus bound for Four Oaks in 1914. 27-seat Birch Bros body.

and the upshot was Frank Searle's LGOC 'B' type, to be built by the thousand and remembered as long as buses shall run.

When the motor-bus returned to Birmingham, however, in 1912 it was the petrol-electric Tilling-Stevens TTA 1, thirteen of which, Nos 0 8200-8212, joined the BMMO fleet. Perhaps the BET, who controlled BMMO, being primarily a tramway combine, looked more favourably on a vehicle driven electrically than one propelled via clutch and gearbox — doubtless they recalled the pre-1907 era and said 'enough is enough'. Evidently the Daimler petrol-electric demonstrator of 1911 had made a good impression, though in many respects it was ahead of its time. The TTA 1 had a 'cheese-cover' bonnet, rather like Renault cars, with the radiator behind the engine ahead of the dash, a position favoured by Austin commercials also. The next addition to the fleet were of the TTA II model, with 40hp engines against the 30hp of the TTA I, with radiator positioned normally, though not yet of the standard Tilling-Stevens type which was to become so familiar everywhere. They gave a very smooth take-off and were reasonably fast on the level, but slow uphill; the weight of the engine, generator and motor came out heavier than clutch and gearbox transmission, and there was very considerable power loss uphill. I realised early that compared with the Daimler 'Y' and AEC 'S' type — this was in the 1920s when the first 30 Midland Tilling-Stevens had been Corporation property since 1914 — the Tillings were slow, because I could catch up with them on my first low-geared boy's bike on the hills in Hamstead Road on the old Handsworth Wood 2 route, impossible with a Daimler or AEC. The great disadvantage with the petrol-electrics was that the engine could not be used to retard the bus downhill as with gearbox transmission; the driver had to rely on rear-wheel brakes only, with narrow solid tyres offering minimal braking area with the road. Today one sweats quietly at the idea of the petrol-electrics up and down Mucklows Hill and Drews Holloway on the Stourbridge service, but they *did* go up and down Mucklows Hill for years. Perhaps faith counted for more than standards in those days.

Although empowered by its 1903 Act to operate motor buses within the city, Birmingham Corporation, as already mentioned, did not figure as a bus operator until 1913 when the Daimlers Nos OA 1601-1610 were put into service on the Bristol Road — another 'first' for Bristol Road. The Corporation now had all the tramways in the city under its control, with through-running Birmingham District trams from Dudley running into Edmund Street and South Staffordshire cars from Darlaston running to Colmore Row, and now turned its attention to the bus services. The BMMO Company had been running the Tilling-Stevens buses since April 1912 on services from New Street to Harborne, Queen's Park, and Moseley and from the Ivy Bush to Handsworth Wood, but in 1914 agreement was reached with the Corporation whereby the Corporation took over these routes,

Above: Tilling-Stevens OA 346 of BMMO Co Ltd beginning the long drag up Mucklows Hill, Halesowen about 1914. Location is just below the canal bridge, utterly unrecognisable today.

with 30 Tilling-Stevens buses and the Tennant Street (Five Ways) garage from the Midland Company. The BMMO Company then moved their headquarters to Bearwood Road where they remained until recently, and continued to run into Birmingham from outside the city; they could still pick up passengers within the city, but at protective fares, double the tram or Corporation bus fare over the section travelled, the Corporation collecting their share of the proceeds. It was a friendly agreement and worked very well for many years. Thus from October 1914 Birmingham Corporation worked all services, trams and bus, within the city.

By this time the fateful date of 4 August 1914 was already past, and things were not long to remain as they now were. The 10 Bristol Road Daimlers, which operated from Dawlish Road tram depot, Selly Oak — actually using the rear of the premises opening into Tiverton Road — were impressed by the War Department, but the Tilling-Stevens petrol-electrics were not required and ten further Tilling-Stevens chassis were obtained, taking registrations of the Daimlers, but carrying fleet numbers 31-40 instead of 1-10. (No 30 was an odd Tilling-Stevens with originally a body by Liversege); the ex-Midland vehicles were Nos 0 8200-8212 (TTA I) and 0 9913-9929 (TTA II). If these had carried fleet numbers when first taken over by BCT they would have been 0-12 and 13-29, and there would have been two lots of 1-10 before the Daimlers were requisitioned by the WD, but accurate information is lacking on this point. When I knew these ex-BMMO vehicles they were mostly no longer buses but Service vehicles, particularly the 0 8200 series. They then had normal Tilling-Stevens radiators. More Daimlers were added to the fleet in 1916, doubtless out of necessity to provide services to

Above: Birmingham Corporation Daimler 'Y' No 7, OA 1607, connecting with the tram service at Selly Oak for Rednal. These 10 Daimlers had a very short run before being commandeered for war service, the bodies being transferred to Tilling-Stevens chassis.

munitions factories. These were Nos 41-46, OB 1569-74, and 47-58, OB 2101-2112. Nos 41-52 had very stylish bodies by Christopher Dodson with some transverse lower decks seats, a distinct improvement, war or no war, on the rather utilitarian LGOC 'B' type bodies of the Tillings. The rest of the Daimlers, 53-58, sported these 'B' type bodies from the 0-8200 series, which were then presumably converted to tower wagons etc. Nos 53-58 did not run long before their Daimler chassis were commandeered, being once again replaced by Tilling-Stevens, but Daimlers Nos 41-52 survived to be rebodied in 1922 with Brush bodies in the style of the LGOC 'K' type, but necessarily shorter as the chassis remained normal-control, instead of the forward-control position beside the engine as on the AEC 'K'. The shapely Dodson bodies from Nos 41-49 were then put on Tilling-Stevens Nos 30-38. I have gone into this at some length, because photographs of all these vehicles have sometimes caused consternation among collectors who find Dodson bodies on a Tilling-Stevens when according to their records they should be Daimlers! I am unaware if this little saga of rebodying, transferring registrations and fleet numbers constitutes a record, but it must be well up in the charts. Mercifully, the practice was not to continue; at the time, it was just a case of making the best of what they had. Incidentally, six of the ex-BMMO Tillings were given single-deck bodies in 1916, five being transferred to 54-58 in 1920.

Faithful to the Tilling-Stevens chassis, Midland Red were able to make some progress during World War I and had opened up garages and services in towns very distant from Birmingham,

Left: Stylish Dodson body on BCT Daimler No 48, OB 2102. These bodies were transferred to Tilling-Stevens chassis when the Daimlers were given new Brush 'K' style bodies in 1922. / *BCT*

and at the close of hostilities were in a more favourable position than many bus operators. The fleet included some charabancs, and I have a very early memory of seeing a Midland Red bus in Weston-super-Mare with a luggage basket on the roof, this being probably 1922. I just couldn't believe my eyes — Birmingham to Weston was for trains, not buses, or so I then thought. (For me it became a cycle trip as well, one which I have done many times and still do, but I didn't reckon with that as I stared unbelievingly at the Midland Red on Beach Road in 1922.)

One of the earliest established BMMO services was from Birmingham to Walsall, mentioned early in this book, which commenced on Christmas Eve 1913, and the company were soon operating in the Sutton Coldfield area, an old-established service being to Sutton via Perry Barr and New Oscott (later the 107) and via Erdington and Wylde Green to Mere Green or Streetly, While double-deckers worked the Walsall service, there was a 'gentlemen's agreement' that double-deck buses should not operate in Sutton Coldfield, and it was not until the late 1930s, when steadily increasing business was making it impossible for single-deckers to handle the service, that the company asked to be released from the agreement. Sutton Coldfield, still rather exclusive today although now included in Birmingham, was almost feudal in those days. The double-deckers which ran Walsall were of the usual pattern of the period, with LGOC style rear-platform 34-seat bodies, but the illustration of No 0 9938 on the Chester Road-Sutton-Four Oaks run has a front-entrance single-deck body showing the beginnings of the individuality which was to stamp the company's vehicles in the post-World

Right: Tilling-Stevens No 33, OA 1603, of BCT with ex-Daimler Dodson body and registration from 1913 Daimler 'Y'. Rebodied 1922. / *BCT*

War I period. The BMMO company had now established their own works at Carlyle Road, Edgbaston, quite close to the Hagley Road behind Edgbaston Reservoir; this sheet of water, where only two miles from the city centre one can see an amazing variety of birds if one gets there early enough — heron, great crested grebe and many marques of duck and geese — was to be the attractive background of any number of official BMMO vehicle photographs. Now completely modernised, they still serve as Midland Red's main works.

Wolverhampton's early motor-bus ventures have already been mentioned; the Wolseleys had ceased to run when replaced by trams in 1909 (I saw one of them in Cleveland Road depot in about 1938, it having been derelict for years, so I was told, at Sedgley depot. It was in a terrible state, but I thought then, when hardly anyone was preserving commercial vehicles, that if it had survived so long, surely it would now be kept for posterity, but I was wrong). In 1911 motor services began again to Compton, Penn and Fallings Park with Albion single-deckers, which were commandeered in 1914, but later released, and some Tilling-Stevens joined the fleet in 1916, and a big expansion programme was put into effect from 1919.

Walsall Corporation obtained an Act in 1914 granting powers to operate motor buses in and outside the borough boundaries, and services to Cannock and Hednesford, from Bloxwich tram terminus, were commenced with Daimler single-deckers. Like Wolverhampton, Walsall developed an enormous 'empire' outside its own boundaries after the World War I. I have been told that only Sheffield developed a larger 'empire', relative to the size of the two towns, than Walsall.

West Bromwich also joined in with four Albion 25-seaters in September 1914. This again proved an unfortunate time — due to circumstances beyond anybody's control — to start bus operation, and like many another, West Bromwich lost its bus chassis to the War Department. Not to be outdone, however, the Corporation obtained four Edison Accumulator chassis and placed the bodies from the Albions on them, transferring the registrations EA 300-303 also. The W. J. Smith bodies had an extra bay built on to the rear, as the front bulkheads were now right at the front of the chassis, and their appearance was odd to say the least of it. They ran on a route from Greets Green to All Saints Church via Dartmouth Square, re-charging the batteries from the Corporation mains while standing at the terminus. It was a brave attempt, partially successful, to keep things going, but the Edisons were not man enough for the job. The climb up to Draper's Bridge, near where the present Oak Lane bus garage stands — not steep, but a climb nevertheless — beat them. There were quite a few of these Edison electrics about on delivery van work which they did very well, lasting well into the 1920s, but a heavy bus body and a full load was much more than they were intended for. Hired Tilling-Stevens from the BMMO helped out, and the upshot was their replacement by Tilling-

Left: Tilling-Stevens No 54, OB 2108, of BCT with Brush single-deck body. Registration from commandeered Daimler. / *BCT*

Below: The first two West Bromwich Corporation (WBCT) Albions, EA 300/301 in 1914. Hardly had they entered service when the chassis were impressed for war service. / *WBCT*

Stevens chassis in 1919, this time the TS3 model. Once again bodies and registrations were transferred, the Tilling-Stevens appearing as Nos 1-4, but registration order was EA 303, 301, 300, 302, and another TS3, No 5, EA 999, with a 29-seat Roberts body, joined the fleet in 1920. The buses operated from the Public Works Department at Hardware Street, in the Cronehills district of West Bromwich. Oak Lane was a long time distant as yet.

This brings the story to the end of World War I period, with one major bus operator destined to become one of the biggest such undertakings in the country, and three municipal tramway operators who also ran some buses but were at this stage not terribly keen about them and who were, certainly as regards Birmingham, thinking of very large-scale tramway development. The Birmingham and Midland Tramways Joint Committee with its associate, the Birmingham and Midland Motor Omnibus Company Limited, it would seem were thinking not at all of tramway development but of the best way open to them of staying in business in an increasingly difficult situation. In the early 1900s they fitted their electric tramways into a long-outmoded road system, and they gave good service in their time. The motor bus is much better at fitting into awkward situations, and doubtless by 1920 the BMTJC could see clearly enough where their future lay. The next few years were to see many of the smaller tramway concerns everywhere fade quickly from the scene, leaving only the 'big boys' to carry on with trams. At this point we might return to the story of Birmingham Corporation Tramways, whom we had left at the beginning of World War I.

Below: A WBCT Edison Electric with WJ Smith body from the Albions, extended at rear. Performance was erratic to say the least, and bodies and registrations were transferred to Tilling-Stevens chassis. / *WBCT*

Birmingham Corporation Tramways 1914–1939

Above: BMMO Co Ltd SOS 'XL' Coach 1929, HA 4966. Chassis and radiators transferred to 'MM' buses 1930, the coach bodies and registrations going to new 'RR' chassis with flat-top radiators.

We left the tramway scene in Birmingham in 1914, by which time the Corporation were in full control not only of the trams but of the bus services as well, with, however, company trams and buses running into the city from destinations outside the boundary. These arrangements were to continue very satisfactorily for many years, though as the Birmingham District and the South Staffs tramway companies' leases ran out Birmingham Corporation tramways took over the entire operation of the Dudley Road and West Bromwich routes, so that we saw only Birmingham Corporation trams and buses, and the buses of Midland Red. Not for Birmingham the joyous kaleidoscope of the London 'Pirates' — though they had as much right on the streets of London as the General — or the Potteries with — was it 58? — independent operators vying with Potteries Motor Traction. That really was something to see!

Like anybody else, Birmingham's tramways suffered during the World War I, both vehicles and track. Kyott's Lake Road Works were engaged on munitions work in addition to keeping the trams and buses going, and a siding was laid in from the Stratford Road Tramway at Camp Hill into the Midland Railway goods yard so that materials and finished goods could be worked to and from Kyott's Lake by tramway vehicles. Although disconnected for many years, it remained *in situ*, and some of it is still visible at the goods yard entrance.

Although some trams had been built by the CBT Company at The Lake, Birmingham Corporation did not build its own cars but had them built by, up to this time, United Electric at Preston. Had BCT built its own cars as some municipal operators did, Liverpool and Manchester among them, perhaps some new construction might have taken place; the neighbouring BMT Joint Committee managed to build quite a few new cars at Tividale during this period. The only noteworthy development at The Lake was the rebuilding of cars Nos 451 and 452, the two large five-bay ex-CBT open-top cars now on Burnley bogies as single-deckers, with a clerestory roof in the case of No 451. This was, I understand, at the instigation of a member of the Tramways Committee who had been impressed with continental practice of running single-deckers with trailers, and to run with Nos 451 and 452 one of the old Bristol Road ex-CBT cars, 509, and No 28 of the 21-70 class were cut down to single-deck trailers. They were put to work on the Washwood Heath and Alum Rock routes, which used the Martineau Street loop terminus in the city centre, but at the outer termini had the usual stub arrangements, necessitating an additional crossover for run-round procedure. Ideally, for trailer operation, a terminal loop is desirable and though proposals were put up for one at Washwood Heath, nothing came of it. (When two Birmingham routes, Yardley and Rednal, did acquire terminal loops it was much later on when any ideas about trailers had been put aside.) Further, it was said that the drivers saw in the trailers a threat to their livelihood and contrived to drop so much time in running round that the trailer period in Birmingham did not last long. Trailer operation was continued on the Nechells route for a little

Below: CBT Co Ltd car No 178 of 1903, built at Kyotts Lake Road on Brush equal-wheel bogies. This car and No 180 became BCT Nos 451 and 452 and were the trial cars for the Burnley Bogie in 1912. / *BCT*

Bottom: BCT car No 451, ex-CBT No 178, rebuilt as clerestory-roof single-decker. Note similarity to a London subway car. / *BCT*

longer, this route having virtually a loop terminus, outwards via Nechells Park Road and inwards via Long Acre, but it is very doubtful if this route ever justified such carrying capacity. The two motor cars were transferred to Rosebery Street depot for use as solo single-deckers on the Hagley Road route, and I have a very clear memory of a ride on No 451 in this condition. Apparently I made such an exhibition of myself that my parents hastily got aboard as the only means of restoring order; I may say that this sort of lapse was very rare as a child with me. I found out very early that I did better by behaving myself than by kicking up, but the sight of a single-decker was too much. I only had the one ride on No 451, and didn't know then that there were two of them. I first met up with No 452 when both cars had been rebuilt yet again with open-balcony top-covers in 1926, but we haven't got to 1926 yet.

During the war route letters, shown on the upper-deck

Below: BCT car No 452, ex-CBT No 180, as rebuilt 1926 with open-balcony top-cover. At Fort Dunlop 1938. / *R. T. Coxon*

Above: BCT 'Aston Bogie' with post-World War I roof numeral indicator boxes, and plain rocker panel. Still open-cab, reverse stairs and on Brill 22E bogies.

bulkheads, were abandoned and route numbers, first shown by stencil numerals on the dash-lamp, replaced them, the geographical destination still being shown by a reversible board on the balcony grille and by side destination boards. The end boards showed the actual destination, 'OXHILL ROAD TO COLMORE ROW' or 'COLMORE ROW TO OXHILL ROAD', whichever way the car was going, and this practice was still in force as my first clear memories developed about 1920. Roller-blind numeral boxes were then fitted to the cars, attached to the upper-deck canopy, and the front boards were then discontinued, though I seem to recall seeing cars on the Oxhill Road route showing both route 26 and the front board, but there is no photographic evidence of this. The side boards, showing only the outer destination, continued in use for some time, the first batch of fully-enclosed cars (637 class) being provided with slots for them. With the loss of the front boards the cars showed only a numeral, and from this time, therefore, dates the lamentable practice of showing only a front route number, and the outer destination on the side. When the side boards were replaced (at first by framed celluloid displays hung from the glazing bar of the window nearest the step showing, for example: 26 OXHILL ROAD 26), then roller blinds showing OXHILL ROAD 26, mounted in the same position, only the outer terminus was shown whichever way the car was going — and this practice was extended to the buses also — so that for half its running time the vehicle was displaying false information, or only informed the passengers where the car was coming from.

Where there was an alternative city terminus, a double-line display showed:

YARDLEY AND
HIGH STREET 15

YARDLEY AND
STATION STREET 16

which was all very well if you were used to the system. Visitors got toted about all over the place, and over the years there was quite a volume of correspondence about it in the local press, but all to no avail. The Department seemed to have a psychological block somewhere on this subject, and the practice has not yet disappeared on the present buses, run by the West Midlands Passenger Transport Executive for the last eight years.

No new cars appeared until 1920, when Nos 587-636 were delivered from the Brush works at Loughborough, mounted on the Brush variant of the Burnley bogie, with an additional vertical member for strength. The Mountain and Gibson Burnleys later had a similar rib added, making them virtually identical to the Brush products. The 587 class were practically identical with 512-586, a detail difference being that whereas on the 512 class the three planes of the angle-dash met at the angle, on the Brush cars the angle was effected through a gentle curve. Moseley Road had the first of the new cars, 587-611, Hockley receiving the rest.

When about five years old I was being taken out to Kings Heath on one of these almost new cars — which even then I realised were bogie cars such as we had on the Handsworth routes — on route 40, Kings Heath via Leopold Street. My mother was a bit concerned over going Leopold Street way, but as a 40 came before a 38 via Balsall Heath we took the risk. Shortly after the car had rounded the corner into Moseley Road the driver brought the car up to a very sudden stop, slid the door back and shouted, 'Aeroplane up!', and every body piled off the car to see the aircraft. What the aircraft was I then had no idea — probably a DH 9A from Castle Bromwich, which design I got to know very well, when, around 1928-1930, I developed strong aircraft leanings and still take great delight in seeing the planes I then knew still taking the air at the Shuttleworth Collection at Old Warden. But this was about 1922, and the combination of a tram ride up Leopold Street and out-of-course stop to see an aeroplane lodged in my memory. A less distinct but still positive memory is of seeing the R 34 come over Birmingham about this period, but I was not riding on a tram at the time or doubtless I should be able to 'fix' the occasion more definitely.

As by now Kyott's Lake was catching up with wartime arrears of painting I got the idea that the Handsworth routes had the best cars and that routes such as Yardley, Washwood Heath and Dudley Road which had old cars with open cabs were not to be mentioned in the same breath at the Hockley routes. As for Perry

Barr, where an uncle of mine lived, well, they had car No 1 on that route which must date back to the Ark: certainly at that date the 1-20 'Aston Bogies' were still on Brill 22Es and were open cab and looked their age. (When, in 1940 during my first months in the Army, I was posted to Eccles and saw the Salford Corporation equal wheel Milnes bogies, still open-cab and with reverse stairs, I got a touch of the 'I-have-been-here-before' feeling and realised that these cars were in the same condition as the Aston bogies as I had known them in the early twenties, and for a moment I slid down a time-crack.)

Unknown to me, since I was only four years old and unlikely to be consulted in the matter, Kyott's Lake had been playing around with two of the 301 class, Nos 342 and 347. This was in 1921. No 342 came out with the balconies enclosed in such a fashion as to be nicknamed 'The Armoured Car' for the rest of its service — a reference to the photograph will serve to show why. The top-deck bulkheads were retained, the balconies being built up with sheet metal; No 347 emerged later in the year, but treated much more acceptably, so that its outward appearance was made the model for the fully enclosed 637-661 bogie class of 1923. Again the top-deck bulkheads were retained, but at least you could see where you were going, which was impossible on No 342. Both cars were rebuilt on temporary licence from the Board of Trade, who were nervous about fully-enclosed single-truck cars on the narrow gauges, but Kyott's Lake thoughtfully forgot to rebuild the two cars back to their original state, and they ran as rebuilt until withdrawn in 1950, both cars clocking up over one million miles. I believe this nervousness on the part of the BOT derives from an accident to a Halifax car which was blown over on the climb up to Catherine Slack; by the same token top-covered cars, be they open-balcony or enclosed, were prohibited on the narrow gauges in coastal areas, or so I understand. Plymouth and Bournemouth on the 3ft 6in gauge had no covered cars, but Southend did, on bogie cars, and late in the day so did Dover Corporation who bought some Birmingham 21 class cars in the thirties and ran them with top-covers and for good measure bought some top covers from the BMTJC and put them on their own open-toppers. And it can certainly blow in Southend or Dover!

All unsuspecting I was walking, or probably running home from school thinking I was a train, in 1923 along Grove Lane on the Oxhill Road route, when I did an emergency stop. I had had a vision — but it was no vision, it was real! It was car No 640 of the new 637 class, which class of 25 cars was being assembled at Hockley depot after delivery from the Midland Railway Carriage and Wagon Company Limited. Since that date, I have seen a number of the world's great sights — sunset on the Jungfrau looking up the Lauterbrunnen valley from Interlaken, Durham Cathedral, the sight of the Orkneys after breasting the last low hill before John o'Groat's after cycling up from the Land's End, and a few others which have made me pause and consider, but

Above: BCT car No 611 of the 587-636 class of 1920, snapped from the balcony of another car near Soho Road Station, Handsworth. Few pictures exist of this class in open-balcony condition. / *The late Wingate H. Bett*

Above right: BCT car No 342, the 'Armoured Car', Birmingham's first attempt at a fully-enclosed car, rebuilt thus in 1921. Quite claustrophobic! Seen at Bearwood terminus 30 September 1939, photographed at great risk in the early days of the 'phoney' war. The 301 class ran on Dudley Road for a few weeks only, this being the last day. / *R. T. Coxon*

Right: BCT car No 347, the second rebuild and much more acceptable than No 342, though top-deck bulkheads were retained in both cases. The fully-enclosed 637 bogie class of 1923 was based on the 347 rebuild. Lickey Road, Longbridge, August 1938. / *R. T. Coxon*

129
RENSONS
TRY "TY·PHOO" TEA for Indigestion
842

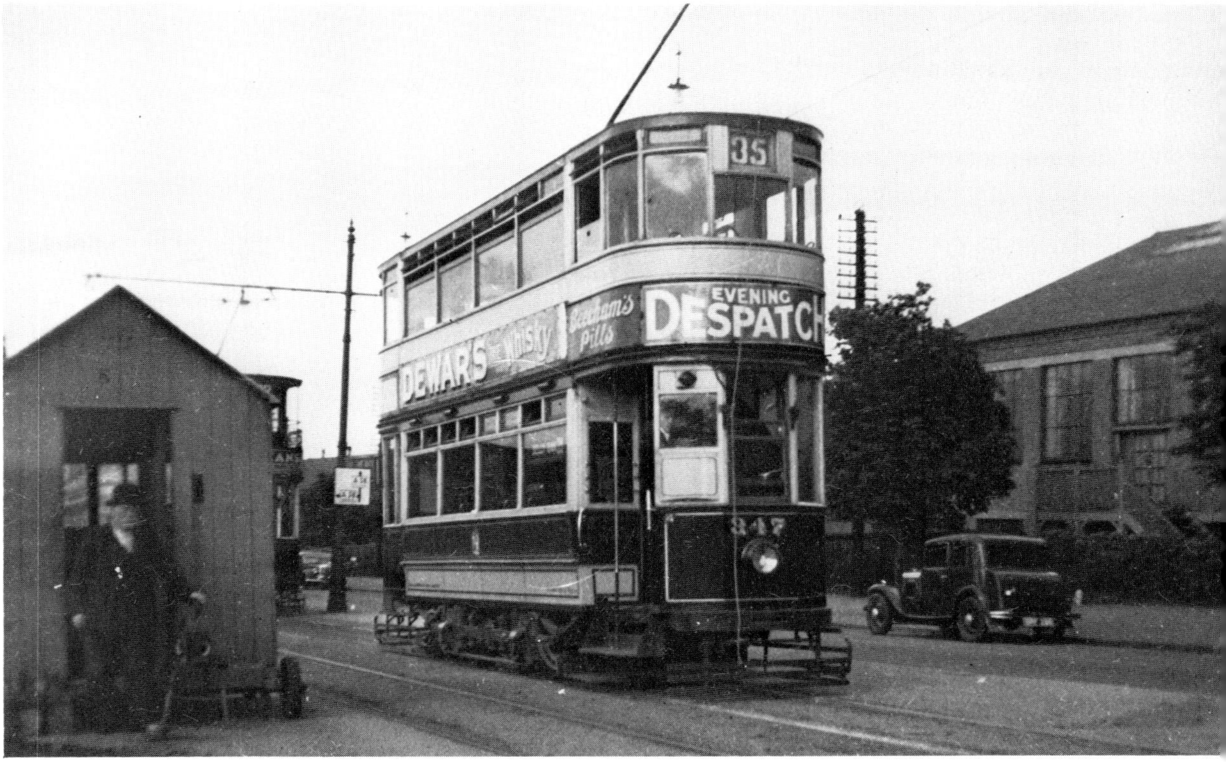

nothing — nothing at all — has ever stopped me in my tracks (I said I thought I was a train) like 640. It was to me the absolute perfection of beauty; to this day the Birmingham standard bogie car remains as my idea of what a tram should be. Yes, I know — Sheffield had a fully-enclosed car, cab and all, in 1907 or thereabouts, London had had fully-enclosed top-decks for years, and Leeds, Liverpool, Glasgow and others were to build cars which would make the 637 class look as dated as I then thought the Aston bogies were. So WHAT? For me, the Birmingham Standards! It would seem, however, that many others, even non-Birmingham folk, think likewise to judge from the number of models of the class, in all scales, which exist. On the model line which I have built myself, there is, of course, a Standard bogie.

I did not know about these cars being put together at Hockley, or I should have brought pressure to bear to be taken there to see what was going on. (Hockley was no place to visit unaccompanied, at age six, but I remember going down there on my scooter, before I had my first bike at age nine.) The 637 class were brought out when Alfred Baker was still general manager, and with them one can see the London influence still at work. The Aston bogies, as first top-covered in 1905, bore a very strong resemblance to the LCC 'D' class bogies with open balconies, but after that the Birmingham cars did not take after the London cars. The 637 class, however, which were a fully-enclosed version of the 512-636 classes, strongly resembled the LCC 'E' or 'E1' classes, and could justly be described as a narrow-gauge version of them. For that matter, the single-decker No 451 bore a strong likeness to a London Subway car, though the platforms were longer and enclosed. To my intense chagrin I found that the 637 class were being moved away from Hockley after being run-

Below: A line-up of BCT football specials at West Bromwich Albion, where two long loops were put in in the mid-twenties giving the aspect of a four-track main line. A line of bow-fitted 21 class cars can be seen, the only photographic evidence of bow cars on the Handsworth routes, and two 637 bogies from Miller Street and a 301 class. About 1926.

in, and were to be seen operating from Steelhouse Lane terminus on the Erdington routes; the fact that they could be seen from the Colmore Row terminus of the Hockley routes only added insult to injury. However, there was plenty of added interest at this time, as some single-deckers, looking as I thought a bit like Great Western Railway carriages — in other words, they had clerestory roofs — were to be seen on Soho Road running in on the Black Country service from Darlaston. Looking back, I wonder if this was something to do with the overturning of a South Staffs double-decker, No 46, outside the Police Station in Holyhead Road. This was due to defective track where a piece of the check-rail was missing, doubtless due to lack of maintenance in the war years, though the track in question had only been relaid in 1911/12 when the electrics took over from the cable cars, and compared with the dire state of the Black Country track it was but a trifle. The single-deckers were not on the service for long, and were in fact some of the Birmingham District Spon Lane cars. Perhaps the SST were just short of cars and borrowed them, as all four companies took in each other's washing in this way. The tall green and cream double-deckers were back on service again after a few weeks, if indeed they had been entirely replaced by the single-deckers during this period. I now noticed that the Black Country cars had small roller-blind indicators on the lower-deck bulkhead behind the driver, which struck me even then as a curious place for an indicator, being practically impossible to read from the footpath. Some of the cars showed BILSTON on the blind, so this must have been in the last year of the SST operating through to Birmingham. The cars now had a very odd arrangement of the trolley rope, the reason for which I did not learn until many years later. From the trolleyhead was

Below: BCT car No 701 of the 637 class at Pype Hayes terminus about 1928. Fitted with plates over the bogies; a few of the class carried these for some years, but later lost them, though the solid panel between the bogies was retained and fitted to all other bogie cars.

suspended a length of bamboo pole, below which was the trolley-rope. The bamboo swung about rather alarmingly, but the trolleys stayed under the wire. The reason for this lash-up was that between Darlaston and Bilston the wires were suspended by bracket arms, involving some quite spectacular side-running by the trolley; trolley-ropes would have become entangled with cars going the other way, and so for this section the conductor went aloft at Darlaston, unhooked the bamboo pole and hung it from a hook on the balcony; I do not know if at Bilston the wire was sufficiently central for the trolley to be hooked down with its own bamboo-cum-trolley-rope or if a full-length bamboo was employed, but on the return trip the procedure was reversed at Darlaston. Birmingham insisted on trolley-ropes inside the city, and this was the SST's ingenious way round the problem. My brother-in-law, the late Wingate Bett, greatly missed by all who knew him, told me of this arrangement long after the Black Country cars had disappeared from the Handsworth tramway scene, and this they were to do at the end of March 1924, when the SST lease in West Bromwich expired. From 1 April, the West Bromwich main routes were worked by Birmingham Corporation, with the difference that the Dudley service, 74, ran through to Colmore Row as did the other service, 75, which now ran only to Wednesbury White Horse instead of to Darlaston and Bilston. It is known that a Birmingham car ran through to Bilston on trial, but probably on account of the side-trolley running and possibly the state of the track, the service went to Wednesbury only. To this day I regret never travelling on a

Below: BCT car No 10, 'Aston Bogie' class, with Milnes top-cover (1-10) rebuilt in mid-1920s with vestibule cab and put on Brush Burnley bogies. Passing the Halfords building in Lancaster Street 1939. / *R. T. Coxon*

Above: BCT car No 11 with United Electric top-cover (11-20), with vestibule cab and EMB Burnley bogies. Perry Barr 1938. Buildings behind the car, though 'got at' still survive. / *R. T. Coxon*

Black Country car. My mother would never travel on one on Soho Road, and was not alone in this; many Handsworth folk would not travel on the 'Darley Nags' as the late Douglas Pritchard called them in an article in *Trams* for July 1964, though I never heard them referred to as such. The Hockley drivers' name for the SST cars was the 'Black Country Whiffers', and the prejudice remained long after the World War II when Handsworth people would let the West Bromwich Corporation buses go by and wait for a Birmingham vehicle — and I can vouch for it that there was nothing amiss with the West Bromwich rolling-stock. They are all the same colour today!

The first I knew of the changeover was the sight of unfamiliar route numbers on Soho Road, 74 and 75, with some 73s to Carters Green. There is a maker's photograph of the last of the new Midland R.C. and W. cars, 661, showing 73 on the front blind, but I don't think these new cars were allowed past the boundary on to the West Bromwich track, which was relaid as far as Carters Green with all speed and the tracks moved in closer to the centre of the road — they had originally been wide-spaced for centre poles. At the same time the famous four-track layout was put in for the football cars at the Albion ground (it wasn't called the Hawthorns then) at the boundary. By the time the relaying was completed the 637-661 cars had migrated to

Miller Street depot. The 74 and 75 cars at first had temporary cardboard destination displays in the windows, but at last — and it was the last depot — Hockley depot had the new side roller blind boxes with the West Bromwich services on the blind in addition to, of course, REDNAL 70 which was carried on the blinds of all depots. Then came another development — car No 223, one of the small single-truck Brill cars, with new vestibule cab and looking very smart indeed. Over the next few years all the 1-20 Aston bogies, all the Radial class 71-220, and all but 28 of the 21-70 and 221-300 Brill cars were given vestibule cabs, the Aston bogies being put on to EMB Burnley bogies as were the 637 class, or Brush Burnleys (4, 9, 10, 16). The Radials were also retrucked, mostly with new P35 trucks which as already mentioned transformed them, or with Conaty or Brush flexible wheelbase trucks ex-CBT cars. Of the CBT open-toppers, most were given open-balcony top-covers and vestibule cabs in 1924-5, just before the 21 class and the Radials, and the final episode was the rebuilding of Nos 451 and 452 in 1926 with open-balcony top-covers. It will be seen that Kyott's Lake Road would have been very busy indeed at this period, which would explain why the 637 cars were assembled at Hockley depot instead of at The Lake, the same applying to further cars 702-731 which were assembled at Moseley depot and worked from there. As Hockley depot was now really pushed for both cars and space the job could no longer be done there anyway, for the new West Bromwich routes were worked from Hockley, the SST depot at the boundary being used now only for football cars. For a time, bogie cars were rarely seen on my route, Oxhill Road, that service and the Lozells circulars 24 and 25 being worked by the rebuilt CBT cars and the newly vestibuled 21 class; in addition, Lodge Road 32 was worked by Hockley at this time.

Somewhere in the mid-twenties another individual Birmingham detail was applied to the cars — the 'Pigtail' for the trolley-rope, fitted to the roof-cantrail just above the end numeral indicator box. This was probably in 1924, as I recall that the first of the 637 class bogies of 1923 did not have pigtails but soon acquired them. Probably these were fitted not just because someone though it looked rather untidy to have trolley-ropes snaking about — though there was already a wire loop above the driver's half-drop cab window through which the conductor threaded the rope, the end of which was then brought into the cab — but to obviate the possibility of ropes getting snarled up with cars going the other way on the reserved-track sections. This was only a remote possibility, however, as the degree of side-trolley running was slight compared with, say, Weston-super-Mare where the wire did not follow the track at loops and the trolley was almost at right-angles to the car. The trolley-rope was flicked into the pigtail by an anti-clockwise motion of the trolley-rope, and out by contrary motion. This was no problem on the standard bogies where the trolley-boom did not overhang the car by very much, but the Radials and more so still the

Right: BCT cars Nos 53, 334 and 634 in Edmund Street, May 1939. No 53 with top-cover, vestibule cab and bow collector was one of the Lodge Road survivors of the 21 class. No 334 was one of the 301 class, displaced from Selly Oak, which ran on Dudley Road briefly in 1939, and No 634 was making a rare appearance of a bogie car on Dudley Road doing a 'short' to Windmill Lane. The picture was something of a scoop. / *R. T. Coxon*

Below: BCT cars Nos 61 and 64 of the rebuilt 21 class at Foundry Lane terminus, Lodge Road route. / *J. S. Webb*

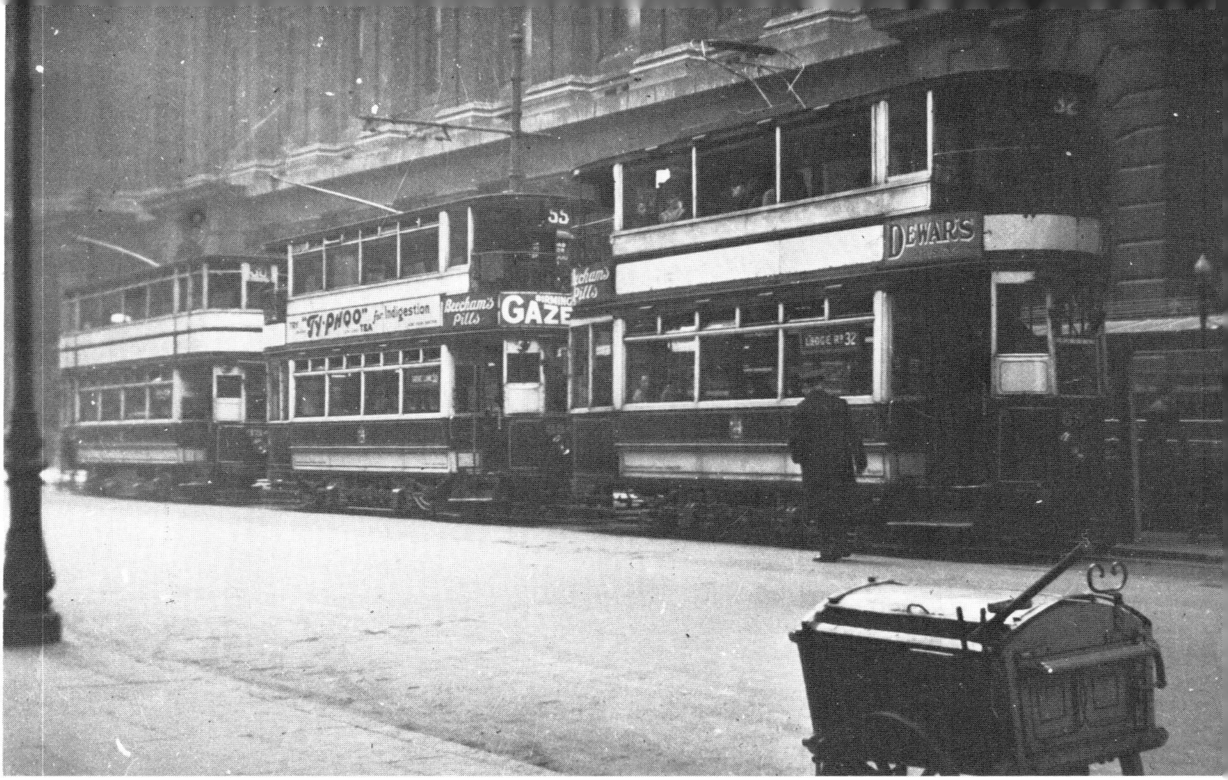
DEWAR'S
"TY-PHOO" TEA for Indigestion
Beecham's Pills
GAZE
55

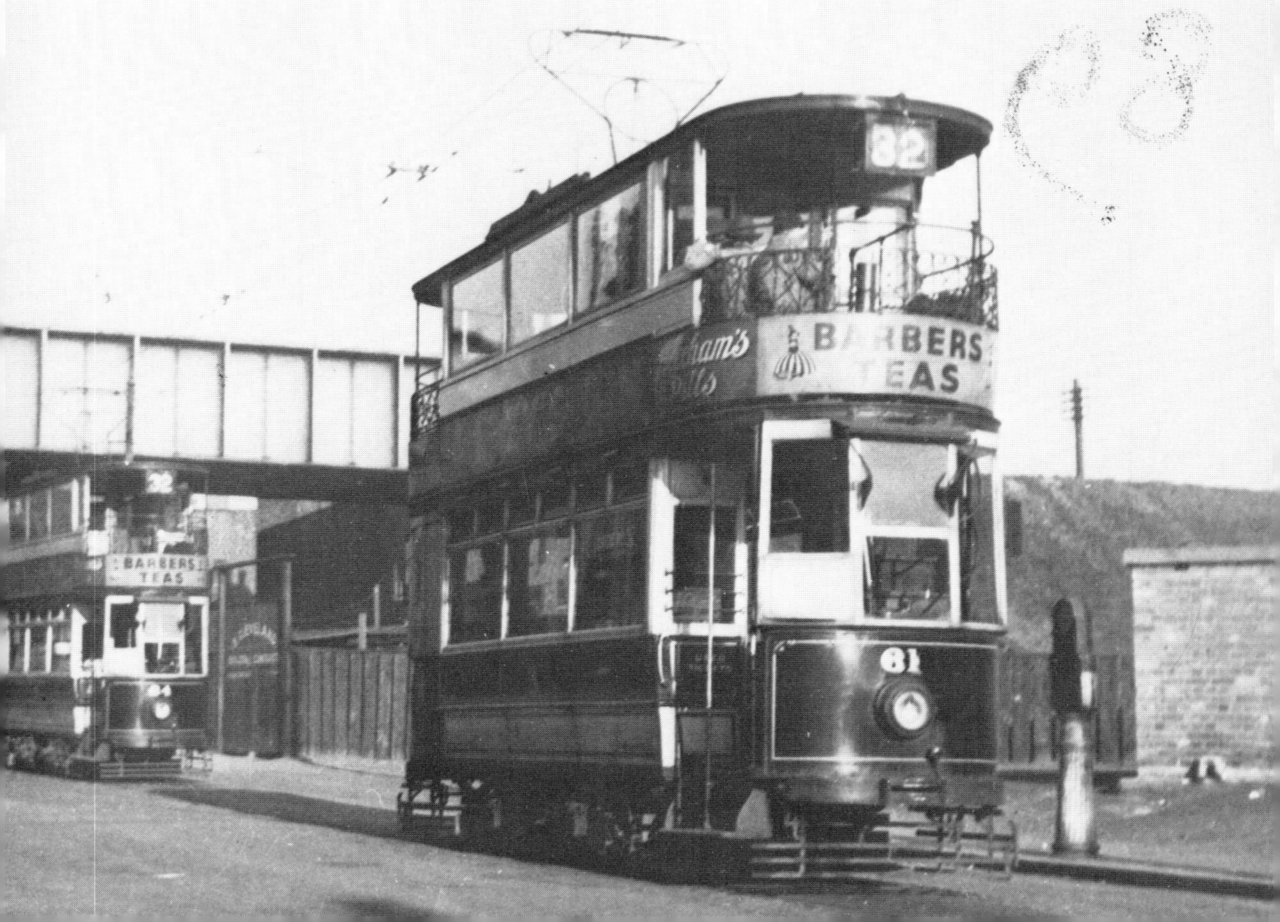
32
BARBERS TEAS
81

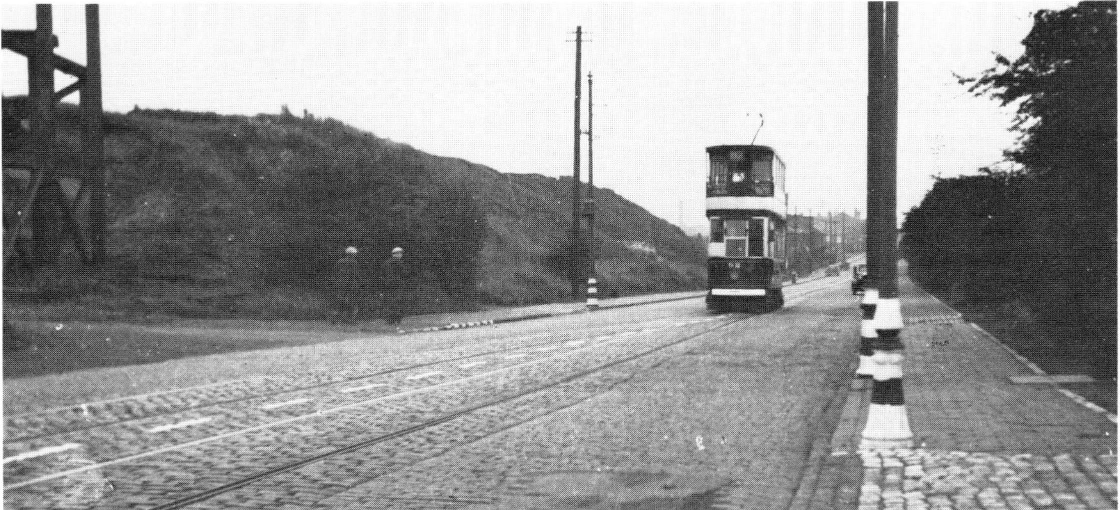

21 class had a considerable overhang; one could usually flick the rope into the pigtail, but getting it out could be difficult, and the conductors of the 87 cars would usually 'de-pigtail' the rope by hand from the balcony between Burnt Tree and Dudley station. It took quite some artistry to get the rope into the pigtail here for the return trip, and some conductors would wait till they were back on the main line again to flick the rope in, either with one hand through the cab window or by the dangerous practice of standing on the rear fender which gave them a better chance with the rope — and quite a good chance of being flung off the car on the very rough track as far as Burnt Tree.

Some time in 1924 I was brought back to Birmingham from a

holiday at Weston (where an aunt of mine lived, hence all these trips to Weston) by car — a bull-nose Morris-Cowley; a great thrill this. It was a Sunday morning when we left Weston, so no trams running there or in Bristol, Gloucester or Worcester, where Sunday tram services did not begin until the afternoon in those days. Suddenly I sat up very straight; we were travelling along a very new road and dual carriageways, and between them were stacks of new tram-rails. We were entering Birmingham, and the new branch to Rubery was in course of being laid. At what I now know to be Longbridge, track and overhead were installed but no trams appeared to be running, but it was Sunday and I may just have been unlucky. However, at Northfield was a tram showing 69 on the blind, but I was puzzled to see that it was a relatively old car of the 301 class. As it was a new route I had expected to see new cars of the fully-enclosed bogie class, but in fact the cars used for many years on the Bristol Road reserved track routes were 301 class single-truck cars displaced from Miller Street depot by the new bogie cars. There was wisdom in this; the single-truck cars were kinder to the sleeper track than the bogies, and anyway the real thrill of a ride out to Rednal was to get on

Above left: BCT car No 255 at Warstone Lane-Frederick Street corner in the Jewellery Quarter, Lodge Road route, with the Chamberlain Clock dominating the scene. Car No 22, going in the opposite direction, ran away down Warstone Lane in 1907 from here. Daimler COG5 bus trying to beat the tram to it into Frederick Street. */ J. S. Webb*

Left: BCT car No 92, rebuilt 'Radial' class, near Brades Locks on the Dudley-Oldbury-Birmingham 87 route, just before closure in September 1939. Typical Black Country 'tramscape'. */ J. S. Webb*

Right: BCT car No 121, with vestibule cab but still on M&G Radial truck at Washwood Heath. P.35 truck fitted in 1927.

Below: BCT car No 125 at Soho station terminus (not to be confused with Soho Road, Handsworth) in September 1939. From Nettlefolds to the terminus was BD territory, though always worked by BCT cars. */ J. S. Webb*

Above left: BCT car No 129 on route 87 at the Boat Inn, Tividale. Note somewhat approximate alignment of track and signal-light on pole, actuated by trolley contactor on the overhead, for the single track over the hump-back canal bridge. Though applying to trams only, motorists sometimes halted on the red! / *R. T. Coxon*

Left: BCT car No 136 passing the former BMTJC works at Tividale. Track and overhead left in for feeder purposes. Note wartime markings on road and vehicles. 30 September 1939, last day of operation. / *R. T. Coxon*

Above: BCT cars Nos 219 and 544 at Dudley station terminus June 1938. No 219, on P.35 truck and with vestibule cab, will travel to Edmund Street via Oldbury, No 544 with enclosed balconies will travel to Colmore Row on service 74 via West Bromwich. / *R. T. Coxon*

the front balcony of a 301 class car. Enormous crowds were taken out to the Lickey Hills — which very considerable area had been presented to the city by the Cadbury family in 1905, I think — at Bank Holidays and weekends, and brought back again, tired but happy. Many other stretches of dual carriageway were now being constructed, obviously with tramway development in mind. Some of them did get their tramways — Short Heath, Tyburn Road, Bordesley Green, Stratford Road — but as the decade progressed ideas changed and the vastly improved buses came on the scene. However, the tramcar was far from finished yet; back on the Handsworth routes I was to experience another pleasant shock — car No 555, of the 512-586 class, appeared on the Oxhill Road route one day with the balconies enclosed as per the 637 class, and was followed quickly by 537 and others. This was in 1926; the rebuilt cars came out at approximately fortnightly intervals, until the last car, No 636, was rebuilt in 1931, to produce a series of 330 cars Nos 512-841 which to the average passenger were identical. There were, of course, many detail differences, but the rebuilds gave no hint outwardly or inside that they were rebuilds; in so many cases it is only too easy to see where something has been added to a car's original configuration, but not so with the 512-636 rebuilds. The new additions matched up perfectly; as for me, the Hockley cars were now as good as those of any other depot, better in fact than some, as the Hockley bogies were now given higher-powered motors and new equipment to give them parity with the new top-

Snow Hill Station. Birmingham.

Above: BCT cars Nos 463 and 499 (ex-CBT Nos 203 and 247), rebuilt with top-covers and vestibule cabs in 1923/4, on Lozells Circular routes 24 (via Wheeler Street) and 25 (via Hamstead Road). In the mid-twenties Hockley depot was short of cars and the ex-CBT cars were in all-day service. Snow Hill station and vintage taxis.

Right: BCT car No 475, ex-CBT No 183, of the 'Yardley Bogie' class, on 'Conaty' single truck. Rebuilt with top-cover and vestibule cab 1925 and shown here at West Smethwick depot for breaking up 1939, with numeral roof-box indicators already removed. / *W. A. Camwell*

covered buses. Nos 512-536 were given two 70hp motors, Nos 537-562, 565 and 566, 587-636 two 63hp motors. The rest of the series, formerly at Cotteridge but now at Highgate Road, retained their 40hp motors as did Nos 637-731. The high-speed cars were primarily for the West Bromwich services, and they made light work of Holloway Bank between Wednesbury and Hill Top, and on the 'open road' stretch between The Hawthorns and Beeches Road they could really open out.

Improvements were not only to the body structure. The first few rebuilds had upholstered longitudinal seating in the lower

Right: BCT car No 512, the first of the class, rebuilt with enclosed balconies to conform with the 637 class, on special wartime Sunday working on route 42, in 1939, to Alcester Lanes End from Hill Street instead of Albert Street. Same location as CBT steam tram. / *W. A. Camwell*

saloon, the trim being in grey moquette, but beginning with car No 554 in 1927 transverse blue leather seats were fitted in the lower saloon, and later car No 516 in 1929 had moquette transverse in the lower saloon and leather transverse upstairs, matching the newest air-brake cars 762 and upwards, with ceilings panelled in bird's-eye maple. As the earlier rebuilds returned to the works they were similarly equipped, certainly in the lower saloons, but a few cars retained their wooden upstairs seating as did some of the 637-731 bogies. The lower saloons of the four-wheel cars were similarly treated, all of the 301-450 classes being re-seated, nearly all the Radials (no longer on Radial trucks but the name stuck to them), two of the large 'Yardley' CBT cars Nos 475 and 478, all the 1-20 'Aston Bogies', and 451 and 452, which also had upholstered seats upstairs, the only balcony cars so treated. The other CBT cars and the 21 class Brills were not re-seated, being now on spare duties except those on Lodge Road.

It was a little easier at Hockley when cars Nos 587-611 were 'posted' there after being displaced at Moseley Road by the new 702-731 batch, followed almost immediately by Nos 512-533 and 535 from Rosebery Street, where new air-braked cars 732-761 had arrived for the Hagley Road service. I knew where these cars had come from as some still bore Edgbaston advertisements. (I deplore advertisements on public vehicles, but they sometimes give valuable clues on photographs.) We had been much intrigued on Oxhill Road by the intermittent appearance of car No 630, with a different pattern of bogie from the rest of the class, fitted up with air-brakes, a throbbing compressor and mysterious dials by the controller. She was the try-out car for the air-brake and left Hockley for Rosebery Street where she kept

Above: BCT car No 351 on Witton route in Dale End just after World War I, passing the corner of Henns Walk. YMCA building, later the Birmingham School of Music, on right.

company with the 732 series and later went to Washwood Heath. The position at Hockley was now much easier, the difficulty now being where to put all the cars. Until Lodge Road was transferred back to Rosebery Street in the mid-thirties many cars had to stay out on the depot fan or on the Ticket Office siding all night. (Hockley had worked Lodge Road since the Ford Street spur from All Saints Bridge had been put in, I believe in 1916, thus completing a ring of track round the central area.)

I had a bad scare one day, probably in 1925, when walking home along Grove Lane. No PW 9 (ex-507) one of the old Bristol Road open toppers, was about its duties cleaning the track when at Chantry Road, dead level with me, there was a terrific flash from under the stairs and the car stopped. I imagine the driver must have had some bad moments too, but I didn't stop. It scared the pants off me and I ran. I had reached the Baths when I heard the devil of a row from somewhere behind, and No PW 9 came hurtling down the hill from Douglas Road, again came up level with me at Hinstock Road and there was stopped on the handbrake. I observed that the trolley was tied down, and waited to see what happened next. This was the arrival of service car No 633, which buffered up behind No PW 9 and with no fuss at all pushed it the rest of the way to Oxhill Road terminus, where it remained until someone from Hockley depot had arrived to replace whatever had blown out. That was the last I saw of that PW 9, or PW 8. Another of the Bristol Road cars, the ex-trailer No 509, which had already been given vestibule cabs in its trailer days, was re-fitted as the new No PW 9, and the former Illuminated Car, No 266, was cut down to single-deck, vestibuled in like manner to the rest of the 21 class except for single-width extrances and given the number PW 8. Both cars

Above: The island shelter in Dale End, 1921-1930, with Radial car No 203. Cars for Martineau Street used the track in foreground and did not stop at this shelter.

were painted in all-over dark blue and lined out, and looked very smart, in contrast to the usual lot of PW and engineers' cars.

Route extensions were going ahead, Short Heath (1926) and Pype Hayes (1927) among them, and for some time the Pype Hayes run to the newly acquired park was very popular. The Tyburn Road route had opened in 1920 as far as Holly Lane for Fort Dunlop, on reserved track laid with Belgian tram-rail. This proved unsatisfactory and was later used, cut up into short lengths, as cross-bearers bedded into the concrete when relaying was carried out, the running rails being clamped to the cross-bearers. There must still be quite a lot of this Belgian rail buried under present road-surfaces all over Birmingham. Tyburn Road at this period was not built up with industrial development between the road and canal, and there were spacious views of the sewage works and Washwood Heath gasholders, but further out the wooded heights of Castle Bromwich came into view. Pype Hayes was one of the first very large municipal housing estates, and this was the real purpose of the tramway extension.

And while on the subject of extensions, mention might be made here of perhaps the most bizarre tramway extension anywhere — Henn's Walk. This was no tree-lined, sleeper-track showpiece running miles out into the country like Rednal and Pype Hayes, but a projection of the incoming Moor Street line from the Bull Ring for about two hundred yards further eastwards along Moor Street, then a sharp left turn to Henn's Walk and left again into Dale End. This was put in in November 1921, and was used by routes 13 (Small Heath Park), 15 (Yardley), 17 (Hall Green) and 19 (St John's Road); the track in Dale End was doubled where the street widened out, the Martineau Street cars keeping right and not using the loading

shelter between the two tracks but carrying on to their own Martineau Street shelters. The Dale End cars kept left and loaded at the shelters, using the front end of the car for loading. This arrangement was doubtless designed to take the pressure off Albert Street, but it caused bunching of cars in the narrow part of Dale End between Henn's Walk and the double track, which short section was used by Washwood Heath, Witton, Perry Barr, and the Digbeth services, and a seized-up axle here would have caused some problems. Henn's Walk itself was the most improbable location for a public tramway route on any undertaking, I would imagine. It was no more than an alley, and I doubt if a standard-gauge car would have got through. There wasn't room to park a bicycle between the track and the kerb. I only traversed it once, and have never seen a photograph of it. When the traffic flow was reversed in 1930 the Henn's Walk extension was abandoned, Digbeth cars then turning left out of Moor Street up Carr's Lane, returning to Moor Street down Albert Street. At the same time the connecting spur from Albert

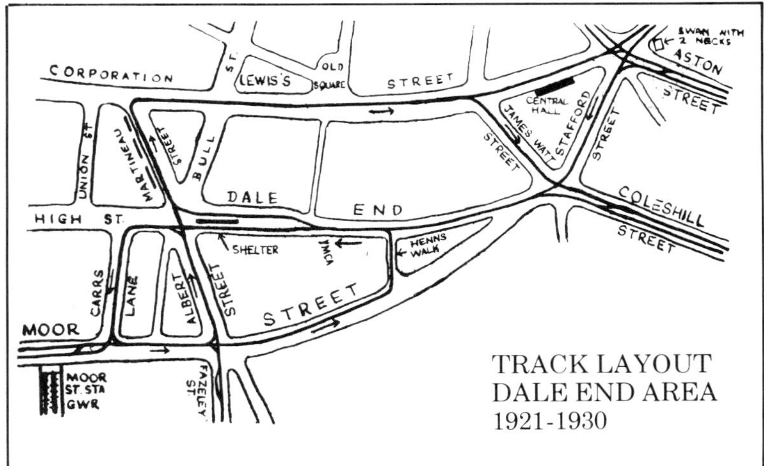

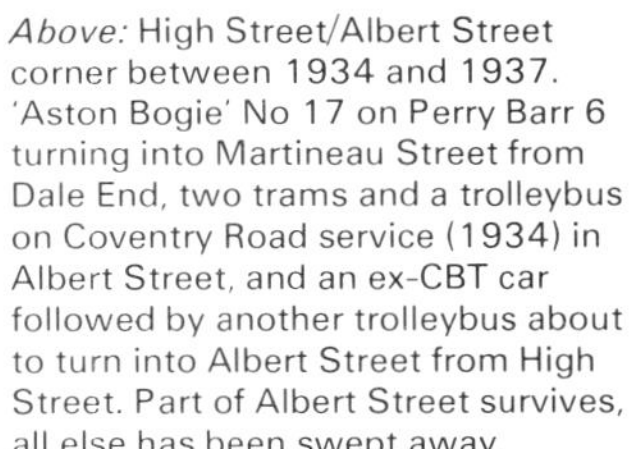

Above: High Street/Albert Street corner between 1934 and 1937. 'Aston Bogie' No 17 on Perry Barr 6 turning into Martineau Street from Dale End, two trams and a trolleybus on Coventry Road service (1934) in Albert Street, and an ex-CBT car followed by another trolleybus about to turn into Albert Street from High Street. Part of Albert Street survives, all else has been swept away.

Above right: Track layout in the Moor Street-Dale End area 1921-1930. In 1930 the traffic flow was altered so that cars ran up Carrs Lane and down Albert Street, and Henns Walk went out of use.

Street up into Martineau Street, once used by pre-1914 cross-city routes, was taken out, but the Dale End-High Street spur was left in for cars going to 'The Lake' and other transfers. The Dale End-Martineau Street curve was eased out and the Dale End shelters removed. The side-blinds on many cars continued to show DALE END for long afterwards.

Another batch of air-brake bogies, Nos 762-811, of 1928 went to Washwood Heath depot to replace Radial cars, which were despatched to West Smethwick depot. Birmingham had now taken over the operation of the Dudley via Oldbury route from the Birmingham District Company, though to begin with BD cars had to be hired back by BCT until sufficient Radials could be released from Washwood Heath.

The new Washwood Heath bogies sported bow-collectors instead of trolleys. Bows had also appeared on the Hockley routes, but only on the small 21 class cars and primarily for the Lodge Road route. The main Hockley routes were rewired for bows as far as Carters Green, and including the Oxhill Road route but not the Lozells circular via Hamstead Road and Wheeler Street. The 21 class cars were not permitted to run beyond Carters Green, and in any case a bow-fitted car would not have cleared the Dudley Port canal aqueduct, so none of the Hockley bogies were fitted with bows except, I believe, 551 for trial purposes. No further routes were converted to bows, which would have been impossible anyway on the low-bridge routes, Dudley Port, Aston station and Selly Oak. When Lodge Road was transferred to Rosebery Street depot the bows were seen no more on the Hockley routes, but Lodge Road and the Washwood Heath routes continued to use them. To reach Kyott's Lake works, cars had to be trolley-fitted, though the Washwood Heath bows could work football specials to the Villa ground. While overhead fittings for bow-collectors, such as 'golf-stick' pull-offs, were appearing in locations where bow-fitted cars never ran, suggesting that a wholesale change from trolleys to bows was envisaged, such a change never materialised. It would have involved converting many miles of overhead on the reserved tracks from bracket-arms involving only one pole to two-pole span-wire construction; with the bracket-arms one wire was off-centre to its track and unusable by bows. It would seemingly have been possible to convert the Moseley routes to bows, where no low bridges or reserved track were involved, and where the severe curves of the 'Chinese Railway' in Balsall Heath would have seemed the ideal location for bows — I understand that the Lodge Road route was converted on account of the heavy wear on trolley wheels due to the curvature. The main Coventry Road route would have been a possibility, but the Stechford route had a long reservation and so some cars would have had to retain trolley-poles. By 1930 the enthusiasm for bows was over, and though they were retained to the end of operation on Lodge Road and the Washwood Heath routes they were not seen elsewhere.

The final batch of cars, air-brake bogies Nos 812-841, although externally the same as previous cars, had bodies by Short Bros Limited who had built a number of bus bodies for Birmingham, and Burnley bogies by Maley & Taunton instead of EMB (Electro-Mechanical Brake) of West Bromwich, who had built the trucks for all cars Nos 637-811. I understand that there was now a degree of coolness between EMB and Birmingham Corporation Tramways, the latter having returned a trolleybus (No 13) of EMB manufacture after having kept it for an extended period — much longer than usual with a 'demonstrator' — and run up quite a big mileage with it. EMB took rather a poor view of this, apparently. Whatever, the 30 bogie cars had M&T Burnley bogies of the same profile as the EMB ones, and went to Cotteridge depot, releasing Nos 563 and 564 and 567-586 to Highgate Road. Two more 'one-off' cars were to complete the story, No 842 with a steel-framed light-weight body by Short on modified English Electric Burnley bogies, and No 843 of 1930, with duralumin-framed Brush body on pressed-steel M&T bogies. Both these cars had domed roofs, and were of very modern appearance, though retaining the traditional Birmingham cab. The saving in weight made it possible to fit them with two 40hp motors to give a performance equal to the heavier standard cars with 63hp or 70hp motors. Both cars were stationed at Cotteridge, No 843 being better liked than 842 as having more room to work on. With No 842 came a 'one-off' bus body in the same style by Shorts, AEC Regent No 368.

With the arrival of these two new cars, we — the few tram devotees of those days — were expecting a whole new fleet of modern lightweight cars, because there was no doubt that No 842 and more especially No 843 were highly successful. They proved to be the last new trams in the fleet. For 10 years it had been a story of extensions and new cars every year and then, in 1930, STOP! The reason? As elsewhere, in those 10 years, and more so still in the last five years since 1925, the motor bus had made phenomenal progress and was now to be considered on equal terms with the tram — even the modern tram.

My first sighting of No 843 was on a date to remember. It was Sunday, 5 October 1930, and the night before the great airship R101 had taken off from Cardington for India; it was a rough night, and early on Sunday morning we heard shouts of 'Special!', but before we had taken the situation in, the newspaper-seller was out of range. Not everyone had radio in 1930 and on occasions of great import special newspapers still appeared. I felt sure that something was amiss with R101, and my father suddenly said, 'Put your coat on — we'll go up town,' which he and I did on the Oxhill Road tram. Sunday visits to the city were very rare and always quite different from weekday trips, but this was different again; something *was* amiss with R101. The tram crew said it had crashed, but I simply could not believe this. As we left the 26 tram in Colmore Row I heard for the very first time the unforgettable sound of a muffled peal on the Cathedral bells, and we walked to Victoria Square, where was a sizeable but silent queue waiting to read the official notice outside the Council House, and as we joined the queue about six or eight RAF planes from 605 Squadron at Castle Bromwich roared overhead, as though reassuring everyone that come disaster or come what may, life goes on and the RAF were still flying. We then did a short walk down Hill Street to New Street Station, and rounding the curve from Navigation Street to John Bright Street was car No 843, which had come into service the previous month. The R101 had flown over Birmingham some time earlier, before being lengthened, and at that time I had the entry to the Midland Aero Club at Castle Bromwich; I had a 'tip-off' from a member who was also in 605 Squadron about the visit of R101, which was treated with much scorn at Handsworth Grammar School when I mentioned the matter. On the day in question, however, during a Latin lesson, a faint rumble,

Below: BCT car No 843, the last car built for Birmingham, approaching Pebble Mill Junction in 1938. */R. T. Coxon*

Above: BCT trolleybus No 17, ON 3261, a Vickers-body AEC, entering Aston Street from Central Place, on the Nechells route, passing tram No 678 on the Pype Hayes service. Swan with Two Necks pub on the left, site now occupied by Central Fire Station.
/ The late Wingate H. Bett

deepening to something like a cathedral organ pedal-note, became audible, and, unable to contain myself, I said, loud and clear, 'R101', and the form, followed by the school, erupted into the yard where we had a memorable view of the great ship. No action was taken against me for daring to violate the silence of that Latin lesson — one did not do that sort of thing then, and I wondered if I should be carpeted, but no. In fact, I now found myself being consulted, not scorned, on matters concerning air or any other transport. And I suppose it's been more or less like that ever since!

I mentioned a trolleybus just now. It had not been tramcars, tramcars all the way. In 1922 the Nechells route, rather a backwater of BCT, was in need of track renewal. Costs of such work were now vastly heavier than pre-1914, and the Tramways Committee looked at the alternatives. The upshot was that Nechells was converted to 'Trackless Trams' — trolleybuses in later parlance — as an experiment, 12 top-covered Railless Limited vehicles being purchased, with Roe bodies, having much tramcar style about them. They performed well, despite their solid tyres and far-from-perfect road surface (never Birmingham's strong point and just as applicable today). They were awe-inspiring things to look at, and failed to overturn as the prophets of doom, always with us, predicted, but they got along. They were driven with one had on the steering wheel and the other on a tramcar-type controller, the days of pedal-controllers being not yet; they were replaced by Leyland vehicles in 1931, based on the Leyland Titan chassis and actually sporting a dummy radiator, the bonnet containing the contactor gear. The original 12 vehicles had been added to with the EMB vehicle already mentioned and four AECs, all these being two-axle vehicles. The Nechells terminus was altered so that Nechells

Park Road was used in both directions instead of returning via Long Acre, a turning circle being put in at Cuckoo Bridge. The trolleybuses worked, as had the trams, from Washwood Heath depot, running without passengers with one trolley on the wire and a string of contactors snaking along behind in the groove of the tramline. It appears that a Guy six-wheel demonstrator arrived in Birmingham this way, being driven to Dudley via Sedgley, then towed down to the Birmingham tram terminus at Dudley station, then driven the rest of the way as per the Nechells arrangement. No doubt due care was exercised under Dudley Port canal aqueduct, but details of the trip are not to hand. The sight of the 1931 Leylands, with a radiator and two trolleys on the roof, was known to have had a sobering effect on at least one person who was somewhat under the influence, and who thought he'd got 'em again! Four AEC 663 six-wheelers joined the Leyland in 1932, and perhaps the performance and capacity of these influenced the decision to convert the Yardley tram-route to trolleybus operation in January 1934 — but this is getting a bit ahead, and we have to return to 1930; for in that year, and before that last tramcar 843 took the road, two tramway abandonments took place — Bolton Road 22, another rather backwoods route, and Hagley Road 34, a main route along Birmingham's most prestigious (then) road. Opened only in 1913, it was the shortest-lived of all the Birmingham routes. Corporation buses had been covering it to Quinton, and when the question arose as to whether to relay it and extend to Quinton or replace with buses, the latter course was adopted. Only two years previously, the last sleeper-track extension to Stechford had been opened, but now the pendulum had begun to swing against the trams.

Above: BCT cars Nos 333 and 358 at Harborne Lane depot, Selly Oak, February 1939. No 333 fitted up with snow-ploughs. Only cars with specially strengthened trucks could carry ploughs. / *R. T. Coxon*

This does not imply that there was to be a sudden and

Above: BCT cars Nos 358 and 327 at Rea Street Junction, Digbeth. Note overhead for trams and trolleybuses. / *J. S. Webb*

Right: BCT cars Nos 524 and 537 (rebuilt with enclosed balconies) at the Scissors Crossover in Colmore Row, opposite the Grand Hotel, in 1928. / *The late Wingate H. Brett*

Above: BCT Hockley Depot in 1938. Car No 546 stands on the siding to the ticket and stationery office. / *R. T. Coxon*

Right: BCT ex-South Staffs depot at Handsworth Boundary, used only by BCT for Football Specials. Standard Bogies Nos 598 and 553, and Stores Van No 6 await the end of a match in 1938. Among the Inspectorate are Messrs Tozer, and Cooper of whistle fame. / *R. T. Coxon*

cataclysmic end to the tramways, but indicates that things went on the change. Standards were maintained, however, and existing trams continued to be improved, and track relaying went on. There was also no reduction as yet in the tramcar fleet, and the programme of fully enclosing the upper decks of the 512-636 classes was completed, but as mentioned, 28 of the small 21 class did not receive platform vestibules and were stored, mostly at Highgate Road and Coventry Road depots. The next abandonment was the Coventry Road line to Yardley, replaced on 7 January 1934 by Leyland-GEC six-wheel trolleybuses, the route later being extended to Sheldon. Now began the first withdrawals, other than former CBT cars not considered worth rebuilding, and the open-cab 21 class and some of the vestibuled ones were withdrawn, some being sold via a dealer to Dover Corporation, and some to the Merthyr Tydfil company in South Wales. Some retained their top-covers in Dover, others, and all those at Merthyr, reverted to open-top.

A curious, almost Keystone Cops accident occurred on Stratford Road, Sparkhill, on Saturday, 28 January 1933. A coal lorry cut in between two tramcars, Nos 579 and 161, approaching from opposite directions. The lorry-driver had badly misjudged things and his lorry was a write-off, but not quite according to the famous Keystone Cops Model T episode; both trams were derailed, and 579's body was so badly distorted that it had to be taken the short distance to Kyott's Lake Road with a tower wagon supporting it each side. It was only in the nature of things that both cars had just come back from the Lake newly repainted. 161 was soon back in service, but 579 was off the road for some time, but it was one of the final survivors in 1953.

I mentioned some way back that the West Bromwich track had been relaid from The Hawthorns to Carters Green. Beyond Carters Green on the Wednesbury and Dudley routes it was still the 1903 track, wide-spaced though the centre poles had long been taken out. (These poles were re-used for span-wire construction on parts of both routes beyond Carters Green, and had huge acorn-shaped finials somewhat resembling those of some of the Berlin tramways; near Swan Village I once saw a lorry which had collided with one of these poles, the finial of which had come through the lorry's cab roof and was sitting beside the driver, who had had a very bad fright indeed.) As to the track, it was easy to see why Birmingham would not allow the four-wheelers beyond Carters Green; it was only the weight of the bogie cars which kept them on the rails. It was in fearful and dangerous condition; check rail missing for yards at a time, rail tread split, wheels running on the bottom of the groove most of the way, rails out of alignment and deeply sunk, and a cloud of yellow dust ground from the granite setts following the tram along. The Birmingham bogie cars, sixteen and a half tons, were much heavier than the South Staffs cars, and the drivers belted them along regardless — one got the impression that the high-speed motors were some sort of insurance against getting grounded. The 512-636 cars took some terrific punishment from this track, which eventually simply had to be relaid in 1935. The only worse track I ever saw was at Walkden on the Bolton system (outside the Bolton boundary) and between Broomstair Bridge and Hyde Market Place on the Manchester 19 route, this being outside the Manchester area, though Manchester's own track was none too good. As the West Bromwich track was relaid, it was moved in closer to the middle of the road; as the relaid sections met the old track, there was quite a difference of alignment. No nonsense about transition curves here — lengths of straight were put in at an angle and the cars took it without any noticeable reduction of speed. I imagine that West Bromwich had hoped to make the old track last the remaining few years of the 15-year agreement with Birmingham; they were lucky not to have had a very bad accident. The agreement was to end in 1939, and the track then hardly had the top worn off it and would have done another 20 years. It says something for the quality of the bodywork of the 512-636 cars, and for the maintenance by Kyott's Lake and Hockley depot, that despite the fearful punishment they took on the West Bromwich track from 1924 to 1935, they were among the cars which saw the whole system close down in 1953.

1935 was also King George V's Silver Jubilee year, and for this occasion car No 63 was transformed into an Illuminated Car — the original Illuminated Car, No 266, was now PW 8. There were no tramway abandonments in this year or in 1936, the policy being that routes would be replaced as their tracks wore out — though 'worn out' in Birmingham would have been considered 'good for another ten years' in many another town. The Stratford Road group was the next on the list — Stoney Lane 4, Acocks Green 44, and Hall Green 17 and 18, the latter with a long sleeper-track extension dating only from 1928. We expected trolleybuses again, but not so. In the four years since the Coventry Road changeover, the Daimler fluid-flywheel bus with Gardner engine had come into service in numbers, and this was to be the replacement vehicle for Stratford Road, which replacement took place as from 6 January 1937. Track and overhead remained along Stratford Road as far as Kyott's Lake Road, and was to remain to the end of the system for cars to reach the works.

At this time, the peace of Europe was becoming threatened; the idea of scrapping further tram-routes to be replaced by buses running on imported fuel was regarded as asking for trouble, and when the Hockley group came up for judgement there was much misgiving. The West Bromwich agreement whereby Birmingham trams worked the main routes to Dudley and Wednesbury ended on 31 March 1939, and the opportunity was taken to close down all the Hockley routes and again replace the trams with diesel buses. West Bromwich Corporation now put in 30 buses on the 'track' routes, as the West Bromwich men still call the Dudley and Wednesbury services, but their buses had been appearing in Birmingham on works specials to Lucas's at Hockley for some years. The whole scheme, with the international situation as it was, now seemed foolhardy, especially as track and cars were in very good shape — the Oxhill Road track was relaid only in the thirties and was good for years, but it went ahead, and the overhead was removed with what seemed indecent haste. This was not all. On 30 September 1939, after World War II had begun, the leases of the Dudley via Oldbury route expired and the Soho Station, Bearwood and Oldbury-Dudley routes went over to buses, though two routes worked by Rosebery Street, Lodge Road and Ladywood, continued to be operated by trams.

As a result of these abandonments, there was now considerable re-allocation of trams; the Coventry Road closure had only resulted in the reduction of the 21 class Brill 21E cars, but Stratford Road caused the withdrawal of the CBT four-wheelers

which were sent to West Smethwick depot, minus roof numeral-blind boxes, for breaking up, and the 40hp No 512 class bogies from Highgate Road went to Miller Street, as did Nos 451 and 452 which had been on Stratford Road for some years. Some ex-Highgate Road Radials went to Hockley as spare cars, displacing the remaining 21 class, leaving only Lodge Road to be worked by those cars. Then came Hockley's turn, and the high-speed bogies were dispersed, some to Bristol Road, some to Moseley Road, some to Witton. As a result, ex-Bristol Road 301 class ran for a few months from Rosebery Street, including Nos 342 and 347 (the only fully-enclosed cars to run on Soho and Bearwood) until the Dudley Road group closed in September. The 301 class also appeared on the Stechford routes, replacing the Coventry Road Radials, which latter class was now put out of business. A reserve fleet of Radials was kept at Rosebery Street, but despite car losses due to air-raids they were never to run again.

At the outbreak of World War II, therefore, Birmingham Corporation was operating trams from the following depots: Harborne Lane (Bristol Road) — Selly Oak, Rednal and Rubery, all now with bogie cars; Rosebery Street, working Lodge Road 32 with the small bow-fitted Brill cars and Ladywood 33 with air-brake bogies; Miller Street working Perry Barr 6 with the Aston bogies and 451/452 and the Erdington group with the ex-Highgate Road 512 class and 637 class bogies, all 40hp motors; Witton working the Witton via Aston Cross 3X and Lozells and Gravelly Hill 5 with bogie and 301 class; Washwood Heath working Alum Rock 8 and Washwood Heath 10 with bow-fitted air-brake bogies; Coventry Road on the Stechford routes 84 and 90 with 301 class; Moseley Road still intact, working the Alcester Lanes End routes and the 'Chinese Railway' in Balsall Heath with the 401-450 class and magnetic-brake bogies; and finally Cotteridge working Pershore Road 36 with the newest cars in the fleet — still a big undertaking. The air-raids which destroyed cars in Miller Street depot and at Washwood Heath lie outside the scope of this book, but despite all the trams kept going and continued so to do until 1953.

The Department ran only a small fleet of permanent way and engineering cars compared with some undertakings, and in later years it was very much reduced. The two 'custom-built' rail-grinders, Nos PW 8 and 9, alias 266 and 509, sufficed, whereas in earlier years there had been several more. At one time there were two welding cars, with the bodies built of corrugated iron and looking as if they had been surreptitiously lifted from the Great Western Railway, looking suspiciously like the GWR's buildings in that material on their 'Halts' and 'Platforms', served by rail-motors. One welder, No PW 16, survived in later years, as the policy evidently was to move materials by motor-lorry, the ex-Tilling-Stevens buses, instead of by rail vehicles which got in the way of service cars. There were some sand vans, one of which was rebuilt into a tower car, No 01, for work on the reserved track sections where motor tower wagons were not practicable. Van

Above left: BCT car No 792 at Washwood Heath, on same location as car No 121. Later version of the Standard Bogie with individual upper-deck windows and air-brakes — observe reservoirs between bogies. Nos 762-811 were allocated to Washwood Heath depot and sported bow collectors.

Below left: BCT 01, the Overhead Tower Wagon converted from a sand van, for use on reserved track sections. This car had just completed removing the overhead from Hockley Depot and was about to leave for its home base at Selly Oak via the Ford Street spur to the Lodge Road route. The last tramway vehicle from Hockley Depot. 18 May 1939. */ R. T. Coxon*

No 10 had vestibule cabs, and usually did the ticket run from Hockley, where the ticket stores were located in the old cable winding engine room. After the service had finished for the night, a van car would leave Hockley and visit all depots with the next day's stocks of tickets, but this duty later was performed by motor van, again ex-bus.

One matter in which BCT never got caught out was the Snow Fiend. I think I am right in claiming that Birmingham was the only tramway undertaking which fitted snowploughs to service cars, though I am open to correction on this point. At each depot, as the snow season came round, certain cars specially fitted for the work would have the lifeguard trays and the 'gates' removed, and diagonal wooden snowploughs slung under the platforms. In falling snow the plough cars would be kept running all night, and the late Chief Inspector Tozer of Hockley told me of an incident when he, then a driver at Rosebery Street, was bringing in the last service car off the Ladywood route one night just before World War I, when snow began to fall. He had a new 512 class bogie with enclosed cab, and as he put the car away in the depot the night foreman hailed him with the news that he had to take the snowplough car out, open-cab No 242 as there was now no one else in the place. There was no use in grumbling — the foreman hadn't made it snow, so out they went, he and his mate, on No 242; they didn't appreciate the open cab one little bit, but they cleared Ladywood and Navigation Street and then went out along Hagley Road, and by this time it was really snowing. Suddenly the car rocked and rolled, lights went out and the snow came up through the floor hatches. 'Off the track?', I asked Mr Tozer. 'Off the track!' said he, 'We were in a bloody front garden!' The car had slewed round and gone straight up the carriage drive of one of the large Victorian villas near Norfolk

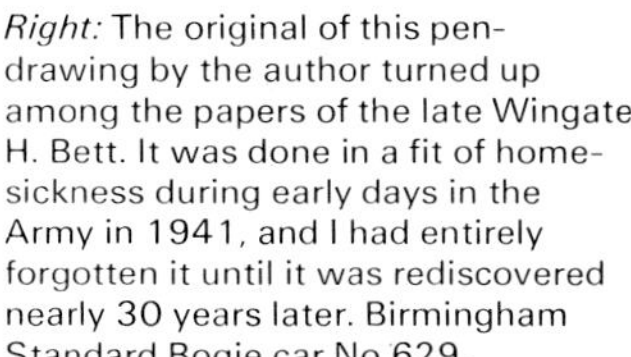

Right: The original of this pen-drawing by the author turned up among the papers of the late Wingate H. Bett. It was done in a fit of home-sickness during early days in the Army in 1941, and I had entirely forgotten it until it was rediscovered nearly 30 years later. Birmingham Standard Bogie car No 629.

Road. When the conductor, after slogging through the snow to the nearest telephone, had reported their plight to the Rosebery Street foreman, he was told that as they were clear of the track they could stay there till morning as he (the foreman) wasn't going to get the breakdown gang out in that weather. Finally they had difficulty with the housemaid as the morning palely dawned when she came out to brush the step and found a tram on it.

I do not recall that the Snow Fiend ever beat the Birmingham trams. What I do recall is on the dual carriageway Bristol Road an occasion when the dual carriageways were blocked, but the reserved tram-tracks were clear and some motorists not only had the unbounded nerve to drive between the special bollards (I don't think commercials would have got between them) on to the reserved track, but to sound their malignant little pipsqueak hooters at the trams on whose territory they were trespassing! I believe that was the 1938/39 winter, when like many other students I was working in the Birmingham GPO on the Christmas mail. I had been on night parcels sorting and came off duty on a bitter morning when there had been snow, turning to rain, then a sudden hard frost — a silver thaw — which coated everything with ice. No buses were operating until quite a bit later on, but the trams were out, and I slithered along Colmore Row and caught the first Oxhill Road car, which was No 544. Ahead was the first 75 to Wednesbury whose lights seemed curiously dim, though 544's lights were somewhat on the blink as well. We reached Grove Lane junction, where was stationed a PW man with a brazier of coal going, keeping hot water handy to stop the points from freezing, but even so No 544 refused the points twice before she got round. Then we had fun. Up to Grove Lane the 75 had been doing the ice-breaking, but now No 544 was on her own, and our lights practically went out. She took the points off the single line at Dawson Road first go — at the caution — and we ground on along Grove Lane, down past Handsworth Park gates and up the hill as far as Hinstock Road, where No PW 9 had come to rest years before, and there she stuck, but not for long. The driver changed ends, drove back wrong line up the other side of the quite steep valley of the Farcroft Brook, which he had just come down, changed ends again and did another run. He just failed to make the Brunswick Road stop, so back again and on the third attempt he got through.

That first 75 would have carried out a drill at Hill Top, West Bromwich, as follows, before descending Holloway Bank to Wednesbury, and I understand this practice was inherited from the South Staffs company. At Hill Top schools the first car out reversed over the crossover and went down Hill Top wrong line, thus breaking the ice or clearing the snow for the return trip up the Bank, which might otherwise have been difficult. The second car out ran right line. This drill was only brought into use in very severe conditions, but West Bromwich lies high and conditions at five hundred feet can be very different from three hundred or two hundred and fifty. I mentioned how snowplough cars on the Lodge Road route had to be careful about curves, but the only time I saw two plough cars get hooked was on the Ladywood route, when two plough-fitted air-brake bogies had a 'cornfield meet' on the corner of Monument Road and Ladywood Road. It was a very slight encounter with just a few splinters of timber off the ploughs, and both cars carried on after one had reversed a few yards.

Only two Birmingham cars had roller-bearings on the axles — one of the Mountain and Gibson trucks of the 401-450 class (No 433 had this truck for a long time, but it appeared under others also) and No 843, the last car built. The late P. W. Lawson told me that though there were slight running economies with roller bearings, these were offset when axles had to go away for wheel re-profiling. Plain bearings could be taken out at the depot by unskilled labour and axles changed there, but roller bearings had to be pressed off and on by skilled labour involving the car visiting the works, and after being pressed on or off the axles two or three times the bearings were then scrap. The Birmingham cars ran very quietly, and perhaps due to the use of track brakes there was little or no rail corrugation — if it occurred, Nos PW 8 or 9 were soon on the spot. Sharp curves were water-lubricated, with a low-pressure jet of water so located in the groove that the water ran down the gradient to the nearest track drain, and there was little squealing of flanges on curves — though I recall doing music examinations in the old Edmund Street building of Birmingham University during hot summer days and hearing cars screeching somewhat round the curve from Edmund Street into Congreve Street; rather odd, this, as it was almost on the doorstep of Head Office. In fact, this curve got into a BBC broadcast one Wednesday. I referred in the railway section to G. D. Cunningham's recitals on the Birmingham Town Hall organ; these were frequently broadcast, and one day, when unable to be in the Town Hall, I was listening to GDC at home, and distinctly heard, in the lull between two pieces, a tram on the Congreve Street curve. GDC like so many organists, if not an out-and-out enthusiast, was certainly very well informed about railways, but I am not sure if he took the trams in as well. Just how much water lubrication helped reduce flange and rail wear on curves was brought home to me when travelling out to Cotteridge one day on one of the 812-841 bogies. At Dogpool I observed another car ahead, but at first didn't attach anything to this, but as we moved up I noticed that the car ahead had its trolley tied down. As my car closed in the driver of the halted car gave my driver the thumbs-down signal, and it seemed that he had a seized-up leading axle. My car buffered up behind, and began to push the other car along an almost level section, but before reaching the British Oak the next car was up behind, so we now had two pushing up through Stirchley. Then came the Breedon Cross climb to Cotteridge terminus with now three cars pushing and things getting a bit warm, but eventually the defective car was pushed on to the terminal stub for the depot. Then an old depot hand came out, took a look at things and stumped back into the depot — he had a 'cay-leg', — and re-appeared with a water can. He liberally sloshed down the rails into the depot with water, got aboard the crippled car and drove it into the depot on one motor, no trouble at all! Needless to say, that axle would have to go away for, I should imagine, re-tyring, but I saw the same car back in service three days later so evidently a spare axle was quickly available and the job done. Many Birmingham cars had helical gears to the driving axles, but I believe that the practice was not unknown, when gears were getting a bit noisy before a works visit became due, of opening the gearcase up and topping up with a mixture of oil and used tickets, which noticeably reduced any 'wow-wow'! Another trick of the trade, at depots with air-brake cars, was to go over the air-line of a car reported for loss or pressure with a shaving mug and lather brush. Where the bubbles were coming up, there was the leak.

A disabled Birmingham tram was a very rare sight, such was the standard of maintenance even if there was to be no new development after 1930. Track maintenance was of an equally high standard, the Department having its own PW section and not, as in some cities, having to rely on the Public Works or similar department of the Council. There was a PW yard in Miller Street on the opposite side to the tram depot, and the Overhead Department was located in adjoining buildings. There was another PW yard at Sampson Road, Sparkbrook, adjacent to the paint shop, with a siding running alongside the Grand Union Canal so that supplies of materials could be unloaded from boats. At Miller Street was also the tramway foundry, where pole-bases, finials, and other articles in cast iron were produced, not only for the Tramways Department but for other Corporation Departments. The familiar Birmingham street nameplates with corded surround, many mounted on pedestals, were produced at Miller Street and many hundreds of them still survive.

At the close of our period the trams were still doing good business, but by the late thirties the 'Rednal Spectaculars' were on the wane. Extra cars certainly had to be put on for the Bank Holidays, but there were now far more private cars around, petrol was by modern standards ridiculously cheap, and people were now doing weekend trips to the coast in their own cars instead of going to the Lickeys by tram, and the famous turning circle was seeing less use. By 1939 circumstances entirely unimagined in 1919 had changed the picture, but that is the whole story of transport. This is perhaps the stage at which we should now look at the rise of the motor bus in Birmingham after World War I, when the bus fleet was a mere half-hundred or so Daimlers and Tillings and the greatest days of the tramcar were yet to come.

The Ascendancy of the Bus 1919–1939

Above: BMMO Co Ltd SOS 'MM' bus 1930 before rebuilding with radiator from 'XL' coach.

We left the buses at the end of World War I; Birmingham at least had some buses, whereas many operators had virtually nothing. London, much more dependent on buses before 1914 than Birmingham, was really pushed, and lorries had to be brought in to help out. That situation did not arise in Birmingham, where there was only a nucleus of a bus system, and as losses of Daimler chassis due to requisitioning had been made good with Tilling-Stevens chassis the 1919 situation was not very different from 1914; fuel shortage rather than vehicle shortage was the problem.

Up to now, Birmingham bus services had served the 'carriage trade' areas of Edgbaston, Harborne, Moseley, and Handsworth Wood, with hourly or half-hourly headway, and neither the public nor the management at this stage foresaw buses taking over on heavy routes, and indeed the vehicles then in use could not have done so. Buses were already getting bigger, however; the Daimlers rebuilt with 'K' style bodywork seated 40 as against 34 of their original bodies, and this was only a beginning. In 1922 a number of demonstrators ran in Birmingham, including a Tilling-Stevens 48-seater, XH 9629, a Leyland which I suspect was an LB, TB 8886 with 42 seats, a bigger Leyland with 54 seats, G7 TC 2128, and an AEC 'S', or 503 model, which took the fleet number 59 with registration OK 3980. Its Fry body seated 54, and it had forward control, the driver sitting alongside the engine; this bus, unlike the 14 which followed, had a windscreen. The others, OK 8002-8015, 60-71 and 89-90, had Brush 54-seat bodies. No 59's body was identical to the LGOC's 'S' buses; the others had detail differences. Eight Leyland A1 type 19-seaters with locally-built bodies by John Buckingham of Bradford Street came into service also in 1922-3, with jack-knife door front entrance for one-man operation, at first numbered 1-8, then 72-79. They were at first on solid tyres, but when I first met up with them had been put on pneumatics. (OK 5482-5489.) A similar Buckingham body was put on No 80, a Daimler CK, OK 9852, followed by OL 1714-1721, the first of which was numbered 82, but renumbered 81; 81 had been temporarily occupied by an AEC demonstrator with Dodson front-and-rear entrances, NO 6856. The Daimlers became 81-88 until, like the Leyland A1s,

Left: Daimler No 48, OB 2102, of BCT with new 1922 Brush 'K' style body with windscreen. Just to complicate the issue further, some of these Daimlers sported AEC radiators later. All were sold to Southdown in 1927. / *BCT*

Below: BCT's sample AEC 503, No 59, OK 3980 of 1923, with Fry body identical to the LGOC 'S' type. / *BCT*

they were renumbered near the end of their time to make way for the Morris Dictators. These small one-man buses were used to open up new services, one being service 11 from Moseley Village to Perry Barr over what became part of the Outer Circle, another part of the Circle being the No 10 from Kings Heath to King's Head, Bearwood. More buses became available as the Bristol Road tramway extensions were opened, and the No 10 was operated by Tilling-Stevens open-top buses. The AEC 503s, which to me seemed huge vehicles at the time, were on the routes running into the city, Moseley 1, Handsworth Wood 2, Queen's Park 3, Harborne 4, and Bartley Green 12.

Probably encouraged by the success of the Nechells 'trackless trams', the Tramways Department was thinking in terms of top-covered buses, and AEC No 62 was fitted up with a temporary top-cover in the works, but never ran with it. Photographs show that the top-deck windows were odd bit of glass taken from withdrawn Tilling-Stevens bodies, as the stencilled registrations

Right: BCT No 2, later No 73, a Leyland A1 19-seater of 1923 with locally-built Buckingham body. Soon put on pneumatics and the 'bible' type indicator replaced with a front numeral box.
/ *John Buckingham Limited*

Below: Daimler CK2 No 82, OL 1715, of BCT at Stockland Green in the early days of the Outer Circle. 637 class tram at Route 1 terminus. The little Leylands and Daimlers were soon quite unable to cope with the tourist trade on the Outer Circle.

Left: AEC 503 No 62, OK 8004, of BCT with temporary mock-up top-cover. No 62 later reverted to open-top. / *BCT*

Below: AEC 504 No 152, OM 9566, of BCT in original condition. / *BCT*

show up, so this was only a mock-up. The outcome was bus 101, an AEC 504 OL 8100, and this was indeed a very historic vehicle. This body was by Brush, and like any other double-decker at this time it was on solids. The 504 would appear to be the same as the 503 with the important difference that the chassis members were channel steel instead of flitched timbers, and doubtless the reason why the 503s were not converted to top-covers or later put on pneumatics was this important difference in the chassis. No 101 antedated the London NS by some months, and I believe can rightly claim to be the first modern top-covered bus. Like the Nechells trolleys, it confounded the Jeremiahs by failing to overturn. Its performance was such that, with the similar 507, 235 examples of this chassis were added to the fleet up to 1929. Evidently the original 503, No 59, had costed better than the Leyland G7 — or could it be the London influence was still at work? Whatever, these open-staircase AECs were a wonderful investment and by 1926 or 1927 their impact was not lost on the Committee.

As far on into the 1920s as 1924 there had been no almighty rush to go over to buses — in fact, the first new vehicles were the

Below: AEC 504 No 101, OL 8100, of BCT the pioneer top-cover bus, put on pneumatics and with front numeral indicator repositioned. Note 'dodger'. These open-cab AECs were favourites with the men. / *BCT*

Above: Guy 6-wheeler No 208, OP 237, of BCT. This bus had a long run on the Outer Circle, but remained a 'one-off'. / *Short Bros Limited*

AEC 503s and Leyland A1s of 1923. Up to then the rebodied Daimlers, Dodson open-top Tillings and the Brush single-deck Tillings were handling the traffic. The new intake in 1923-1924 was therefore 15 AEC 503s, eight Leyland A1s and nine Daimler CK2s, a not very considerable increase compared with the expansion of the tram fleet. It was really No 101 which changed all that, and an order for 30 more 504s with Short Bros bodies, 102-131, OM 201-230, followed, making it possible to run most existing routes with top-covered buses. A new route to Handsworth Wood, 16, opened in January 1925, running direct via Snow Hill instead of via Monument Road and Hagley Road. This was the first new route with top-covered buses, and its immediate popularity hit the trade of the No 2 route via Monument Road, and more so still the circular railway service at Handsworth Wood station. Undoubtedly, however, the biggest impact the bus has ever made in Birmingham was still to come, and it came in April 1926 with the completion of the Outer Circle. Route 11 from Moseley to Perry Barr was extended westwards via Handsworth and City Road to the King's Head where it met the No 10 from Kings Heath, and the Moseley Village to Acocks Green section was altered to Kings Heath-Acocks Green, thus completing the circle. Acocks Green to Moseley was added to the No 1 service from the city, becoming 1A.

The complete circle took the Department by surprise. Everyone went joy-riding round the Outer Circle. It became as popular as the tram ride to the Lickeys, and the little Leyland and Daimler 20-seaters just couldn't handle it. Everything the Department could spare ran the Outer Circle, and an order for more top-covered 504s went in, but they, of course, had to be built. In the meantime, about a dozen LGOC 'B' type open-toppers were hired from AEC (11 are known, but there may have been more) to cope with the situation — which they did, albeit at the continuous boil, for the Outer Circle had some formidable hills, and those 'Old Bills' were far past their prime. They were still in LGOC red; one could discern the 'GENERAL' transfer under the red-painted side panel. They carried the LGOC stencil numerals 11 front and rear. I travelled on them several times; I didn't think very much of them at the time, but am happy now to think that I did travel on the 'B' type, even if not in London. Eventually the new 504 arrived, 132-161, OM 9546-9575 and 162-171, ON 1313-1322, all with Short bodies, and the 'B' types went to their long home. Alas, no photograph of them on the Outer Circle has come to light so far. They died well.

Further 504s took the fleet numbers up to 207, and then came a prodigy, or so we thought. It was a 56-seat normal-control Guy six-wheeler with Daimler engine, Shorts putting the body on it. The following year, 1927, another six-wheeler appeared, this time a half-cab Karrier 60-seater, Shorts again being the bodybuilder, and about this time a Leyland Titanic, TE 1128,

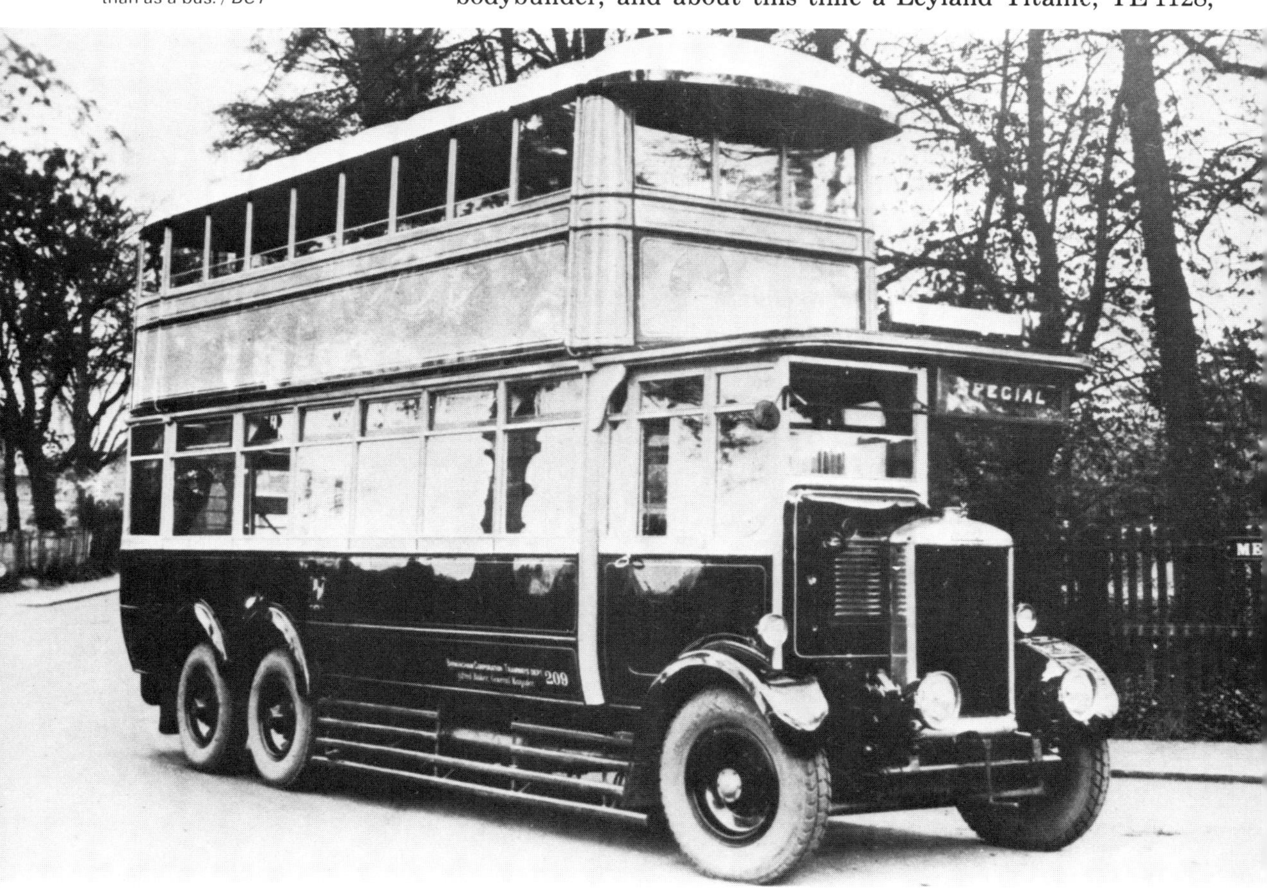

Below: Karrier half-cab 6-wheeler No 209, OP 238, of BCT. It had a longer career as a breakdown crane than as a bus. / *BCT*

with body finished in polished aluminium, ran on the Outer Circle on demonstration. The Guy and Karrier were tried on various city routes, but soon became part of the regular Outer Circle roster, where indeed they were very useful. Birmingham apparently found them too unwieldy in the city centre, though nearby Wolverhampton went in for them in a big way. The Karrier proved troublesome and its days as a bus were limited. The body remained in Harborne Lane garage for a long time, and the chassis was used for a breakdown crane. The Guy, however, ran until 1934, always on the clockwise Outer Circle. No 208 (OP 237) was the Guy's number, the Karrier being 209, OP 238. Both these fleet numbers were to be re-used by 'one-off' jobs later.

1926 saw another innovation, and an important one. While waiting for a 16 bus at the top of Snow Hill, I saw an AEC 504 on Harborne 4 turn out of Bull Street into Colmore Row. I could see there was something different from head-on as it came along Bull Street, and as it made the turn I saw what it was. The bus was on pneumatics, and I just made out its number, 122. It was on trials with 'blow-ups', obviously successful, for all the AEC 504s were put on pneumatics in a very short time, but not the open-top 503s. They were still in full-time service, but they were soon to be relegated to tree-cutting and running Sunday afternoon specials to Witton Cemetery, some becoming service lorries. The Guy six-wheeler 208 was the first new double-decker on pneumatics, as were all subsequent buses. In two years the double-deck bus had taken two giant strides — the top cover, and blow-up tyres, and it had the capacity of the smaller tramcars — more, in effect, as nobody travelled on the balcony seats in wet or winter weather. Just as the increased earnings of the fully-enclosed 637 class tramcars justified the expense of rebuilding the 512-636 cars to fully-enclosed condition, so the greatly increased earnings of the top-cover buses justified their increased first cost. The two six-wheelers 208 and 209 were the first buses with enclosed cabs and staircases, but the next 10 504s, 210-219, were open-cab. 220 was the first of the Inner Circle low-loaders, which had enclosed cabs: first a word about the Inner Circle.

The Outer Circle having proved a money-spinner, the idea of an Inner Circle came up. There was a problem on this route, Icknield Street bridge under the GWR at Hockley station. The standard top-covered 504s could not pass this bridge, and indeed notices on each side reading *'Passengers must remain seated while passing under this bridge'* told their own tale. To negotiate this obstacle, some very odd-looking bodies on Associated Daimler 507 (virtually the 504, but with rear platform bearers added) chassis were built by Shorts, 220-234, OP 7863-7877. The roof of the lower saloon was of 'camel-back' section, the upper deck seats being individual bucket seats set at an angle on each side of the arch, with a perimeter gangway all round. It was rather like riding side-saddle, and they were a gift to

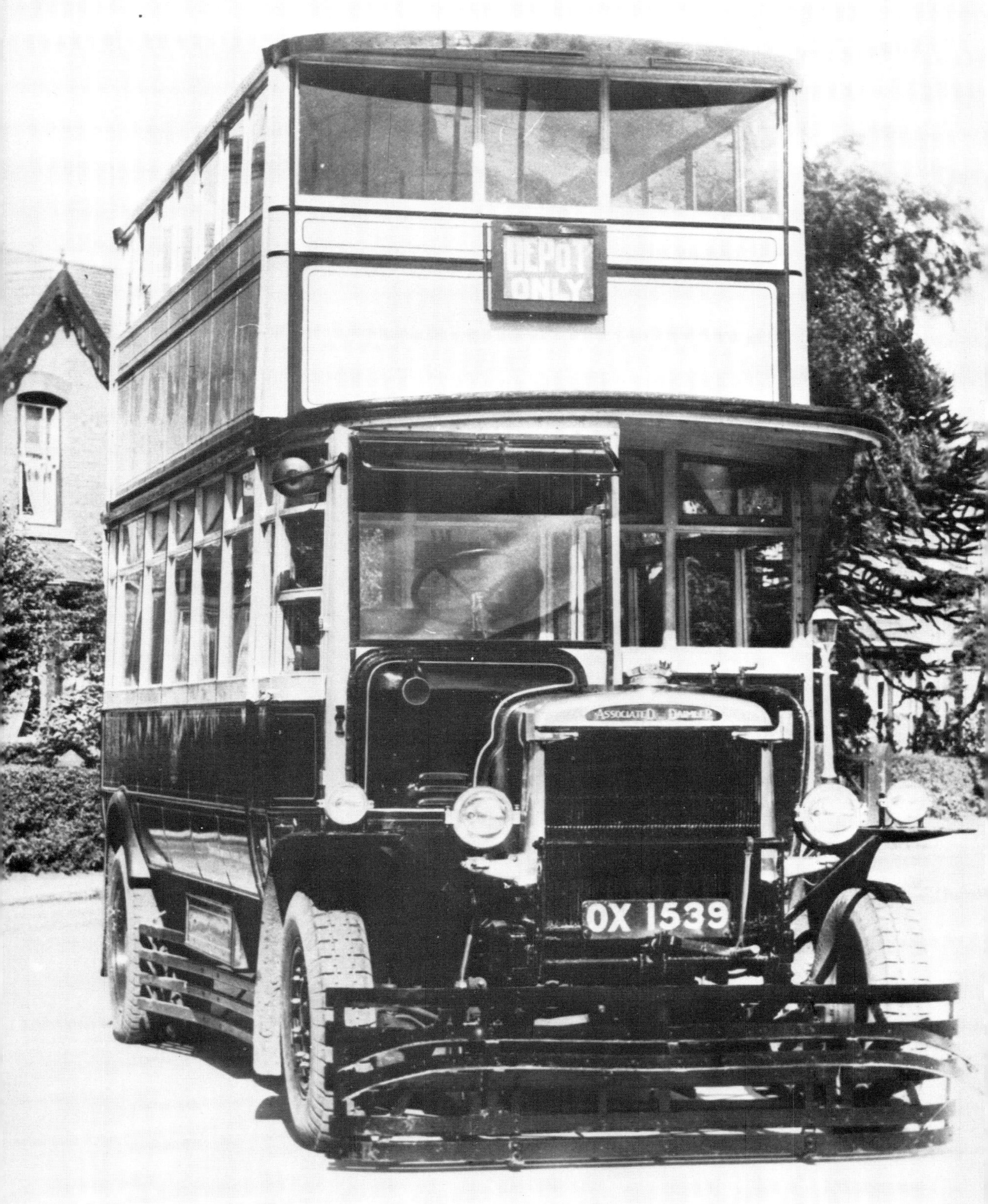
DEPOT
ONLY
ASSOCIATED DAIMLER
OX 1539

Left: Associated Daimler 507 No 263, OX 1539, of BCT with cab-fitted Buckingham body and carrying an experimental lifeguard. / *BCT*

Above: ADC 507 No 295, VP 1159, of BCT — an Inner Circle 'Pickpocket Special' metal low-height body by Short Bros Limited. Regarded unfavourably by passengers and conductors. A London AEC 'NS' would probably have been a better solution to the low-bridge restriction on Route 8. / *BCT*

pickpockets, and became known as 'Pickpocket Specials'. Passengers and conductors alike hated them, and it does seem a little odd that a London NS should not have been tried on the Inner Circle, and there is no evidence that one ever was. The NS was certainly in production at this date. Perhaps Birmingham looked askance at the right-angle drop in the chassis behind the engine, as a possible source of frame fracture, and more so still perhaps they did not like the NS final drive, which was really a reincarnation of the gear-ring and pinion drive of the old Milnes-Daimler. For all these possible sources of trouble, the AEC NS gave years of good service in London, and as their roof-height came out the same as the Regent STs they would have been a better proposition on the Inner Circle than 220-234, and the metal-body batch which came in 1928, 286-295. However, Birmingham seemed set on the straight chassis, and that is how it was.

The Inner Circle, which began to operate in February 1928, was, of course, not the tourist attraction which the Outer Circle was in those days, when much of it was still rural. It is quite as useful a service, however, and still loads well even when so many industrial workers today travel in their own transport. It is less well liked by drivers, for whereas on the Outer Circle one can easily make up time lost trying to get across one of the radial roads at a peak hour (and in a trip round the Outer Circle one is bound to hit one of the rush hours, and things are never the same twice running at any one place), on the Inner Circle the bus is no sooner clear of one radial road than the next one is coming up,

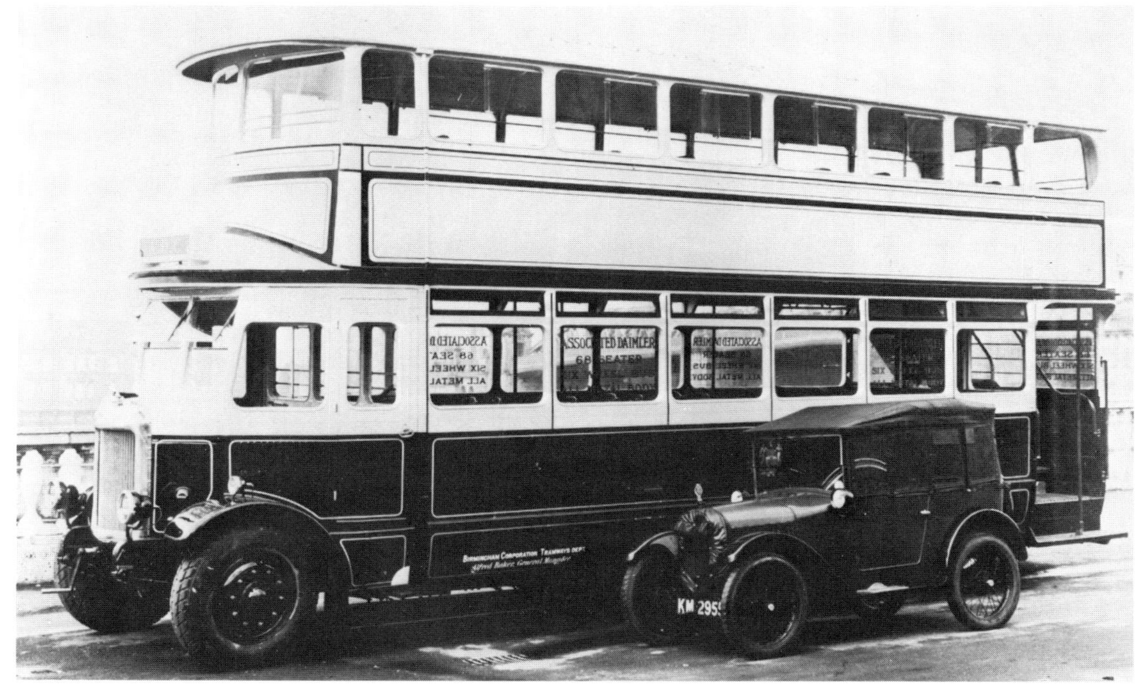

Above: ADC 802 (LS) 6-wheeler 1928, No 286, OX 4594, of BCT. Stylish all-metal body by Shorts, but the type did not catch on either in Birmingham or London. One of the original 'Baby' Austins is alongside. / *Short Bros Limited*

Above right: One of BCT's first batch of AEC Regents, No 340, OF 3972, with Brush body, of 1929. An enormous advance on No 101 of 1924. / *BCT*

Right: Guy Conquest of 1929, No 57, OF 3966, of BCT. These imposing vehicles were rebuilt by Guy as half-cab 32-seaters. / *BCT*

and there is far less chance of recouping time lost. On the Outer Circle, to allow for these changing conditions timings have always been liberal, and at times the bus will just die for a bit while the running time catches up with it. On most tram and bus routes the Bundy clock was in evidence, many of them still surviving, and on the Circle routes these temporary states of 'limbo' would occur just before the next Bundy clock; if the driver's key number on the paper roll showed a late departure, that could be explained by traffic delays, but an early departure would mean a carpeting. In the early twenties I must have had dozens of key numbers impressed on my wrist by Oxhill Road tram-drivers who had just clocked in; I think many of them came to regard me as an honorary checker.

More full-height ADC 507s came into the fleet, all with enclosed cabs, then came a one-off, 285, OX 1570, with Short Bros all-metal body but, oddly, reverting to open-cab. Then came 286, an ADC 'LS' six-wheeler, OX 4594, with Short Bros fully-enclosed metal body. Like the other six-wheelers, she took to the Outer Circle, but her stay was short and she went south-west to operate in the Plymouth area; on return, her number had been taken by the first of the 10 metal-body Inner Circle low-loaders, and she became No 100. I believe she was only on demonstration and was not BCT property. The London 'LS' class, a mere handful for London, had very dated open-staircase bodies and, of course, open-cabs, since windscreens were not permitted by the Metropolitan Police until about 1930. No 286

MOSELEY AND ACOCKS GREEN 1A
340

SPECIAL
SPECIAL
PLEASE PAY AS YOU ENTER
57

was a very attractive and impressive vehicle, and had quite a hint of the style of tram 842 and bus 368 about it. Evidently, however, the six-wheeler was not for Birmingham, and further 507s followed bringing the fleet numbers up to 337.

Then came the next giant stride in the shape of the six-cylinder dropped-frame AEC Regent, fully-enclosed and with the upper deck built over the engine canopy in a 'piano-front'. The first batch of 1929 were 338-367, OF 3970-3999, though the first two chassis were later replaced by OG 3638-3639, and then came the one-off Short Bros body to match tramcar 842, the bus being 368, OF 8368; this last bus was the first in the fleet to have the registration coinciding with the fleet number, which now became standard BCT practice. Just before the Regents arrived, some Guy 'Conquest' 26-seat single-deckers joined the fleet to replace the Leyland and Daimler 20-seaters. These were 51-60, OF 3960-3969, followed by another 20, 61-80, OF 6071-6090 (the last figure of the registration coincides here, and it did on 507s 210-219, but 368 was the real beginning of the practice.) These were very impressive-looking vehicles with a great bonnet like the Leyland Lioness, and they could certainly move; with their petrol consumption so they should, too — they were certainly thirsty vehicles. It seem a little odd, looking back, that the Department should not have ordered the AEC Regal single-decker as they were investing in Regents, but as it was we had 'feathers in our cap' on the Ivy Bush and Handsworth Wood No 2 as it had now become. They were not to remain in their bonneted 26-seater state for long. New regulations laid down 20 seats as the maximum for one-man operation (how circumstances alter cases!) and BCT were faced with what to do with 30 new 26-seaters which would be uneconomical with a conductor; equally wasteful would be to take out six seats; sell them? — nobody would want them as they were. The answer was to send them back to Guys at Wolverhmapton, who lengthened the chassis and rebuilt them as half-cab 32-seaters, in which condition they were viable with a conductor, and thus it was. They remained expensive buses to run, however, and were replaced relatively early, but like most Guy products they were good to look at and certainly could get moving. There had to be some single-deckers in the fleet for private hire work and later for service 27, involving the low canal aqueduct in Bournville Lane.

A solitary low-bridge Leyland Titan with side-gangway body put in an appearance on the Inner Circle (any demonstrators etc seemed to gravitate to the No 8). This was 99, OF 3959. She stayed for some time, but was highly unpopular with conductors and passengers (the drivers liked it!) and eventually passed out of the fleet to Preston Corporation. Evidently Birmingham was keeping the London tradition (the Birmingham Regents were based on the London STs) for the present. One of the OF batch of Regents, 344, had a straight staircase, which was to become a Birmingham standard feature. The rest of the batch had angle stairs. Before another batch arrived, a one-off turned up, taking

Right: Guy Conquest No 60, OF 3969, of BCT as rebuilt and converted to run on town's gas — quite successfully, but only No 60 was so treated. / *BCT*

Below right: A 1930 Regent, No 402, OG 402, of BCT with English Electric body, at Hamstead Road, Handsworth in 1938. / *R. T. Coxon*

Right: A 1931 Regent, No 486, OV 4486, of BCT at the beginning of its restoration in 1977. A lot to do, but it will run again! / *R. Archer*

the fleet number of the now long-withdrawn Karrier, 209, OG 209. This AEC Regent had a Metro-Cammell metal body, which firm were to build hundreds of bus bodies for the city. The next lot of Regents, however, OG 369-443, had bodies by English Electric and Vulcan, and Vulcan put a similar 'piano-front' body on a Vulcan Emperor, WM 5621, No 98, and sent it to Birmingham. A BCT driving instructor once told me that it was the nicest bus he had ever driven. Any demonstrators at this period were numbered in the 90s, and quite a few came and went. More Regents arrived in 1931, 444-503, OV 4444-4503, with bodies by Short and Metro-Cammell; the bus fleet numbers were now catching up on the trams, though they still had some way to go. Another 'piano-front' demonstrator was a TSM (Tilling-Stevens in disguise) No 95, KJ 2918. It ran, of course, on the Inner Circle.

Contemporary with the OV Regents was a solitary six-wheel AEC Renown, No 92, MV 489, obviously from its registration a demonstrator. It was taken into the fleet and worked from Perry Barr garage, usually on route 29, Highfield Road-Kingstanding. It had 'piano-front' bodywork like the Regents and had a long run as a bus, and a further career as a breakdown crane, receiving the crane off the Karrier OP 238. Another six-wheeler was a Guy, UK 8911, with the large 'Invincible' radiator like 97 — or 208 (II) and numbered 96. This ran its brief career in Birmingham on the Outer Circle with the first Guy six-wheeler, 208 (I). Evidently the Renown made the best impression of all the six-wheelers, but it seemed that the Regent, in its petrol-engine form, was what Birmingham required.

These AEC Regents made No 101, the much-publicised top-

Above: BCT No 90, OV 4090, a 1931 Morris Dictator with MCW body, at Hamstead in 1938. This bus also has survived and awaits full restoration. */ R. T. Coxon*

cover bus of 1924, look as dated as 101 had outdated pre-1914 Tillings, and all in five years. In those momentous five years the bus had caught up with the tram to the extent that it was now on equal terms. Nobody could have foreseen such developments even in 1920 — those who had said in the early 1900s that buses would eventually oust the trams were laughed to scorn — and road developments in Birmingham, planned in the early twenties or even before, were obviously enough thought of in terms of dual carriageways with trams on central reservations, as witness the many instances of quite unnecessarily wide reservations. There was now nothing to choose in passenger comfort between the AEC Regent and the latest in trams, 842 and 843. Moreover, the Regents could now outpace even the 70hp bogie trams, and even before the Regents came on the scene the 504s and 507s had proved capable of containing the trade on the new outlying routes to Perry Common, Kingstanding, Yardley Wood, etc. With the Regents now available, the fate of the Hagley Road tram route was sealed and it was combined with the Quinton-Kingstanding service, still retaining the tram service number, 34, in one direction. From now, it was to be road vehicles. Only one major tramway work was undertaken, apart from routine relaying — the diversion of the trams from High Street, Erdington, to the Sutton New Road in 1938. The buses were in the ascendant, the double-decker having attained the all-enclosed profile which it was to retain for 30 years before rear-engine buses displaced them in the 1960s.

More single-deckers were required, and this time another local manufacturer got the order, Morris-Commercial, who built two batches of the Dictator chassis with Metropolitan-Cammell

Above: BCT No 555, OC 555, a Daimler CP6 of 1933 at Hamstead Hill in 1939. Ten of these petrol-engine fluid-flywheel buses were ordered after a demonstrator, VC 7519, had made a very favourable impression. / *R. T. Coxon*

metal bodywork — a bit utilitarian in appearance, but they did well and came out more economical than the Guy Conquests. One, OV 4090, survives, but at the time of writing awaits complete restoration as a runner. These were followed by an order for 50 Morris 'Imperial' double-deckers, after a demonstrator, No 91, OV 4848, had put in a brief spell. No 91 had a 'semi-piano-front', but the production batch had a front profile flush with the cab windscreen; Birmingham had been rather slow to adopt this style which was well established elsewhere, but this was to be the order of things for the future. These Imperials were 504-553, the first three having bodies by Brush, English Electric and Gloucester RC and W, the rest MCW. They went to Perry Barr garage, then working the Handsworth Wood-Yardley services 15 and 16, and I got to know them well. Admittedly they were fast, but they were about the roughest-riding double-deckers I have ever encountered, solid-tyre period included, and the gearbox was evidently very difficult. More than once I have known drivers have to stop, 'go back to square 1', and go through the box again. A feature of the design was that the engined was mounted on a sub-frame attached to the front axle, and could be wheeled out on the front axle — after, of course, jacking up the rest of the bus — for inspection and repairs. Whatever, they were not liked and there were no repeat orders. They were followed by 10 Daimler CP6s, with fluid-flywheel and petrol engines, after a demonstrator, the second No 100, VC 7519, had worked from Perry Barr for a time. These were 554-563, with BRCW bodies differing rather from the

Morris batch. These were beautiful vehicles to travel on and to drive and I understand the drivers even preferred them to the Regents, which says a great deal for them. The came another one-off, the second 208, OC 8208, whose chassis was a reincarnation of 97, a Guy Invincible demonstrator, UK 8047. This had a Gardner 5LW engine and a MCW body of the same pattern as those on the Morris Imperials. It would then appear that someone probably at Tyburn Road works or Congreve Street said, 'Aha! What we want is something with a fluid flywheel *and* a Gardner engine' — and that was the next order, for 30 Daimler COG5 double-deckers, 564-593, AOG 564-593, bodies, 15 apiece, by Birmingham RC and W and MCW. These were not the first diesels in the Birmingham fleet, as a few of the Regents had been converted with Leyland oil engines, and 442's chassis had been replaced by a Crossley 'Condor', OJ 5442. The COG5s were highly successful, and with improved bodywork were ordered by the hundred. As the STL Regents became the standard London bus to the late 1930s, so the COG5s became the Birmingham standard. With 594 came the well-known Birmingham style of bodywork with beaded waistlines, that at indicator level being downswept each side of the front indicator and this style lasted until the MOF registration buses of 1954 — some are still in service on the Outer Circle as I write this. These bold waistlines were probably suggested by an AEC 'Q' double-decker, No 93, AHX 63, which ran on the Acocks Green via Moseley route for quite some years. Its body had such waistlines, and as applied to AOG 594 *et seq* the style impressed me as being amongst the most handsome and dignified of all double-deck vehicles. At this time, 'streamlining' was in vogue, and some disastrous examples of this style of painting were around, particularly on coaches, but not only on coaches.

Evidently the Daimler COG5's reliability and economy was taken into account with regard to the next stage of the tramway conversion, this being the Stratford Road group in 1937, for this group of lines, based on Highgate Road depot, was replaced by COG5s instead of trolley-buses as on Coventry Road, and there were to be no more trolleybus conversions in Birmingham. One solitary front-entrance double-deck COG5, No 94, BOP 94, was built with MCW body, probably as a result of Midland Red having gone over to front-entrance deckers, but she was a one-off and kept company with 'Q' 93 on the 1A service. Birmingham did a bit of shopping around, and put five Leyland Titan TD5s with torque-converter transmission in service in 1937, 964-968, with Leyland bodies. These worked the Inner Circle and were instantly recognisable by their bodywork not conforming to the deep waistline style of the Daimlers, and they also had angle stairs.

If the Daimler COG5 had a fault it was that of being under-powered uphill; the Hockley group of tramways were next due for replacement, and Birmingham ordered more Leylands with MCW bodies for their share. West Bromwich Corporation, after

Above: BCT No 94, BOP 94, a 'one-off' front entrance Daimler COG5 at Five Ways on the Acocks Green 1A route in 1939. / *R. T. Coxon*

trying out some COG5s and two COG6s, a Regent and a Leyland TD5C, ordered Daimler COG6s, for their share of the service, and these, with AEA registration, were always known as the 'Track' buses. They, of course, had the advantage over the COG5 uphill and were equal in performance to the Birmingham Leylands, with the advantage that the engine could be used as a retarder downhill, whereas the Converter Leylands could not so be used. While more COG5s were ordered by Birmingham, more Leylands also were ordered, this time with Leyland bodies, for the Dudley Road tram conversion. These bodies were basically the same as on 964-968, but with the Birmingham straight staircase and body-styling to conform with the Daimlers. Five AEC oil-engine Regents, 1034-1038, had appeared in 1938 — the chassis presumably conforming to the London STL Regents — but no more were bought. Some of the orginal Regents were now being withdrawn, as in those days 10 years was considered to be the lifespan of a bus; the last of the 507s were taken off in 1937, though several continued as service trucks. To the end, if the drivers could take out one of the open-cab 504s they would do so in preference to a cab 507, which had a reputation for draughts. If the weather cut up rough on an open 504 they rigged

Above: BCT No 290, EOG 290, a torque-converter Leyland TD5C in 1938. These were the replacement vehicles for the Hockley trams. / *BCT*

up a tarpaulin dodger and drove on. What they did not like was a split turn starting with a cab bus and having to finish on an open one. Only a few Regents had been withdrawn by 1939, and the rest continued through World War II, many with the bodies rebuilt to Utility standard.

The first 230 COG5 double-deckers, and the first of two batches of single-deckers, had the engine mounted solid in the frames, but beginning with the BOL registration single-deckers and BOP doubles the engines had flexible rubber mountings. The vibration was not too bad on the solid-mounted buses, but it was there; with the rubber mountings virtually no engine vibration came through and they were very pleasant and beautifully sprung vehicles to ride on. A 1937 example, 1107, with a 1939 body, has survived in preservation and is well known at vintage commercial rallies, and some of those converted after World War II to service vans and trucks are still extant. Neither the COG5 or COG6 had fans, the theory being that a slow-running diesel did not need fan cooling. West Bromwich found with the 'track' buses that on the Wednesbury 75 service they got very warm in the one direction and cooled off on the way back; if they were running into the wind, that kept them cool, but with

Above: BCT No 1034, CVP 134, one of five oil-engine Regents ordered in 1937, at Aston Villa in 1939. / *R. T. Coxon*

the wind behind them no wind was going though the radiator and they could boil coming up Holloway Bank. Probably Birmingham's choice of torque-converter Leylands for the ex-tram drivers at Hockley and Rosebery Street was that they were much more like a tram to drive. Apparently some of the older Highgate Road tram-drivers had found the combination of having to steer the bus and go through the box, even with fluid-flywheel, none too easy. As was quite usual, the ex-tram men could easily be spotted on the road — they still drove down the middle, track or no track! By 1937 the fleet numbers of the Birmingham buses were in four figures and the buses now outnumbered the trams. For the 1937 Coronation, since the tramway map was now so much reduced, the Department (which about now dropped the ponderous title of Birmingham Corporation Tramway and Omnibus Department and became

Birmingham City Transport) brought out Illuminated Tramcar 63 again, and for the first time an Illuminated Bus, based on a new COG5 chassis, CVP 118, which later duly became bus 1018. Some of the COG5s were still running — as buses — in 1960; their postwar successors ran up some equally long records and as mentioned some of the JOJ and MOF CVG6s of 1950 and 1954 are still going in 1977, having been built for a 15-year life!

Thus Birmingham in 1939: predominantly, though not exclusively, Daimler. In 20 years a situation had come about which not even the most optimistic bus protagonist would have imagined in 1920, but again different from what we thought around 1930, when it seemed that it was to be AEC for ever. Nevertheless, while all voted the Daimlers to be first-class vehicles, there were those drivers who still considered the petrol Regents to be the best ever. Happily, one of them, 486, has been rescued; already a great amount of restoration has been carried out on its MCW body, but it will be some time yet before, once again, a 'piano-front' Regent delights our eyes on the streets of Birmingham. How I wish now I had thought of preserving one of the old 504s, about a dozen of which were jammed into a scrapyard in Wellington Road, Handsworth; jammed so tightly, in fact, that the wooden bodies swelled with being exposed to the weather and it was quite a job to get at them for the final insult. No one then had thought about preserving buses and commercials — they just came and went.

Wolverhampton, as might be expected, supported home industries and built up a fleet of Guy vehicles, both motor and trolley, with the other local trolleybus builder, Sunbeam, well represented and putting in some motor examples too, but in the mid-thirties Daimler COG5s came into the fleet here also. As already mentioned, Wolverhampton operated an extensive bus 'empire' outside the borough boundary, and so did Walsall, who were strong Dennis supporters. Walsall had a big fleet of Dennis 'E' single-deckers and some of the corresponding 'H' double-deckers, though in the early twenties there were Daimlers, Tilling-Stevens and Guy vehicles in use. Many of the Dennis 'Es' were rebodied in the mid-thirties and the 'H' double-deckers had the bodies very cleverly rebuilt, with modern front-end built out over the canopy, and deeper side-panels. One had to look very hard to detect that they were still the 1927 bodies, but Walsall has always been very good at rebuilds. Petrol-engine Dennis Lancets followed, and later some with Dennis diesel engines which did very well, and there were also some 'Flying Pigs', or 20-seater Dennis Aces which did very useful work in the remote parts of Cannock Chase where the Walsall empire extended. The Walsall pre-war colour scheme was most attractive, being light blue with deep dark-blue waistlines. At one time tyres were painted white; this was not just bull — I understand that if a driver came in with his tyres marked where he had hit the kerb somewhere, he lost a bonus! Those certainly were the days!

West Bromwich also became strong Dennis supporters, after

Above: West Bromwich Corporation Guy BB No 12, EA 3334, at St Paul's Road, Smethwick, 1938. Three of these buses came into the fleet 1927/8. / *R. T. Coxon*

early days with Tilling-Stevens, one or two Morris-Commercials, and Guys. The Guy FBB half-cab single-decker was very much like the Birmingham Guy Conquests, but with a smaller radiator. The change to Dennis came, as I understand it, due to joint running on the Walsall-West Bromwich service where West Bromwich used Guys and Walsall the Dennis 'E's The Dennises not only kept better time but did the job much more economically, so West Bromwich went in for the five Dennis 'E' type already referred to; certainly preserved No 32 still does 10mpg if not slightly better, whereas 6mpg with a Guy was about the best you could expect. These were followed by some Dennis 'EV's, with the same Dennis four-cylinder petrol engine as the 'E', but with left-hand gear-stick and chromium radiator, and the first double-deck vehicles in the fleet were three Dennis 'HVs' with Massey bodies sporting the same 'Pickpocket Special' layout as the Birmingham Inner Circle AECs. Further double-deckers were of conventional layout on Dennis Lancet chassis, the first, No 42, EA 5202, having a locally-built body by

Above: WBCT No 46, EA 6301, a Dennis Ace, inevitably known as a 'Flying Pig'. One of these handy little buses almost got preserved, after a career as a mobile 'chippy', but the vandals got in first. / *WBCT*

Dixon of West Bromwich, who had put the bodies on the 'E's. This body outlived the chassis and was put on to post-war Daimler 132. Some 'Flying Pigs' were in evidence, and one nearly got preserved at about the same time as 32 was rescued, having been in use as a mobile fish-and-chip emporium. But the vandals got in first, and the Pig was no more.

Then, as in Birmingham and Wolverhampton, a Daimler COG5 was tried out, No 53, EA 6308. The change to Daimler was not immediate, as more Dennis Lances were added, but the change was inevitable. As mentioned earlier, a Regent and a Leyland Titan were costed against the Daimler COG6, which West Bromwich preferred to the COG5, but the big order for the tramway replacement buses was for the Daimlers. To house this big addition to the fleet, the garage at Oak Lane was extended, the extension having what I believe is still the greatest roof span in the country without any floor supports. Structural engineers still come to see it, and the whole fleet could be housed under this most impressive roof. I have more than once heard the opinion expressed by responsible people that the West Bromwich fleet of about one hundred and twenty buses was just about ideal. For many years the general manager was A. Witcomb Smith, and it is said that he knew everybody employed by the undertaking, crews, garage staff and office and had a 'good morning' for all, being quite upset if the greeting was not returned. It is also said that when the first petrol buses with starters, the Dennis Lancets, came into the fleet, he had the starters taken off. He said it made the men idle! I may say that although No 32 generally starts easily enough on the handle, there have been times in cold and wet weather when she doesn't want to know and a starter would be very acceptable!

In these 20 years between the wars traffic conditions had changed enormously. There was plenty of traffic before 1914, and London photographs in those days reveal some very interesting tangles long before even the electric tram came on the scene. It was less severe in Birmingham, and photographs of the early twenties depict a fairly leisurely way of life, with plenty of space between the vehicles and people crossing the road with a fair degree of safety. The view-cards of those days always had a tram in the picture if possible, and how those cards are prized today! By 1930 it was another story, and in Birmingham a one-way system was brought into being, most of it in 1933 when the Hockley trams had to vacate the Cathedral terminus and all cars used the Livery Street loop terminal. With these loop terminals it was important that incoming cars should be in the right order for their loading bays, and where routes converged on the way in, such as at Grove Lane junction where the Oxhill Road route rejoined the main route, drivers would signal to each other, by a display on the fingers, their time of departure from Colmore Row. The Dudley 74 loading point was ahead of that for Oxhill Road, which was the rearmost, so if a 74 was due away at, say, 3.31pm and the Oxhill Road car left at 3.32pm the drivers would put up the appropriate tic-tac on their fingers and the 74 would precede the 26. Once past the junction they could not overtake. This sometimes led people who did not understand what was going on to think that the drivers were making derisory gestures at each other, and I believe complaints were sometimes sent in. For all I know, there may have been a standard letter at Congreve Street to deal with this matter — ('Send this guy the bug letter') — but this is mere guesswork. One recalls, however, the fearful ruckus not so long ago when one of our most celebrated show-jumpers indulged in a similar display of tic-tac, though in this case he was probably not signalling his time of departure. This practice, of course, came to an end with the trams, as the buses can and do overtake each other, and if drivers go in for such displays today they probably *are* making derisory gestures at somebody. It should always be borne in mind, I feel, that a gentleman is never rude unintentionally.

It may have been observed that this chapter has been a survey of the municipal bus operators in our area, with no mention of the Birmingham and Midland Motor Omnibus Company Limited. This is by design and not by accident, because in the inter-war period the character of the Midland Red as an operator was to undergo changes quite as profound as those of the four Corporation concerns, though necessarily different. The next chapter will be devoted, therefore, to the Midland Red and some of the companies with whom the BMMO ran in association.

The Upsurge of the Midland Red

Above: BMMO Co Ltd SOS rear-entrance double-deck bus 1932, HA 8017.

The Birmingham and Midland Motor Omnibus Company Limited which had been formed largely to compete with and then absorb the Birmingham Motor Express Company, reverted to horse traction until 1912 as a more practical method of operating a bus service. Hardly had the motor-bus been re-established by the company in Birmingham than Birmingham Corporation exercised its right to operate all services in the city and the BMMO moved out to Bearwood — though on perfectly amicable terms with Birmingham Corporation. Then came World War I — almost as if the 'Natural Cussedness of Things in General' (Carter Dickson's Sir Henry Merrivale) was doing everything it could to stop this bus company ever doing any business. There were some tenacious men on BMMO, however, and the company throve on adversity. At least they had buses now which would go, and continue to go, these of course, being the Tilling-Stevens petrol-electrics. As previously remarked, as the BMMO was a BET tramway associate, the electric system may have been favourably regarded by the tramway-minded management, but be that as it may the Tilling-Stevens was a very good bus indeed.

After World War I the Midland Red was still a small concern, compared with what it was to be in 1930 and after. It had commenced in 1913 running to Walsall and Coventry from Birmingham, and in 1914, before the outbreak of war, was running to Redditch and Astwood Bank, Stourbridge, Bewdley, Malvern, Warwick, and Shenstone, and despite the war the network of services continued to grow, spreading as far afield as Shrewsbury, Tamworth and Nuneaton, and if these tentacles were not extended far enough, really long-distance services began in 1921 to Weston-super-Mare and Llandudno. Without going into further detail it can be see that even in the early twenties Midland Red thinking was very ambitious indeed, and I first became aware that long-distance buses, or coaches as they now were, were really in business when I saw the North-Western Leyland Tiger coach on the Manchester-Birmingham-London service, operated jointly by Midland Red and North-Western, every day on Soho Road, Handsworth, while waiting for my Oxhill Road tram after school, about 1930. By that date the

Digbeth Coach Station had been opened and the vehicles were highly-appointed luxury coaches. The days of solid-tyred Tillings going down to Weston with the luggage in a roof basket were long past.

This chapter is not intended, however, as a survey of the whole of Midland Red's activities between the wars, but only as concerns the Midland and Black Country area, but obviously there must be some interweaving, especially as sometimes a long-distance coach might turn up on a purely local trip, though this was only in an emergency. To begin with, about 1920, there were no coaches as such, but a few Tilling-Stevens chassis were given charabanc bodies, with cross-bench seats with individual doors on the nearside, and a canvas hood for bad weather; likewise some of the first SOS 'S' type had charabanc bodies also. These were the first vehicles to point the difference between bus and coach; one certainly could not use a charabanc for a stage service, but one could use a bus for an excursion or distance run if necessary. Charabancs disappeared from the scene everywhere very early; the American style 'Safety Coach', with front entrance, centre gangway, solid sides and back and permanent glass windows and sunshine roof swept them off the road in a very short time. In the coach business, only the very latest will do, and this still holds. A modern coach will only do about two years on first-class jobs like continental tours, and then it is football and works services and the place thereof knows it no more. Some present-day coach firms change their fleet every year and let someone else do the heavy maintenance on them. By 1930 one saw no more charabancs on the sea-front at Weston or Bournemouth, etc. They wouldn't have got any business. It was the sleek Reo and Chevrolet and other makes of safety coaches who were taking the trippers to Wells Cathedral and Stonehenge, and today I believe the only true charabanc in preservation is Lord Montagu's Maxwell, an American 18-seater. So on the Midland Red two fleets began to emerge, the bread-and-butter fleet of buses and the more exotic charabancs and coaches, with, however, quite early on, some dual-purpose vehicles.

One of the first, and most interesting, vehicle developments on Midland Red was the appearance in 1922 of some forward-control (half-cab) Tilling-Stevens double-deckers, open-top, of course, at that date and on solids, but with front entrance and staircase and knife-board seating, ie longitudinal benches placed back-to-back on the crown of the 'camel-back' arch to the lower saloon roof, of which the later Birmingham Inner Circle 'Pickpocket Specials' were a derivative. The idea of the knife-board seating was to reduce height and to lessen the chances of passengers being struck by tree-branches on country routes; for the latter reason the advertisement panels or 'decency boards' were very high and the view from the top deck rather restricted. They were not pretty vehicles, perhaps, but they did well and doubtless had much to do with BMMO adopting front entrance

Above: Angel Place, Worcester, 1923, with BMMO Co Ltd Knifeboard and single-deck Tilling-Stevens buses. The double-deckers are on the Birmingham-Malvern service. / *Alec G. Jenson*

for much later double-deckers. They ran the Birmingham-Walsall service, also Coventry and Worcester, but had a relatively short innings, as evidently double-deckers were not approved of on the BMMO at this time, and with the advent of the SOS types in 1923 it was to be single-deckers for a long time.

The initials 'SOS', it was popularly reported stood for 'Shire's Own Specification', the company's talented engineer being L. G. Wyndham Shire. The first model was the 'S', a normal-control single-decker which nevertheless seated 32 (reduced to 31 by removing the folding seat on the rear emergency door). Registered HA 2330 with bonnet number 330 it was on Tilling-Stevens chassis frame, mounted on spoked pneumatic-tyred wheels, the rear wheels being only singles. Like the LGOC 'K' and 'S' types, quite a bit of World War I aircraft technology had gone into the body design. It was a light-weight and a flyer, leaving the Tilling-Stevens, even the gearbox TS3s, absolutely nowhere. It was a great treat to be taken to Sutton Park on a Bank Holiday from Perry Barr, having first got to Perry Barr on the new Outer Circle on whatever bus Birmingham Corporation could spare. At Perry Barr one queued at the Aldridge Road stop where spare Midland Reds were shuttling between Perry Barr and Sutton, and hoped that the bus would be an SOS; such was the queue that we bundled aboard the first bus which could take us, however. I approved of Sutton Park, as the admission tickets were of railway type (Edmundson) cards, and I collected as many as I could and ran my own booking office at home with them. Beyond the Boar's Head, where now the M6 crosses the dual-carriageway College Road, it was country; one did not meet the houses again until the Beggar's Bush, and the Midland Red drivers invariably knocked the gear-stick 'out of cog' on the long hill beyond Perry Common and let her roll. (It would be a foolhardy driver who would do this on Mucklows Hill, Halesowen, however.)

I next saw the SOS charabancs not in Birmingham but, yes, at Weston-super-Mare, at about the same time that I realised that the Bristol Tramways and Carriage Company Limited were also building their own vehicles. Then down at Perry Barr one day, where I had probably gone to see if any more of the 'Aston Bogies' had been rebuilt, I saw a half-cab SOS on the Walsall service, one of the 'FS' type. It did not dawn on me for some time that the front-entrance Tilling-Stevens double-deckers were not around any more, but they vanished quickly as more FS and Q single-deckers, the latter seating 37, took up service. What I did not know until much later was that the lower saloons of the double-deck bodies had in some cases been rebuilt with new roof-sticks and put back into service as single-deckers on SOS chassis and classified 'OD', but I had a suspicion that somehow these bodies had been 'got at'.

Some very superior-looking BMMO coaches were now to be seen, bonneted safety-coach type, these being the 'QC' variety and really handsome vehicles. By this time the older Tilling-Stevens single-deckers with very box-like bodies were almost extinct as still more new SOS vehicles came on the road, a significant newcomer being the QL type in 1928, with twin rear wheels and lower-built body, though still of the traditional BMMO straight-side, cut away on the angle profile. Some coaches, similar to the QCs but designated QLC, with twin rears, followed and had a long life, but the biggest break-through in coaches came in 1929 with the RR series, HA 4956-5006. I first met with this type when taken by my father on a works visit to the new Hams Hall Power Station (recently closed down as outdated — how that sort of thing knocks one as age advances!). There were four of these spandy-new coaches waiting for us in

Below: BMMO 'FS' HA 3584 of 1926 which replaced the Knifeboards. Their unladen weight was only 3tons 15cwt. Performance sprightly. / *Brush EE Co Ltd*

Paradise Street, and I remember that my reaction was, 'That'll make Bristol Tramways sit up!', as by now I was comparing anything BMMO with anything Bristol. Certainly the RR was a first-class vehicle, and Midland Red's long-distance business was really built up with them. They had a long life and the design was repeated with the BRR HA 5123, the SRR HA 6174/6175 all with similar bodywork, and the LRR, HA 9051, AHA 587-611 with modified bodywork reflecting mid-thirties trend but without the horrific streamlining then in vogue. (There were some Coronation Coaches around then, enough to cause a traffic accident!) These variants of the RR design were to be seen in and out of Birmingham on the main roads, but were also part of the scene in London, Cheltenham and south-west, and North Wales. BMMO were in any case 'exporting' to other operators, and SOS buses were to be seen in the fleets of Potteries, Trent, Northern General, Llandudno Coaching and Carriage Company, and others. The RR was a dual-purpose design, primarily for coach work, but suitable for stage also.

Prestigious though the coaches were, it was the buses which earned the dividends, and the BMMO empire was by 1930 really far-flung. It was without doubt, however, the former Black Country tram routes with their punishing gradients and

Above left: BMMO 'QL' HA 4892 awaits the Austin Works turnout at Longbridge. With twin rears they came out a little heavier than the FS and Q types and were highly successful vehicles. HA 4892 was one of about ten QLs which lasted until 1950. / *R. T. Coxon*

Left: BMMO 'RR' coach HA 4967 of 1930. Midland Red's long distance coach services were built up with these handsome and highly competent vehicles. / *Alec G. Jenson*

awkward, narrow and congested traffic situations which proved the SOS types, and they came out well. The BMMO were also called upon to replace the Worcester and Kidderminster tramways and still more QLs rolled out of the Carlyle Road works, Edgbaston, followed in 1929 by the M, basically the same bus but with curved side panels, and then a six-cylinder job, the MM. Up to now the radiator for the single-deckers had been similar to, but smaller than, the Tilling-Stevens, but with only the top tank ribbed. With the MM, the ribbed top tank was dropped, and on the RR coach a new radiator appeared with a distinctive flat top tank, and this radiator profile was to remain standard throughout most of the thirties. The next batch of single-deckers, an improved 'M' known as the IM4, with some six-cylinder IM6s, all with various improvements in bodywork, followed, and then came rumours of a Midland Red top-covered double-decker in 1931, at first openly disbelieved. However, one day I was travelling out along the Bristol Road on a tram when a BMMO double-decker — carrying advertisements, to my disgust — surged past us very much in the manner of the later petrol catch-phrase — 'That's Shell — that was'. It was HA 7329, the prototype rear-entrance double-decker, and there was no doubt at all that it could move. It was out of sight before I'd got my breath back. It had no indicator in the front panel, nor did it acquire one, but the production batch HA 8001-8050 did have a roller blind geographical indicator surmounted by the BMMO stencil numeral box, and all double-deckers up to World War II were similarly equipped. Only the RR coaches and their derivatives had had roller-blinds before this, and single-deck service buses continued to carry only a board on the half-bulkhead, not easy to see at night, and stencil numerals. These double-deckers were rear-entrance, and they were to be the only pre-war examples. In 1933 a very curious vehicle appeared on the

Below: BMMO rear-entrance double-decker HA 8003 of 1932 at Dudley station in 1938, with Birmingham trams in background. Fifty were built, after which BMMO adopted the front entrance layout, most unusual for double-deckers at that time. */ R. T. Coxon*

118 Walsall run — possibly because Walsall Corporation had invested in a front-entrance Tilling-Stevens (TSM) double-decker, DH 9043, No 101? This was HA 9000, carrying bonnet No 1000, a front-entrance decker with top deck commencing behind the front bulkhead — in other words, the cab projecting forward of the top deck. This prototype did have front indicators, but its very 'one-off' front end was not rebuilt, and it spent most of its time on the Walsall run. It was followed in 1934 by 50 front-entrance deckers, this time with flush or nearly flush front, and then by several more batches up to the FHA batch of 1939, which were allocated to Oldbury garage for replacing the last Black Country tram routes, Birmingham Corporation's 87 Dudley via Oldbury. They were notable vehicles indeed but unhappily none has survived.

Equally famous were the ON series of single-deckers which followed the first 50 FEDDs (HA 9401-9450). HA 9451 was the first ON, with a broad beaded waistline somewhat in the Birmingham style, and with variations the type ran into hundreds. Like the FEDDs, the earlier examples were petrol, the later ones diesel with many conversions. With these ONs the distinction between coach and bus was considerably reduced, and at holiday times they would be put on as duplicates to seaside destinations. I once travelled to Weston on an ON with the two rear seats taken out for luggage space; certainly no commercial vehicles passed us and not many cars. The conductor was sitting at the back keeping a discreet eye on what was following, presumably to give the driver a bell signal should a police car evince too much interest. Incidentally, some coach drivers — I am not sure if this applied to BMMO, but I certainly saw this done on a Yorkshire Woollen District Coach — carried their own rear-view mirrors which they would screw into the coachwork above the windscreen so as to give them a view

Left: BMMO prototype front-entrance double-decker HA 9000 at the Scott Arms, Birmingham-Walsall service 1938. Definitely a curiosity. */ R. T. Coxon*

through the rear window of the coach. Normally only side-mounted mirrors were fitted at this period, but some drivers preferred to know exactly who was on their tail; at the end of the run the mirror would be taken off to be used on the next vehicle! Some lorry drivers resorted to taking up one of the cab floorboards and fixing a mirror on the front axle for the same reason.

In the thirties the usual good relations with Birmingham Corporation were maintained, and at Bank Holiday periods Birmingham buses would be hired to run local Midland Red routes so as to release BMMO vehicles for long-distance duplicates, but on one occasion I saw two Birmingham Daimler COG5 single-deckers in, of course, Weston, bearing 'On Hire to Midland Red' stickers. By this time, vehicles from far away were daily visitors in the Digbeth Coach Station, where one could see Red and White, Black and White, Crosville (then in chocolate livery), Standerwick, Scout, Ribble and many more, while at Bank Holidays independent vehicles on hire to the big companies would turn up and there really was some variety. On one occasion a Cheltenham District Guy Conquest came in on a Black and White duplicate. That must have been an expensive trip!

For extended tours BMMO built a batch of very handsome bonneted normal-control coaches, the OLRs, with 29 seats, AHA 612-636. These were of the same parentage as the QC and QLC coaches of the late twenties and were probably the last of their type, though Grey Cars of Torquay had some AEC Rangers

Below: SOS 'OLR' touring coach AHA 634 of BMMO at Quedgeley, Glos, on Birmingham-Weston run 1938. Among the last 'safety coaches' built. They were rebuilt during World War II as half-cab buses with solid roof. / *R. T. Coxon*

Right: BMMO's SOS rear-engine bus CHA 3 of 1936 and looking 20 years ahead of its time, at the Oxhill Road terminus of the short-lived extension of route 213 from New Inns. Cut back to New Inns on the outbreak of war and not reinstated. Summer 1939. / *R. T. Coxon*

Below right: BMMO's SOS 'SLR' touring coach of 1937, CHA 996, at Weston-super-Mare with a Leyland Cub of Auty of Bury behind. Very trendy for their time, they proved too big for the restricted lanes of the far West. / *R. T. Coxon*

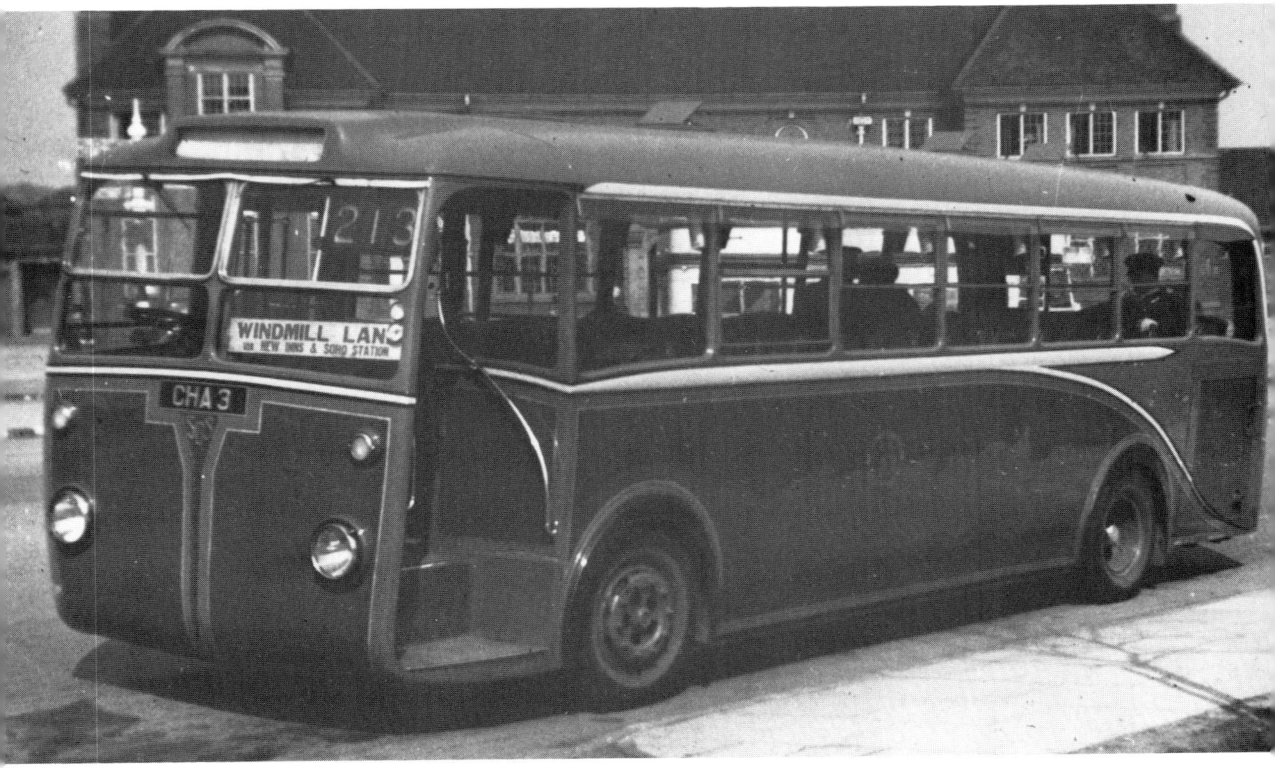
213
WINDMILL LAN
VIA NEW INNS & SOHO STATION
CHA 3

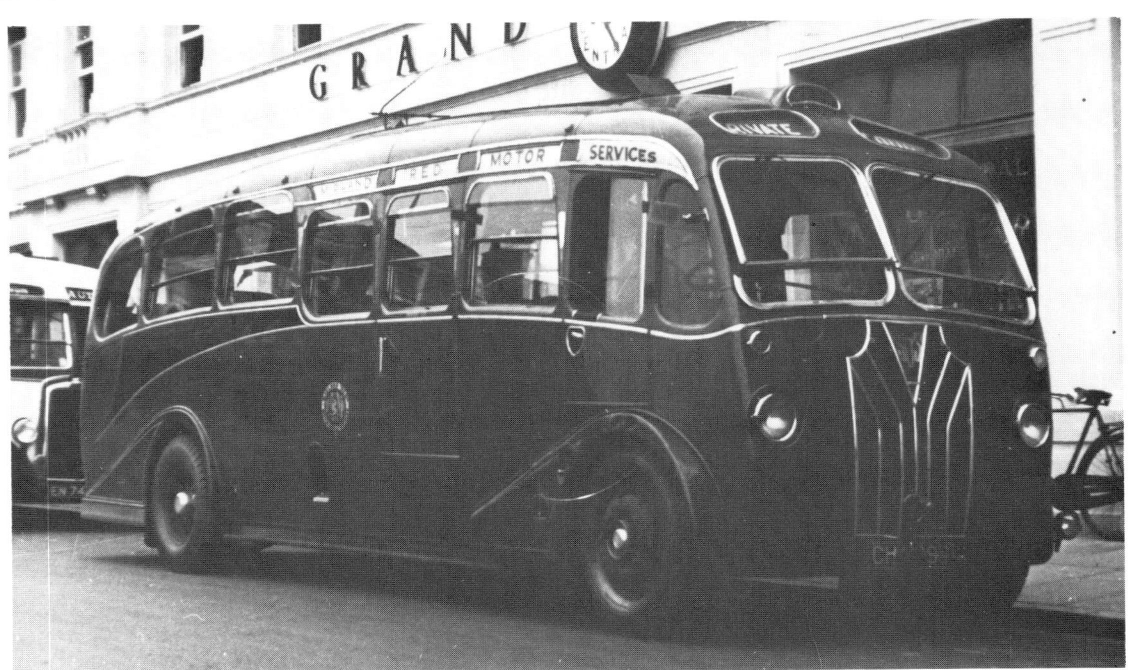

GRAND
MOTOR
SERVICES

Right: SOS front-entrance decker EHA 290 of BMMO at Dudley on Wolverhampton-Birmingham service 1938. The full-front cab was soon converted to normal half-cab.
/ R. T. Coxon

at about the same time. Before the next batch of touring coaches came out, Carlyle Road had turned out four very revolutionary machines, three buses, BHA 1, CHA 2-3, and CHA 1, a coach, all with rear engine and looking far more like products of the 1950s than 1936. Being experimental vehicles, they were not without their troubles and were kept on local routes, though the coach certainly ran some London turns. Midland Red were not alone in this sort of project — Northern General were building some side-engine coaches at this period. Eventually these four vehicles were rebuilt with underfloor engines, but that is outside our terms of reference.

The SLR coaches of 1937 were far in advance of the OLRs of 1935. They were full-front jobs, streamlined, but moderately compared with some then current vehicles. There were 50 of them, CHA 950-999, and though mechanically successful enough they proved too big for the then narrow roads of the far West, on which the OLRs had to be kept. Before the final batch of inter-war coaches came out in 1939, a stranger appeared in the fleet, a Dennis Lancet II, DHA 200, with an ON bus body. Various oil engines were being tried out at this time, and apparently the only way to do a trial with a Dennis engine was to buy the whole chassis. It was not around for long, and I failed to get a photograph of it. The only other vehicles in the fleet not of SOS make were some Albions from the Leicester and District (Leicester Green) which remained with BMMO, still in green but with MIDLAND transfers, for a short time in 1936-7.

More variants on the ON theme, DONs and SONs were added, and more front-entrance deckers. The ONs had a full canopy over the engine, whereas earlier SOS half-cab single-deckers had the canopy swept back in a curve from the cab to the nearside of the bulkhead. Provision was made in the ON canopy profile for an indicator, and used for that purpose on some 'exported' ONs on the Sunderland District, but BMMO retained the bulkhead board-in-slot. The final variants on the ON chassis were FHA 401-425, the ONC full-front diesel coaches, which hardly had a chance to show what they could do when World War II broke out. Of the EHA batch of double-deckers, EHA 290, 292 and 297 were built with full-front bodies, but reverted to half-cab in 1940. These also carried a new pattern radiator with the initials 'SOS', the MIDLAND RED inscription being dropped.

BMMO vehicles for the most part remained as built, unlike some operators who rebodied chassis sometimes more than once, such as Southern and Western National. The exception to this rule was the original SOS 'S' type, some 50 of which were given new low-built bus bodies seating 26 in 1929 and 1930 and known as type ODD. They were pretty little buses and I would like to have seen one survive. However, as 'S' type with original body, HA 3505 has made a most improbable come-back and is being restored by the Birmingham Omnibus Preservation Society, who also own a 'Q' type operated by Northern General. One of the original batch of ONs, HA 9483, also survives, and though much remains to be done on the 'S' and the 'Q', much has been done, including, of course, the most essential fact of actually saving them, far gone as they were. Their present owners are a determined body of people and one day these representatives of the great days of the Midland Red will take the road again. And they were great days, those inter-war years. The reputation of Midland Red stood very high indeed, not only in the industry but with the public, for possibly two main reasons, the reliability of their vehicles and the fact that the company cultivated its public. They aimed to give service and worked at it, as a study of official directives to staff in the 1920s demonstrates. The emphasis was on crews looking out for passengers and working a new service up, which evidently they did. As to reliability, one just did not see broken-down Midland Reds. One heard that Wyndham Shire would not have a vehicle towed in, unless it had been involved in a collision, and that a BMMO driver was not allowed to lift the bonnet cover in the street. Evidently the buses themselves took this seriously; and in all seriousness I can say that I never saw a failed SOS.

For many years BMMO fitted a hand klaxon on the cab door; it was used sparingly but with effect. I recall seeing a man crossing New Street, engrossed in the *Sports Argus* — it could have been when I was moving across to New Street station from Snow Hill on a Saturday night — and his attention certainly wasn't on crossing the road. A BMMO 'Q' or possible 'QL' came ghosting down on him, and the driver really did let go with the klaxon. The man appeared to rise several feet vertically into the air and made the pavement in one almighty bound. Rarely have I seen a faster take-off!

Until the advent of the SOS 'QL', the name MIDLAND was carried on the side panel in Roman gold-block letters, rather like the pre-1914 GENERAL of the LGOC. London General adopted, apparently with the AEC 'K' type in 1919, the better-known insciption with the G and L in large letters, with a gold leaf line below the intervening letters; BMMO, much later in 1928, turned out the later QLs with the MIDLAND transfer (I am pretty sure that the earlier QLs had the older transfer) and this remained standard up to 1939. Coaches carried a garter title on the side panel, and the ONs and front-entrance deckers carried it on the half-cab dash. Lining out in the 1920s was again rather in the LGOC style, in black, but with the 'QL's', and probably at the same time as the new underlined transfer, the lining out was simplified and in gold-leaf. Needless to say, vehicle turn-out was impeccable. One batch of SONs, the DHA-registered batch, had a slight touch of streamlining on their side panels and some rather tawdry fillets of chromium-plate on the pillars, but they soon lost these rather regrettable embellishments. The Midland Red didn't need things like that!

One delightful custom the company had was to grace their timetable books, handbills etc with a block illustration of one of their vehicles. They didn't have to do this, of course, but it was just one more facet of their capacity to take trouble over anything they did, and these little vignettes were very eye-catching. The earliest example in my possession is one of the 'S' type bus and charabanc, but they came out right up to the time of the 'SLR' coaches and front-entrance deckers. BMMO were not alone in this practice, but I don't think any other operator went in for it quite so comprehensively. The company also published a magazine, and late in the 1930s, if not before, an official list of attractions and events. To my delighted surprise, a series of articles began to appear in 'Attractions and Events' called 'Travel in Other Times', and quite fortuitously when asking for one of these publications in the excursion office in Great Charles Street, from where many of the BMMO's tours started, I was put in touch with the author of these articles, Alec G. Jenson, then living in Solihull. As a transport historian Alec Jenson is known today as of the first order; it seemed to me back in those days quite incredible that one man should have amassed such a wealth of information, and in such a highly-ordered manner, on any subject, particularly this subject of transport of which I was now a confirmed addict. He told me then that he didn't know anyone else was interested, and indeed there were few of us who took stock of road vehicles and services — the railway side was well catered for; the *Railway Magazine* has been going since 1897. However, there were a few of us who kept an eye on things, including Peter Hardy, with a mind like a computer, who could quote from memory the fleet and history of independent operators in obscure parts of the Welsh Marches or the Western Islands for that matter — and he'd be right. I did a bus-hunting holiday with Peter in, I think, 1937 in his Morris Minor, and among other innumerable visits on that trip we fetched up in South Shields at the Northern General garage. We breezed in, though politely enough — it always pays off — and, explaining that we were from Birmingham, asked if we could see their SOS buses. The foreman — I think — assumed that we were from BMMO, and put everything at our disposal; he did more. In the garage was one of the new Northern General SE6 side-engine jobs, and evidently the foreman thought it would be nice to show these Birmingham chaps what NGT had come up with. 'Joe, hinny, start it oop', he called to a garage hand, and start it up he did. We got aboard, and were taken, not just for a trip round the block, but for a run down the coast road to Marsden; that SE6 could certainly move, and I am glad that one of these notable vehicles has survived, though now converted to two-axle layout. Up to now the engine had always been at the front of a motor vehicle, because that was where the horse used to be. BMMO's rear-engine vehicles and Northern's side-engine examples — not forgetting the AEC 'Q' — were among the earliest to break away from the front-engine tradition. In retrospect, which is what this book is all about, the advance in design in those few years — less than two decades — was quite astounding. The 'Q', the SOS rear-engine jobs, the Northern SEs and the Maudslay SF 40 would not look unduly dated today, if a bit on the small side. They made the designs even of the late twenties look quite archaic, and set the pattern for designs many years in the future. I realised quite early just how much things had moved on when I saw the driver-training vehicle, HA 2250, rebuilt as a full-front single-decker from one of the knife-board Tilling-Stevens open-toppers, parked alongside one of the RE buses near Bearwood garage. HA 2250 very rarely made a public appearance, usually being parked just inside the garage out of camera range — and in those days photographers were not encouraged around BMMO garages. On this occasion, of course, I hadn't got the camera with me.

At the end of our survey Midland Red was absolutely up in front. Their standard designs were fast, competent and reliable and have become legendary. They really were something special and out of the ordinary; their advanced experimental designs put the company in a position years ahead of the rest after World War II, but that is another story, belonging to another world.

Traffic

Above: BMMO Co Ltd SOS 'IM4' bus 1932.

'Things which move are more interesting than things which stand still.' Traffic gives life to places — towns, at all events. Traffic is offensive in some circumstances; juggernaut lorries pounding the life out of rural villages rather than giving life to them; motor-cycles snarling round a cathedral close — and plenty more such could be quoted, but enough. When we visit a town, we look at the guide-book items, the cathedral, the guildhall, the castle and so on, because our attention is directed to them. We also take in, perhaps subconsciously, the traffic. Even people not particularly interested in transport were quick to notice the open-platform Paris buses, attractive by their very ugliness; schoolchildren, and adults, visiting this country always want to ride upstairs on our double-deckers and so forth. But traffic is not just buses and trams — indeed, they are relative newcomers. The horse was the motive power for everything for long ages and survived in numbers until well into our period, and though in my boyhood passenger transport was mechanical, the horse still did most of the goods work — bakers' vans, milk carts (I must have ridden quite a mileage on a milk-float which used to serve us), coal carts and railway delivery carts or drays, not to mention any number of general carriers and odd-job men. Funeral vehicles were also horse-operated and some people did not like the idea of motor corteges at first, though it would no longer be a matter for concern for the person mainly involved.

Many visitors to London take away an impression, not only of the Abbey and Trafalgar Square, but of red buses everywhere — and taxis. Photographs taken before 1900 show London streets crowded with horse vehicles, many of them being Hansoms (named after their inventor, who was also the architect of Birmingham Town Hall). Photographs of the pre-1914 period show the motor-taxi taking over; those of the twenties show passenger transport entirely mechanical and not many horses even on goods work. But everywhere the taxis, and doing good business. I would imagine that a great proportion of the taxi business in London is inter-station journeys. Had London's railways all used one huge unimaginable station it might have been a different matter, and perhaps that is why the taxi has never been such a feature of Birmingham traffic. Birmingham had only two main railway stations, with little interchange traffic, and in pre-World War II days there were few, if any, cruising taxis; there are some today, though at nothing like the London frequency. Both stations had taxi-stands, and there were others at strategic locations round the central area. As the twenties came into the photographs, more private cars are to be seen, mainly the more opulent examples, but as the age moved into the thirties the Austin Sevens and Twelves,the Morrises of all varieties and so many other marques which contributed to the variety of the scene all helped to thicken up the traffic situation so that in 1933 the famous (notorious?) Birmingham one-way system was brought into being. Notorious perhaps because people were not used to the idea, but it worked. At first, Victoria Square operated clockwise, and this certainly did not work; moreover, strangers were apt to get into a 'stack' situation, rather like aircraft trying to get into airports today, and went round and round Victoria Square with little hope of ever getting out again. A variety artiste at a now-vanished Birmingham theatre put over a gag about the statue of King Edward VII, who then kept company with Queen Victoria on the central island of the square, leaning over to address a motorist who had gone round several time, 'I say, sir, will you please go away — you're making my mother giddy.' When the traffic flow round the square was reversed, things were much better, though care had to be exercised on the steep down-gradient, paved with wood blocks, from Colmore Row round into New Street. I saw a piano-front Regent do a broadside skid on these blocks one wet day and go into New Street back-end first; the only practical way out of that one was to continue to reverse down New Street into Ethel Street and then come out the right way, after which the wood blocks were ripped out and a bitumen surface put down. Those wood blocks survived long past their time on many Birmingham roads, as did the granite setts. The trams were excepted from the one-way system in Corporation Street past Lewis's, between Bull Street and Old Square, and in Steelhouse Lane. As few people would care to argue with a tram, they went through against the traffic without any great difficulty. The railway heavy cartage horse-drays were around for a long time, their drivers quite impervious to tramcar gongs, Midland Red klaxons, or anything else except a fire-engine bell, and then things did scatter. The old fire-station was in the Old Square, and turn-out from there was impressive indeed. When the present Central Fire Station was opened in 1936, near the General Hospital, quite a bit of old Birmingham was erased, including a pub by the name of the Swan with Two Necks; some rearrangement of the tramway junctions was done at the same time, making for much easier movement. Central Place, as it was then called, was one of Birmingham's biggest junctions and though not to be compared with London's Elephant and Castle or Salford's Cross Lane 'Grand Union', it was quite a place. Crossovers were put in just short of the junction in Aston Street and Lancaster Street, so that in case of some sort of obstruction in the city centre cars could be turned there. This was standard BCT policy on all routes entering the city; crossovers were few and far between, but there was always one just short of the centre. Certainly during the air-raids of World War II a few more crossovers would not have come amiss.

Handcarts were quite a feature of Birmingham traffic at one time, of course, round the fruit and vegetable markets, but also in the Jewellery Quarter of Hockley, where many three-wheeled basket trolleys were to be seen, likewise delivery bicycles built with front end carriers. The Jewellery Quarter, little of which now remains, was certainly unique. Most of its business premises had been quite large early Victorian houses, the jewellers living where they worked, but as they prospered and needed more work-space they moved out to the then exclusive area of Handsworth Wood outside the city boundary. The area retained its shabby-genteel appearance for most of our period, and one can still find the occasional Regency or Georgian house or terrace. It was served by the Lodge Road tram and the Handsworth routes along Great Hampton Street until the advent of the City Circle bus (19) in 1932 — a typically misleading Birmingham destination as some people naturally imagined it ran round the central streets of the city. The 19 soon became a peak-hour service only and traversed some streets in the Jewellery Quarter not much wider than Henn's Walk, and I once 'did' the route on a Regent — baffling the conductor not a little when I asked for a ticket all the way round — when, in Powell Street the bus, having shed some of its passengers at the stop, keeled over to the nearside where all the remaining top-deck passengers now were and leaned up against a street gas-lamp, doing the gas-lantern not very much good. There was a steep camber and clearances were very tight and the crew had quite a time 'getting her off'.

For a long time a feature of Birmingham traffic was the fleet of green battery-electric refuse lorries operated by the Salvage Department. Some Edisons were running in the early twenties, followed by more modern Morrisons and Garretts; at Brookvale, Witton, on the corner of Moor Lane (now obliterated by the M6) was a salvage depot which generated its own power from boilers fired by the refuse brought in by the electrics, which power was used to recharge the electrics for the next day. Gradually, as the increasing range of the rounds outgrew the electrics' capabilities they were replaced by motor vehicles, but happily one has survived and is in the Birmingham Science Museum. In their time they did well. They were slow, and unlike a small milk or bread battery-electric, their load increased as the day went on and they were sometimes hard put to it to crawl up the concrete ramp to discharge their load. One of these refuse wagons crawling home could cause quite some problems on the Outer Circle when the Witton factories, such as Imperial Chemical Industries, were turning out, though they were as nothing to present-day problems with everyone trying to get home in his own car.

Birmingham's traffic pattern has long been that of two main peaks, morning and evening, requiring a huge fleet of vehicles, most of which are not required during the rest of the day. This doubtless is not exceptional. In nearby West Bromwich the pattern was quite different — the buses stayed out most of the day and ran up quite a figure. The Birmingham pattern has doubtless been brought about by the building of the vast municipal housing estates miles out from the centre, though in more recent years the factories have tended to move out also. In our period, however, the factories were mainly in the inner ring, a notable exception being Fort Dunlop to the east, and the Austin works at Longbridge to the south-west. The daily Longbridge tip-out involved a large contingent of trams for the Birmingham workers and fleets of coaches, ancient and modern, from Bromsgrove, Redditch and the Black Country, with a fair number of Midland Reds and the 'ghost train' to Halesowen and Old Hill. It was quite a sight. Fort Dunlop, on the other side of Birmingham, had been served since 1930 by a double-track branch off the Pype Hayes tram route along Holly Lane, part of the road, I believe, being the property of the Dunlop Rubber Company Limited. Loading shelters were provided, and cars for the works traffic carried the display TYBURN ROAD 63. Probably the only time before World War II that a car other than works specials used the the branch was the famous occasion in 1938 when car No 843 was used by the Light Railway Transport League on a run from Dudley to Rednal, quite a few more places of interest being worked into the itinerary as well. The two 'Titanics' Nos 451 and 452 occasionally worked out to Dunlop, but so tight was the clearance with these two cars under Aston station that on return to service from re-tyring at 'The Lake' they had to be checked for height. They were used only rarely on the Erdington group of routes, for had they suffered a seized-up or broken axle north of Aston station they could not have been brought home to Miller Street with the 'jockey' bogie under the platform, whereas a standard bogie car would still have cleared the bridge on the jockey truck. They were mostly to be seen on Perry Barr, and I must have waited for one of them, if I saw it in the queue of cars at the terminus, many times.

There were no independent stage operators in Birmingham, but plenty of coach firms with excursions and tours licences, a few of whom are still in business, though the character of the business has changed. Many subsisted on works trips during our period, with weekend trips to Blackpool and other resorts, also hiring vehicles to BMMO when they were pushed, as they sometimes were in the late thirties at Bank Holidays. There are few works services today and the coach business seems to lie in Continental tours, only just beginning in our period.

By the late thirties traffic in our area was thick enough to make pedestrian crossings — with Belisha Beacons — a necessity, and they are still with us. What is perhaps not realised today, because the process is so gradual, is how much minor road improvement has been carried out over the years — easing out awkward corners, reducing bad gradients and cambers and re-aligning junctions which were certainly not laid out for motor traffic — they just happened. Of course, these improvements never catch up with the traffic situation, because as soon as roads are improved somebody wants to put bigger and heavier vehicles on them. Certainly today's monstrous goods — and passenger — vehicles would never have got through in the 1920s. The first Scammell articulated six-wheeler lorries of about 1922, with a canvas hood over the open cab, seemed colossal to me as I saw them in MacNamara's fleet passing along parts of the Outer Circle. They seem quite tiny today, but they were as big as the roads would then take, and the term Juggernaut was used in letters to the press about them in those days. Occasionally the roads would not take them and would fall in. For a time in 1927 the Outer Circle was diverted from Church Lane, Handsworth, while a sewer was put in at some depth; it was diverted via Somerset Road and Handworth Wood Road. One day, after one of Pat Collins's huge engines with two box trailers in tow had gone up Somerset Road, the road surface resigned and collapsed under the rear offside wheel of the next Outer Circle AEC 504. The bus took quite a list to starboard but did not capsize, and a gang from Perry Barr garage (then the old tram depot in Birchfield Road) were soon on the spot and had her out. There was a quite alarming void where the road had gone in, and I recall that there was no foundation under the surface, which was simply years of 'tar-and-feathers', certainly not designed for showmen's engines and top-cover buses.

In the middle thirties Birmingham went in for roundabouts, or 'merry-go-rounds' as they were sometimes called, then regarded as the answer to all traffic problems. They are the answer in some cases, but time has shown that they by no means solve all the problems; in those days there was still some road space between vehicles and everybody got his chance. Today there can be an unending flow in one direction and nobody else can get in, and on Birmingham's Outer Circle (particularly infested with roundabouts) are some dating from our period which did well enough in their time but which are now a positive menace and ought to have been replaced with traffic lights long ago. Two such, at the King's Head, Bearwood, and the Fox and Goose, Washwood Heath, have now been so treated but others remain. At the Robin Hood island on Stratford Road and at the Chester Road-Sutton Road junction at Erdington the trams refused to be diverted from their course and went straight across the middle of the island!

It is possible that the idea of the central one-way system was suggested by the practice of sending the buses from the Broad Street direction round the central loop, carrying a 'via' destination board reading either 'VIA NEW STREET TO

COLMORE ROW' or 'VIA COLMORE ROW TO NEW STREET'. This practice of alternate buses traversing the central loop in opposite directions began in 1923 and lasted until the one-way scheme of 1933, when everything went anti-clockwise. Loop terminals for the trams had long been the general practice, the only exceptions being Steelhouse Lane for the Erdington routes, Navigation Street (Stephenson Street), Hill Street and Colmore Row (Cathedral). As a result of local alterations the Fazeley Street routes (11 and 90) used Seymour Street as a dead-end terminus from 1930, and as previously mentioned the Cathedral terminus was disused when the 1933 central scheme came in and all Hockley tram services used the Livery Street-Colmore Row-Snow Hill loop. Although the trams went against the Colmore Row traffic flow, they were separated from it by a narrow island — which could be tricky for pedestrians crossing from the station to the Great Western Arcade who faced the hazards of trams from the right, then buses and everything else from the left a few inches further out. Today's pedestrians face other hazards in the city centre's subways. It was perhaps safer up on top in the thirties.

Still With Us

Above: BMMO Co Ltd SOS 'LRR' coach 1934, HA 9398.

When people today tell me that I'm living in the past I take it as a compliment, as do the rest of the now quite considerable body of us who preserve old passenger vehicles; it may have been surmised from earlier stages of this book that I am thus involved. Preservation in all directions is very much in people's minds today, and rightly so. I long ago realised that history is not in books — they are just for the record, and highly important as such, but the real history is on the ground — Stone Age forts, earthworks, roads, bridges, buildings and what not else; more recently attention has been focused on how people lived and worked; one could do no better in this respect than visit York's truly marvellous Castle Museum where the figures working at their various trades almost come alive; this impression is strengthened by a look at the Heritage Centre in the former St Mary's Church, Castle Street, to see mediaeval builders at their work. After this one may be permitted to visit the Railway Museum! The thousands of visitors tell their own tale of how much people are interested in history, even if not between the covers of books, and this is further borne out by the fantastic numbers of passengers at the Crich Tramway Museum. And all over the country are people — mostly men, but some women — who devote much time, care, love and money to bringing back to life cars, traction engines, fire engines and commercials, and as one of these persons myself I find it exceedingly difficult to say just why. There is the very real thrill and challenge of driving an old-timer; the satisfaction of coaxing old machinery into life again; meeting like-minded people at rallies, etc; but perhaps the greatest reward is in the pleasure these old vehicles give to quite ordinary folk, old and young, but particularly the more elderly, at seeing something which they knew, perhaps rode on, perhaps drove, half a lifetime away.

Half, or even a whole, lifetime is no time at all and our preserved trams and buses count for nothing compared with Stonehenge or Hadrian's Wall. The commonplace of today, however, is the historic of tomorrow; this has only been realised as regards commercial vehicles when earlier generations had already long departed for the scrapyard, and the few survivors of our period are in many cases largely replicas; one could argue about this the length of this book, but it seems to me that a replica is better than nothing. For that matter, how much of the ancient cathedrals and stately homes is original? The original fabric would long ago have crumbled but for the continual process of restoration of stonework and timbers, until really only the design remains, and that seems to me to be the focal point of the whole subject.

In the middle thirties as a teenager I realised that things were changing fast and set about assembling a pictorial record of transport in the area. I had a box Brownie camera but little money for films, but 'snapped' as many vehicles and scenes as I could — the demand for these photographs today has quite amazed me — and in addition visited just about every newsagent and stationer in the district asking for old viewcards showing trams and buses, and sometimes surprising results came up. Once or twice I was told that someone else had recently been in and forestalled me, and I later met up with this person, who was none other than Arthur Camwell ('Cam'), who though scornful of buses in those days was like myself busily recording the tramway and railway scene, and who is known as one of our foremost railway photographers. He is known to have given some branch-line engine-drivers quite a jolt by photographing a train at one station, then arriving by car at the next station *before* the train and shooting it again. I must have gone round the Birmingham newsagents about three weeks ahead of Arthur and in many cases scooped him, though we have long ago shared our scoops. I am happy to include his photographs in this survey.

I had been a model railway — 'O' gauge, of course — operator when about 11 to 14 years old, though my rolling-stock of Hornby, Bing and some of Bassett-Lowke manufacture would perhaps not qualify as models today, but at least the line was properly run. Crude toy buses were about (though I was given a tinplate LGOC 'B' type bus which certainly was far from crude and would fetch some incredible price today), but apart from occasional German or Czech-made single-deck trams, model tramcars were scarce, and I always had a feeling that I would one

Below: BMMO Co Ltd SOS front-entrance double-decker 1934, HA 9429.

Below right: BMMO Co Ltd SOS 'OLR' coach 1935, AHA 612.

day make my own, which, of course, would be Birmingham cars. It was not until after the close of our period that I put the idea into practice; I could already draw vehicles and buildings fairly competently and I argued that if one could draw a tram one could model it, and proceeded to do so during off-duty periods in the Army, using such scrap materials as came to hand. These were built to a curious and possibly unique scale, running on 'O' gauge track representing not the standard gauge but the Birmingham 3ft 6in, so the scale comes out at around 9mm instead of 7mm. At first these models were not motored, and for years remained in their boxes doing nothing, until one day I spotted a Triang XT60 motor and realised that it would fit into the Burnley bogie of one of my models. It did, and I motored the rest of the fleet which now numbers eight cars running on a track 18ft long, against a background of typical Birmingham 'tramscape'; a miniature Birmingham tramway museum, in a way, helping to preserve for me in concrete form those unforgettable inter-war days when the real trams were still with us. Many people have seen the models, as each summer the model tramway goes up to the Crich Tramway Museum on display, and the evident delight of the Birmingham visitors at seeing models of 'their' trams makes up for their disappointment at not seeing a real Birmingham car there.

One day in 1939 I was in High Street, West Bromwich, when I saw one of the five Dennis 'E' single-deckers approaching on the 'Lanes' service to Oldbury. I had the camera with me, turned the bike round and shot her in St Michael's Street. It was No 32, and if anyone then had prophesied that nearly 40 years later the bus would still be around and that I should be driving it, I would have considered him fit for certifying. But that is how it has turned out. The Dennis 'E's were then on spare duties and I thought I'd better get a shot while I could. When war broke out, instead of being replaced they, of course, slogged on like everything else, and 32 — probably because it was in the poorest condition of the five 'E's, was converted for ambulance work, like so many single-deckers at the time. It did little mileage as such, and by the end of the war was in better shape than Nos 28-31, which were withdrawn in 1946. No 32 was put back into passenger service until 1948, when new vehicles were beginning to be available, but her end was not yet. Out came the seats again and banks of batteries were put in; a canvas-covered framework was built over the body, Father Christmas and the reindeer went up on top and she became the 'Christmas Lights' bus, emerging at Christmas and Coronation and Charter Week and so on, until 1962, when she was declared past it. The proposal was then made to West Bromwich Transport Department that she should be restored for the Department's Golden Jubilee in 1964, but the ruling was that as they were then only just breaking even (many undertakings were by then in the red) no money could be spent on the Dennis, but if a group were interested in restoring it from its now derelict condition, they

Above: West Bromwich CT Dennis 'E' No 32, EA 4181 with Dixon body of 1929 on 'The Lanes' (Spon Lane, Bromford Lane) service in St Michael's Street, West Bromwich in 1939, then on spare duties and apparently near the end of its career. Events turned out otherwise and the bus is still very much in evidence. */ R. T. Coxon*

Left: WBCT No 32 on the graveyard at the back of Oak Lane Garage at the end of its 'Christmas Lights' phase. The last of the 'track' buses, AEA 88, is alongside and quite some material from 88 was worked into 32's restoration.

could have the bus as it was. That is how No 32 came to be restored, roughly perhaps in 1965, to as near to its original condition as possible. She has improved since then, and has become very well known where preserved vehicles are seen — Brighton, the Trans-Pennine Run, the Crich Tramway Museum, Old Warden Aerodrome, and many more. She is very far from past it!

Above: WBCT No 32 as restored at Worcester (Pitchcroft) in 1972. / *G. Dowling*

Quite a few Birmingham Corporation buses are now preserved, but only one pre-war example is a runner, Daimler COG5 No 1107. Originally bought from a scrap dealer by Barry Ware, still in practically running order, No 1107 is the only survivor as a bus of the eight-hundred-odd examples of this chassis operated by Birmingham. Others, converted by BCT to service lorries survive, one being AOG 679, now the property of Arthur Whitehouse, whose capacity for keeping old-timers moving is something like genius. No 679 was converted to a Bank Van, with roller-shutter side doors and the service No 83.

The body of an ex-BMMO Tilling-Stevens, No 0 9926, is owned by the Birmingham Omnibus Preservation Society, who also have BCT No 90 (II). a 1931 Morris Dictator single-decker, and 486, the piano-front Regent already mentioned, together with an SOS 'S' normal-control single-decker and a 'Q' type half-cab. An enormous amount of work will be entailed before these vehicles come back on the road, but if I know the BOPS aright, they will!

Only No 395 survives of Birmingham's tram fleet, in the Museum of Science and Industry in Newhall Street. The Black Country Museum Transport Group have a 'Tividale' type single-decker body and have a suitable truck for it, and also have two Wolverhampton double-deck tramcar bodies. Some day,

Above: SOS 'S' type HA 3505 of BMMO in the early stages of restoration. / *Arthur Whitehouse*

Left: BMMO Co Ltd SOS 'SLR' coach 1937, CHA 998.

perhaps, there will be some 3ft 6in gauge cars on service at their Dudley museum site, and another incredible come-back will have been achieved, and another piece of history come alive. It is when history does come alive that it makes its greatest impact; if roads are historically important, as, of course, they are, so are the vehicles which travel along them. Railway locomotives have been preserved for many years, and so have motor-cars. For trams and buses, however, it was a near thing. We were only just in time.

Index

Above: BMMO Co Ltd SOS 'SON' bus 1936, CHA 509.